Political Economy of Development in India

In the Global South, indigenous people have been continuously subjected to top-down, and often violent, processes of post-colonial state and nation building. This book examines the development dilemmas of the indigenous people (*adivasis*) of the Indian state of Kerala. It explores the different facets of change in their lives and livelihoods in the context of modernisation under different political regimes.

As part of the Indian Union, Kerala followed a development approach in tune with the government of India with regard to indigenous communities. However, within the framework of India's quasi-federal polity, the state of Kerala has been tracing a development path of its own, which has come to be known as the 'Kerala model of development'. Adopting a historical–political–economic approach, the book locates the *adivasi* communities in the larger contextual shifts from late colonialism through the post-independence years and critically analyses the Kerala model of development with particular reference to the *adivasis*' changing political status and rights to land. It pays special attention to policy dynamics in the neoliberal phase and the actual practices of decentralisation as a way of including the socially excluded and marginalised.

Offering a theoretical elaboration of the interaction between class and indigeneity based on intensive fieldwork in Kerala, the book addresses *adivasi* development in relation to the general development experience of Kerala and goes on to relate this particular study to the global context of indigenous people's struggles. It will be of interest to those working in the fields of South Asian development, political economy and South Asian politics.

Darley Jose Kjosavik is Associate Professor of International Development Studies at the Department of International Environment and Development Studies, Norwegian University of Life Sciences, Norway.

Nadarajah Shanmugaratnam is Professor Emeritus of International Development Studies at the Department of International Environment and Development Studies, Norwegian University of Life Sciences, Norway.

Routledge Contemporary South Asia Series

1 **Pakistan**
Social and cultural transformations in a Muslim nation
Mohammad A. Qadeer

2 **Labor, Democratization and Development in India and Pakistan**
Christopher Candland

3 **China–India Relations**
Contemporary dynamics
Amardeep Athwal

4 **Madrasas in South Asia**
Teaching terror?
Jamal Malik

5 **Labor, Globalization and the State**
Workers, women and migrants confront neoliberalism
Edited by Debdas Banerjee and Michael Goldfield

6 **Indian Literature and Popular Cinema**
Recasting classics
Edited by Heidi R. M. Pauwels

7 **Islamist Militancy in Bangladesh**
A complex web
Ali Riaz

8 **Regionalism in South Asia**
Negotiating cooperation, institutional structures
Kishore C. Dash

9 **Federalism, Nationalism and Development**
India and the Punjab economy
Pritam Singh

10 **Human Development and Social Power**
Perspectives from South Asia
Ananya Mukherjee Reed

11 **The South Asian Diaspora**
Transnational networks and changing identities
Edited by Rajesh Rai and Peter Reeves

12 **Pakistan–Japan Relations**
Continuity and change in economic relations and security interests
Ahmad Rashid Malik

13 **Himalayan Frontiers of India**
Historical, geo-political and strategic perspectives
K. Warikoo

14 **India's Open-Economy Policy**
Globalism, rivalry, continuity
Jalal Alamgir

15 **The Separatist Conflict in Sri Lanka**
Terrorism, ethnicity, political economy
Asoka Bandarage

16 **India's Energy Security**
Edited by Ligia Noronha and Anant Sudarshan

17 **Globalization and the Middle Classes in India**
The social and cultural impact of neoliberal reforms
Ruchira Ganguly-Scrase and Timothy J. Scrase

18 **Water Policy Processes in India**
Discourses of power and resistance
Vandana Asthana

19 **Minority Governments in India**
The puzzle of elusive majorities
Csaba Nikolenyi

20 **The Maoist Insurgency in Nepal**
Revolution in the twenty-first century
Edited by Mahendra Lawoti and Anup K. Pahari

21 **Global Capital and Peripheral Labour**
The history and political economy of plantation workers in India
K. Ravi Raman

22 **Maoism in India**
Reincarnation of ultra-left wing extremism in the twenty-first century
Bidyut Chakrabarty and Rajat Kujur

23 **Economic and Human Development in Contemporary India**
Cronyism and fragility
Debdas Banerjee

24 **Culture and the Environment in the Himalaya**
Arjun Guneratne

25 **The Rise of Ethnic Politics in Nepal**
Democracy in the margins
Susan I. Hangen

26 **The Multiplex in India**
A cultural economy of urban leisure
Adrian Athique and Douglas Hill

27 **Tsunami Recovery in Sri Lanka**
Ethnic and regional dimensions
Dennis B. McGilvray and Michele R. Gamburd

28 **Development, Democracy and the State**
Critiquing the Kerala model of development
K. Ravi Raman

29 **Mohajir Militancy in Pakistan**
Violence and transformation in the Karachi conflict
Nichola Khan

30 **Nationbuilding, Gender and War Crimes in South Asia**
Bina D'Costa

31 **The State in India after Liberalization**
Interdisciplinary perspectives
Edited by Akhil Gupta and K. Sivaramakrishnan

32 **National Identities in Pakistan**
The 1971 war in contemporary Pakistani fiction
Cara Cilano

33 **Political Islam and Governance in Bangladesh**
Edited by Ali Riaz and C. Christine Fair

34 **Bengali Cinema**
'An other nation'
Sharmistha Gooptu

35 **NGOs in India**
The challenges of women's empowerment and accountability
Patrick Kilby

36 **The Labour Movement in the Global South**
Trade unions in Sri Lanka
S. Janaka Biyanwila

37 **Building Bangalore**
Architecture and urban transformation in India's Silicon Valley
John C. Stallmeyer

38 **Conflict and Peacebuilding in Sri Lanka**
Caught in the peace trap?
Edited by Jonathan Goodhand, Jonathan Spencer and Benedict Korf

39 **Microcredit and Women's Empowerment**
A case study of Bangladesh
Amunui Faraizi, Jim McAllister and Taskinur Rahman

40 **South Asia in the New World Order**
The role of regional cooperation
Shahid Javed Burki

41 **Explaining Pakistan's Foreign Policy**
Escaping India
Aparna Pande

42 **Development-induced Displacement, Rehabilitation and Resettlement in India**
Current issues and challenges
Edited by Sakarama Somayaji and Smrithi Talwar

43 **The Politics of Belonging in India**
Becoming *Adivasi*
Edited by Daniel J. Rycroft and Sangeeta Dasgupta

44 **Re-Orientalism and South Asian Identity Politics**
The oriental Other within
Edited by Lisa Lau and Ana Cristina Mendes

45 **Islamic Revival in Nepal**
Religion and a new nation
Megan Adamson Sijapati

46 **Education and Inequality in India**
A classroom view
Manabi Majumdar and Jos Mooij

47 **The Culturalization of Caste in India**
Identity and inequality in a multicultural age
Balmurli Natrajan

48 **Corporate Social Responsibility in India**
Bidyut Chakrabarty

49 **Pakistan's Stability Paradox**
Domestic, regional and international dimensions
Edited by Ashutosh Misra and Michael E. Clarke

50 **Transforming Urban Water Supplies in India**
The role of reform and partnerships in globalization
Govind Gopakumar

51 **South Asian Security**
Twenty-first-century discourse
Sagarika Dutt and Alok Bansal

52 **Non-discrimination and Equality in India**
Contesting boundaries of social justice
Vidhu Verma

53 **Being Middle-class in India**
A way of life
Henrike Donner

54 **Kashmir's Right to Secede**
A critical examination of contemporary theories of secession
Matthew J. Webb

55 **Bollywood Travels**
Culture, diaspora and border crossings in popular Hindi cinema
Rajinder Dudrah

56 **Nation, Territory, and Globalization in Pakistan**
Traversing the margins
Chad Haines

57 **The Politics of Ethnicity in Pakistan**
The Baloch, Sindhi and Mohajir ethnic movements
Farhan Hanif Siddiqi

58 **Nationalism and Ethnic Conflict**
Identities and mobilization after 1990
Edited by Mahendra Lawoti and Susan Hangen

59 **Islam and Higher Education**
Concepts, challenges and opportunities
Marodsilton Muborakshoeva

60 **Religious Freedom in India**
Sovereignty and (anti) conversion
Goldie Osuri

61 **Everyday Ethnicity in Sri Lanka**
Up-country Tamil identity politics
Daniel Bass

62 **Ritual and Recovery in Post-Conflict Sri Lanka**
Eloquent bodies
Jane Derges

63 **Bollywood and Globalisation**
The global power of popular Hindi cinema
Edited by David J. Schaefer and Kavita Karan

64 **Regional Economic Integration in South Asia**
Trapped in conflict?
Amita Batra

65 **Architecture and Nationalism in Sri Lanka**
The trouser under the cloth
Anoma Pieris

66 Civil Society and Democratization in India
Institutions, ideologies and interests
Sarbeswar Sahoo

67 Contemporary Pakistani Fiction in English
Idea, nation, state
Cara N. Cilano

68 Transitional Justice in South Asia
A study of Afghanistan and Nepal
Tazreena Sajjad

69 Displacement and Resettlement in India
The human cost of development
Hari Mohan Mathur

70 Water, Democracy and Neoliberalism in India
The power to reform
Vicky Walters

71 Capitalist Development in India's Informal Economy
Elisabetta Basile

72 Nation, Constitutionalism and Buddhism in Sri Lanka
Roshan de Silva Wijeyeratne

73 Counterinsurgency, Democracy, and the Politics of Identity in India
From warfare to welfare?
Mona Bhan

74 Enterprise Culture in Neoliberal India
Studies in youth, class, work and media
Edited by Nandini Gooptu

75 The Politics of Economic Restructuring in India
Economic governance and state spatial rescaling
Loraine Kennedy

76 The Other in South Asian Religion, Literature and Film
Perspectives on Otherism and Otherness
Edited by Diana Dimitrova

77 Being Bengali
At home and in the world
Edited by Mridula Nath Chakraborty

78 The Political Economy of Ethnic Conflict in Sri Lanka
Nikolaos Biziouras

79 Indian Arranged Marriages
A social psychological perspective
Tulika Jaiswal

80 Writing the City in British Asian Diasporas
Edited by Seán McLoughlin, William Gould, Ananya Jahanara Kabir and Emma Tomalin

81 Post-9/11 Espionage Fiction in the US and Pakistan
Spies and 'terrorists'
Cara Cilano

82 Left Radicalism in India
Bidyut Chakrabarty

83 "Nation-State" and Minority Rights in India
Comparative perspectives on Muslim and Sikh identities
Tanweer Fazal

84 **Pakistan's Nuclear Policy**
A minimum credible deterrence
Zafar Khan

85 **Imagining Muslims in South Asia and the Diaspora**
Secularism, religion, representations
Claire Chambers and Caroline Herbert

86 **Indian Foreign Policy in Transition**
Relations with South Asia
Arijit Mazumdar

87 **Corporate Social Responsibility and Development in Pakistan**
Nadeem Malik

88 **Indian Capitalism in Development**
Barbara Harriss-White and Judith Heyer

89 **Bangladesh Cinema and National Identity**
In search of the modern?
Zakir Hossain Raju

90 **Suicide in Sri Lanka**
The anthropology of an epidemic
Tom Widger

91 **Epigraphy and Islamic Culture**
Arabic and Persian inscriptions of Bengal and their historical and cultural implications
Mohammad Yusuf Siddiq

92 **Reshaping City Governance**
London, Mumbai, Kolkata, Hyderabad
Nirmala Rao

93 **The Indian Partition in Literature and Films**
History, politics, and aesthetics
Rini Bhattacharya Mehta and Debali Mookerjea-Leonard

94 **Development, Poverty and Power in Pakistan**
The impact of state and donor interventions on farmers
Syed Mohammad Ali

95 **Ethnic Subnationalist Insurgencies in South Asia**
Identities, interests and challenges to state authority
Edited by Jugdep S. Chima

96 **International Migration and Development in South Asia**
Edited by Md Mizanur Rahman and Tan Tai Yong

97 **Twenty-First-Century Bollywood**
Ajay Gehlawat

98 **Political Economy of Development in India**
Indigeneity in transition in the state of Kerala
Darley Kjosavik and Nadarajah Shanmugaratnam

Political Economy of Development in India

Indigeneity in transition in the state of Kerala

Darley Jose Kjosavik and Nadarajah Shanmugaratnam

LONDON AND NEW YORK

First published 2015 by Routledge

2 Park Square, Milton Park, Abingdon, Oxfordshire OX14 4RN
711 Third Avenue, New York, NY 10017

Routledge is an imprint of the Taylor & Francis Group, an informa business

First issued in paperback 2018

Copyright © 2015 Darley Jose Kjosavik and Nadarajah Shanmugaratnam

The right of Darley Jose Kjosavik and Nadarajah Shanmugaratnam to be identified as authors of this work has been asserted by them in accordance with sections 77 and 78 of the Copyright, Designs and Patents Act 1988.

All rights reserved. No part of this book may be reprinted or reproduced or utilised in any form or by any electronic, mechanical, or other means, now known or hereafter invented, including photocopying and recording, or in any information storage or retrieval system, without permission in writing from the publishers.

Notice:
Product or corporate names may be trademarks or registered trademarks, and are used only for identification and explanation without intent to infringe.

British Library Cataloguing in Publication Data
A catalogue record for this book is available from the British Library

Library of Congress Cataloging-in-Publication Data
A catalog record for this book has been applied for

ISBN: 978-1-138-84456-8 (hbk)
ISBN: 978-1-138-31960-8 (pbk)

Typeset in Times New Roman
by Apex CoVantage, LLC

Contents

List of tables — xii
Preface — xiii
Acknowledgements — xv

1. Indigeneity in transition: Locating indigenous people (*adivasis*) in the indigeneity–class intersection — 1

2. Property rights transitions and alienation of indigenous people's (*adivasis'*) land: Pre-colonial period — 19

3. Pauperisation and proletarianisation of *adivasis*: Colonial and post-colonial property relations — 36

4. Not a frozen class: Indigenous people (*adivasis*) in the Kerala model of development — 69

5. *Adivasis* in a development triangle: Decentralisation, neoliberalism and the Kerala model — 96

6. Contested frontiers: *Adivasi* land restitution law and settler narratives — 114

7. Re-articulating *adivasi* land rights and identities: Tensions in the indigeneity–class intersection — 128

8. Epilogue
The struggle continues: Indigeneity and social change — 145

Index — 159

Tables

2.1	Property rights in Wayanad during the Kottayam–Kurumbranad regime	30
3.1	Property rights to agricultural land in Wayanad (1805–1930)	44
3.2	Property rights to forests in Wayanad (1805–1930)	48
3.3	Property rights to agricultural land in Wayanad (1930–1947)	54
3.4	Decadal variation in the populations of Wayanad and Kerala from 1951–1991	57
3.5	Property rights to agricultural land in Wayanad (post-independence period)	60
4.1	Literacy and education levels in Kerala by population categories	73
4.2	Disaggregated data on school enrolment in Kerala (2000)	74
4.3	Landlessness among the *adivasi* households in rural Kerala	75
4.4	Extent of landlessness among *adivasis* in northern and southern Kerala	77
4.5	Restitution effected by March 1991	78

Preface

Indigeneity emerged as an analytical category with the rise of the indigenous peoples' movements in different parts of the world. As a politically loaded term, it has inspired considerable debate and competing interpretations. Nevertheless, it remains a key concept in studies of indigenous peoples' struggles for recognition and political, social and economic rights. We understand indigeneity as a dynamic concept with reference to processes of change driven by capitalist transitions under diverse national and local conditions in a globalising world. Indigeneity is in transition indeed. In this book, we theorise on the transition of indigeneity in terms of indigeneity–class intersection, while locating the processes in the larger political economy of change. In our view, it is important to move from the global to specific national and sub-national contexts to grasp how indigeneity is constructed and articulated as a political strategy and how it relates back to the global.

Informed by this perspective, this study examines the conditions of the *adivasis* of the south Indian state of Kerala. It provides an analysis of the history of dispossession of the *adivasis* of Wayanad in Kerala from pre-colonial through colonial and post-colonial times. Further, it analyses the *adivasis*' resistance to dispossession and marginalisation and the outcomes of struggles to reclaim land rights and for socio-economic advancement. We critically look at the impact of the Kerala model of development and the contradictions of neoliberalisation on the lives and livelihoods of the *adivasis*. A central argument of this book is that given the material deprivation and inability to be competitive in the labour market, the *adivasis* would fall back on land as the main demand for their socio-economic advancement, as shown by the widespread land occupation struggles in Wayanad and other *adivasi* areas in Kerala. At the same time, there are compelling objective reasons for them to find a common cause with other subordinate groups such as the working class, whose demands include higher wages, better working conditions, freedoms and opportunities for human development and social mobility. This issue deserves the serious attention of the Left and other emancipatory movements in Kerala.

Our research has drawn inspiration from the sustained struggles of the *adivasis* of Wayanad. We are ever grateful to them for sharing their experiences.

Darley Jose Kjosavik and
N. Shanmugaratnam
Department of International
Environment and Development Studies
Norwegian University of Life
Sciences (NMBU)
December 2014

Acknowledgements

This book has drawn upon material from within Darley Jose Kjosavik and N. Shanmugaratnam, 2007, "Property Rights Dynamics and Indigenous Communities in Highland Kerala, South India: An Institutional-Historical Perspective", *Modern Asian Studies*, 41: 1183–1260, published by Cambridge University Press and reproduced with permission.

We acknowledge the permission granted by Taylor & Francis to draw upon and reproduce material from the following publications:

Kjosavik, D. J. and Shanmugaratnam, N., 2004, 'Integration or Exclusion? Locating Indigenous Peoples in the Development Process of Kerala, South India'. *Forum for Development Studies,* 31(2): 231–273.

Kjosavik, D. J., 2010, 'Politicising Development: Re-Imagining Indigenous Peoples Land Rights and Identities in Highland Kerala, South India'. *Forum for Development Studies*, 37(2): 243–268.

The permission granted by John Wiley & Sons to draw upon and reproduce material from Kjosavik, D. J. and Shanmugaratnam, N., 2006, 'Between Decentralized Planning and Neoliberalism: Challenges for the Survival of the Indigenous People of Kerala, India', *Social Policy and Administration*, 40(6): 632–651 is duly acknowledged.

We acknowledge the permission granted by John Wiley & Sons to draw upon and reproduce material from Kjosavik, D. J. and Shanmugaratnam, N., 2007, 'Between Decentralized Planning and Neoliberalism: Challenges for the Survival of the Indigenous People of Kerala, India', in Giarchi, G. G. (ed.), *Challenging Welfare Issues in the Global Countryside*: 53–71.

Darley Jose Kjosavik and
N. Shanmugaratnam

1 Indigeneity in transition

Locating indigenous people (*adivasis*) in the indigeneity–class intersection

Introduction

Indigenous peoples comprise more than 370 million persons living in more than 90 countries across the globe today. They account for 5% of the world's population. However, in the absence of a universally accepted definition of indigenous peoples, their current population estimates are based on self-identification and the formal recognition of certain groups as indigenous peoples or tribes by governments. The issue of defining indigenous peoples remains contentious, and we shall be addressing it later in this chapter.

In spite of their historical, cultural and geographic diversities, communities recognised as indigenous and tribal peoples share common experiences of conquest and resistance in modern times. Their histories are marked by colonisation, dispossession, deprivation and suppression of their collective identities. On the other hand, they have also been resisting the overpowering invasive forces, though with the predictable outcomes of unequal contests. In the Global South, indigenous and tribal communities have been continuously subjected to top-down, and often violent, processes of post-colonial state and nation building and uneven development and underdevelopment. They were drawn by these processes into complex and contradictory dynamics of assimilation, ethnic differentiation, changing landscapes, class formation, marginalisation and exclusion. These communities are not isolated entities, and indigeneity itself has become a dynamic and contested category in a globalising world.

However, the problems of indigenous peoples received little attention from the international community until the advent and rise of indigenous peoples' organisations and the indigenous peoples' movement in the 1970s. Before this, there was the ILO Convention No. 107 of 1957 'Concerning the Protection and Integration of Indigenous and Other Tribal and Semi Tribal Populations in Independent Countries', which was criticised as assimilationist by the indigenous movement (UN, 2009). Subsequently, in 1989 the International Labour Organization (ILO) adopted Convention No. 169 which more specifically addressed issues such as citizenship and human rights by focusing on non-discrimination, recognition of the cultural and other specificities of indigenous and tribal peoples, consultation and participation and the right to decide priorities for development (ILO, 1989).

2 Indigeneity in transition

In 2007, the UN General Assembly adopted the 'Declaration on the Rights of Indigenous Peoples' in response to sustained actions by indigenous people's movements. Significantly, representatives of indigenous peoples had an opportunity to participate in the drafting of the declaration, which affirms that 'indigenous people are equal to all other people' and incorporates a wide range of rights and fundamental freedoms in forty-six articles. While recognising their right to self-determination, the declaration states that 'control by indigenous peoples over developments affecting them and their lands, territories and resources will enable them to maintain and strengthen their institutions, cultures, traditions, and to promote their development in accordance with their aspirations and needs' (UN, 2007: 13). A leader of an indigenous peoples' organisation praised the declaration as 'the most comprehensive international instrument addressing the rights of indigenous peoples' (ibid: 41).

Indeed, the UN Declaration represents an important milestone in the struggles of the indigenous peoples of the world. However, its effectiveness as an instrument in achieving desired results depends on the political environment and the real extent of enfranchisement of the indigenous peoples in particular national contexts. In the South today, many indigenous communities lack protection against powerful global and local forces of primitive accumulation, or accumulation by dispossession (Harvey, 2005), while they are still struggling to overcome their historical disadvantages. Even before the recent trend of large-scale land grabbing, indigenous peoples in many countries of the South were dispossessed and displaced by major dam building and development projects and enclosures of tracts of land as nature reserves and protected areas. The following finding of the World Commission on Dams (WCD) is also generally applicable to the impact of other major development projects and land acquisitions on the lives of indigenous peoples:

> Due to neglect and lack of capacity to secure justice because of structural inequities, cultural dissonance, discrimination and economic and political marginalisation, indigenous and tribal peoples have suffered disproportionately from the negative impacts of large dams, while often being excluded from sharing in the benefits.
> (WCD, 2000: 144)

The outcome of mass dispossession and displacement caused by colonialism and post-colonial development and modernisation can best be described as a combination of pauperisation and proletarianisation, a phenomenon experienced not only by indigenous peoples but also by peasants and other land-based communities (Shanmugaratnam, 1985).[1] Dispossession and displacement deprived the affected indigenous communities of their means of livelihood and habitat, but did not necessarily throw all of them into a labour market created by the demand for labour from potential employers. Large sections of the victims generally found themselves struggling to eke out an existence from cultivating the marginal lands and from hunting and gathering in forests they could find access to (often 'illegally'), while some joined the growing ranks of the footloose proletariat dependent on casual employment as lowly paid, unskilled and unorganised rural and urban workers. Dispossession and displacement caused livelihood loss and disintegration of their communal life without integrating the vast majority of them into the mainstream of social change and development. Such a situation may better be described as pauperisation or emiseration. Their conditions showed some signs of improvement in terms of livelihood opportunities and social advancement when they were targeted as beneficiaries of affirmative action.

These and other changes in the states of being of indigenous people have compelled researchers to revisit the discourse on indigeneity (Beteille, 1998; Karlsson and Subba, 2006; Kjosavik, 2011). We shall presently address this issue with reference to the Indian context. It is worth noting that the problems highlighted so far expose the real obstacles to the indigenous and tribal peoples' freedom to exercise the rights enshrined in the UN Declaration of 2007 or in the national constitutions and legal enactments of certain countries. The experience so far shows that the existence of legal provisions to protect the interests of the indigenous people is a necessary, but not a sufficient, condition to ensure their sustained socio-economic advancement.

Indigeneity – A contested yet politically significant category

Indigeneity has been characterised as 'a travelling discourse that has emerged and developed in dialogue with various social movements and non-indigenous actors, and not something that reach us straight from the mud-hut, bush or wherever one is to locate the "authentic" tribal spokesperson' (Karlsson, 2006: 55). The discourse has given the term 'indigenous peoples' a certain conceptuality that serves as a powerful basis for political mobilisation and collective action, international standard setting, transnational networking and programming the activities of inter-governmental and non-governmental bodies (Kingsbury, 1998).

Indigeneity is a term that emerged in the process of constructing the identity of the indigenous peoples in their political struggle in a particular historical context. The context was a moment when the voices of millions of people 'without history' were being heard and taken note of by the world. The most fundamental claim of these peoples was that they were the first or original settlers and, hence, the collective owners of the territory they inhabited and governed through their own institutions and that their lands had been appropriated by colonialists and post-colonial states and corporate interests with far-reaching consequences for their identity, autonomy and way of life. The UN Declaration cast the demands of the indigenous peoples in a paradigm of rights, including the highly politically charged collective right to self-determination. The various discussions and debates on the meanings and possible definitions of terms such as indigenousness and indigenous peoples led to the conclusion by the Working Group on Indigenous Populations in its fifteenth session in 1997 that it was 'neither desirable nor necessary to elaborate a universal definition of indigenous peoples' and that such a definition was not necessary for the adoption of the UN Declaration, which actually underlined the importance of self-identification, 'that indigenous people themselves define their own identity as indigenous' (UN, 2009: 5).

Thus it is imperative to move from the global to specific national and subnational contexts to understand how indigeneity is constructed and articulated as a political strategy and how it relates back to the global. Indigeneity is a dynamic category, and its strategic use and importance vary, depending on several factors. Of fundamental importance is the legal status of groups self-identifying themselves as indigenous peoples and the availability of democratic space for them to act collectively to pursue their interests. This depends on the nature of the country's political system, particularly on the processes of state building and nation formation in ethnically diverse societies. Of equal significance are the development policies and processes that impact the social institutions, livelihoods and territoriality of indigenous peoples. These sets of factors are interrelated and are connected in various ways to other factors operating globally, such as the hegemonic models of state building or state restructuring and development, and the workings of transnational capital.

The rise of neoliberal globalisation has contributed to social differentiation characterised by widespread pauperisation and proletarianisation of indigenous communities through dispossession and displacement in the Global South. It is not accidental that indigenous movements gathered momentum as the adverse socio-economic consequences of neoliberal economic policies increased in recent decades. The political articulation of indigeneity in terms of human rights, territoriality and identity is the response of the affected indigenous peoples to this disenfranchisement in their particular national contexts. There is evidence that indigenous groups often form strategic political alliances with other disenfranchised groups, which suggests that claims based on indigeneity can be expressed in non-sectarian terms to make common cause with other marginalised social groups affected by the same internal and external forces. On the positive side, globalisation has been facilitating the internationalisation of the demands and struggles of its indigenous victims. On the other hand, governments and multilateral organisations seek to draw indigenous communities into the mainstream of market-friendly development through special programmes linked to the Millennium Development Goals (MDGs) and similar programmes. Apparently, the overall objective of these programmes is to endow marginalised sections of society with capacities to meet their needs through participation in the market economy. In reality, however, these interventions have not been able to counter the exclusionary forces of neoliberalisation.

The global and local political economic contexts in which indigenous people find themselves are dynamic and complex indeed. And the dynamics of these contexts are principally driven by forces of capitalist transition characterised by changes in property relations, social differentiation, commodification and accumulation. In such a situation, as a dynamic category, indigeneity is in transition too.

Indigeneity in transition: Intersection with class

The identity construction of indigenous people is taking place in a context of transition in which indigeneity intersects with class, ethnicity and nation. In the South, indigenous people are being incorporated into ongoing projects of post-colonial state and nation building. Construction of ethnic and other collective identities takes place within this larger setting of change. In this chapter, we explore in some detail the indigeneity–class intersection with a view to understanding the political economy of indigeneity's transition. With a rather long history of state interventions addressing the problems of 'Scheduled Tribes' (ST) (*adivasis*), and many development and conservation projects impacting their lives and livelihoods, India provides a good example to examine the transitional character of indigeneity. Before looking at the Indian experience with reference to the case of Kerala, we briefly discuss the concept of intersectionality.

The concept of intersectionality was used by black feminists such as Patricia Hill Collins (Collins, 1998a,b) and Kimberle Crenshaw (Crenshaw (1991) to understand the social location of African-American women in the United States. The argument is that within unjust power relations, markers of power such as race, gender and ethnicity intersect to give rise to social institutions that construct groups, which in turn become defined by these characteristics. These groups are hierarchically related in the sense that some groups define and rule other groups Collins (1998a). 'As a heuristic device, intersectionality references the ability of social phenomena such as race, class, and gender to mutually construct one another' (Collins, 1998a: 205). Drawing on the notion of intersectionality, Kjosavik (2011) argues that indigenous people are situated in a social location at the intersection of class and indigeneity, and this social location is key to understanding the current development dilemmas of these peoples.

> Intersectionality thus provides an interpretive framework for thinking through how intersections of class and indigeneity shape the experiences of indigenous people across social and geographical contexts. It is to be emphasised that the communities that exist at this intersection are not theoretical categories but are historically constructed through material-social processes.
>
> (Kjosavik, 2011: 121)

The existence of indigenous people at the class-indigeneity intersection is subject to processes leading to a state of double alienation in the sense of separation from their own means of production (land, forests and other natural resources) and alienation from the product of their labour consequent to their insertion in market relations (Kjosavik, 2005, 2011). In reality, however, this trend involves a range of observable social locations that characterise the transition, which is not a linear process. Indigenous people displaced from their habitat and deprived of livelihood opportunities may turn into migrant workers, sex workers and beggars. Some may even take to petty crimes to survive. There are those who stay on in their native areas and engage in seasonal wage labour and farming on accessible marginal lands and gathering for subsistence. A minority may have moved permanently into the ranks of the industrial proletariat and share their fellow workers' concerns about employment security, real wages and conditions of labour. Some may have managed to achieve upward social mobility into the 'middle class' through access to education and skill development. However, unemployment, livelihood insecurity and deprivation are general conditions of existence for the vast majority who are thrown into the combined processes of pauperisation and proletarianisation. Such conditions reinforce the indigenous people's desire and determination to struggle for their lost land rights and livelihoods. This is indeed the general case with indigenous people in the South, including India. On the other hand, the same conditions may drive them to join hands with other marginalised groups, particularly in rural areas, in organised collective action. Political mobilisation plays a key role in shaping the alliances, directions and modes of struggle. We shall be addressing this aspect with reference to the Kerala context in a moment. Our contention is that indigenous people's material and social experiences at the indigeneity–class intersection are critical to an understanding of indigeneity's transition.

The Indian context

The term '*adivasi*' commonly used in all the Indian languages, originates from Sanskrit – *adi* meaning 'beginning' or 'earlier times', and *vasi* meaning 'resident of'. It is in a way similar to the word 'aborigine' or 'indigenous', meaning 'existed from the beginning' in a territory, landscape or geographic formation. In colonial times, the *adivasis* were officially grouped under a general category of 'backward classes'. The Indian Constitution does not use the term indigenous but recognises *adivasis* as STs. There are more than 700 STs in India at present. However, the word *adivasi* was first articulated by political activists in central India in the 1930s (Bates, 1995), in the livelihood struggles of the so-called tribal communities against the colonial state and its colluders, that is, the dominant classes. The *adivasi* ideology – that is, in today's terms, the ideology of indigeneity, was articulated into the tribal movement. This was an act intended to help them make sense of the historical marginalisation process and its linkages to the existing socio-economic conditions of the *adivasis*, thereby constituting them as political subjects. The articulation of this term by the *adivasis* and the activists could be interpreted as a political tactic to forge alliances and solidarities among the various tribal groups that inhabited the fragmented landscape of India. The subsequent struggles of the tribal peoples in the colonial and post-colonial periods were orchestrated around their identity articulated as *adivasis*. In a similar vein, the concept of 'indigenous peoples' was first articulated in the 1970s by the North American Indians in their struggle for self-reliance and access and control over land and other natural resources (Gray, 1997; Tauli-Corpuz, 1997).

Officially, the classification of oppressed castes as Scheduled Castes (SCs) and *adivasis* as Scheduled Tribes (STs) in the Indian Constitution was meant to target them for affirmative action and to integrate them into the socio-economic mainstream through special development programmes.[2] Articles 342 and 366 of the Indian Constitution have provisions for the designation and legalisation of particular communities as STs,[3] although the constitution does not state the criteria for defining a community as an ST. However, according to the Ministry of Tribal Affairs, the criteria 'for specification of a community as scheduled tribes are indications of primitive traits, distinctive culture, geographical isolation, shyness of contact with the community at large, and backwardness.'[4] Obviously, these criteria define *adivasis* as isolated 'pre-modern' people who do not fit into a 'modern' society, and affirmative action is viewed as a means to facilitate their modernisation and integration. The ground realities, however, are riddled with contradictions. In their self-identification, *adivasis* see themselves as the original, or first inhabitants of the lands that have been taken away or are being taken away from them. The articulation of their identity in their struggle for land is a response to dispossession and disempowerment caused by the processes of modernisation. Politically, their strategies are meant to reclaim their land, but not to return to a life of isolation. In reality, their social exclusion isolates and denies them the opportunity to participate in modernisation as free subjects and enhance their capabilities. The centrality of land in the *adivasis*' struggle may set them apart from social groups such as the urban working class, whose struggles are in general centred on better wages and working and living conditions. The *adivasis*' demand for land is impelled by their state of dispossession and pauperisation in a situation of unfinished proletarianisation. Their aspiration is not to become wage workers, but to secure land-based livelihoods for their further socio-economic advancement.

Policies of affirmative action and democratisation have opened up spaces for *adivasis* to raise their voice in organised ways and exercise collective agency. The positive effects of affirmative action need to be weighed against the adverse consequences of displacement and dispossession and uneven development of capitalism in India. There are, however, variations between states in the actual implementation of affirmative action and the socio-economic impact of development processes on the lives and livelihoods of *adivasis*, as well as the latter's capacity for mobilisation and alliance formation to struggle for their rights. We now turn to the Kerala context to elaborate on this.

The Kerala model of development

Kerala, as part of the Indian Union, followed a development approach in tune with the government of India in regard to indigenous communities. However, within the framework of India's quasi-federal polity, the state of Kerala has been tracing a development path of its own, which has come to be known as the 'Kerala model of development'. The Kerala model was a product of radical reforms carefully designed and institutionalised by the Communist Party of India during its tenure as the state's democratically elected government during various terms since 1957. These reforms enjoyed the support of the workers' and peasants' movements, led by the Communist Party, which had been demanding radical reforms, and of other civil society organisations, especially the Left-oriented progressive writers' and artists' groups, teachers and other intellectuals who were either active party supporters or sympathisers.

Much has been written and debated on the Kerala model of development by social scientists and development practitioners. The literature generally focuses on the development impacts of the model at the macro level – that is, the state level. Kerala has a stratified socio-economic structure with regard to class, caste,

8   *Indigeneity in transition*

ethnicity (indigenous peoples/tribes/*adivasis*) and gender. Studies of how the development model, as conceived and practised, impacted specific social categories – particularly indigenous peoples – are rare. Existing studies confine themselves to selected policies and their impact on these communities.[5]

Kerala embarked on her new 'tryst with destiny' in 1957 when the Communist Party of India was elected to power in this South Indian state.[6] The government launched a series of radical reforms with the objectives of achieving equity and social justice, together with economic growth. Large-scale investments in the social sector and a radical redistribution of agricultural land – the principal means of production in rural Kerala, where the vast majority of the state's people lived – have resulted in exceptional achievements in social development, although economic growth remained relatively low. This development pattern, characterised by high levels of social development and low levels of economic growth and per-capita income, came to be known as the 'Kerala model of development' in international development debates. The point of departure for scholarly debates on Kerala's development experience was a study by the Centre for Development Studies (CDS), Trivandrum. The study highlighted that Kerala had achieved a relatively high degree of human development and quality of life, in spite of low per-capita incomes and consumer expenditure, and this was attributed to the development policies followed by the state, with a thrust on redistribution (United Nations, 1975; CDS, 1977). Since then, the subject has been debated at national and international forums.

Franke and Chasin (1989) sought to place the Kerala experience in the context of theoretical debates on development. Using four indicators of 'quality of life' (adult literacy rate, life expectancy, infant mortality rate and birth rate) vis-à-vis per-capita Gross State Domestic Product (GSDP),[7] they compared Kerala with India, other low-income countries and the United States, and concluded that Kerala's indicators are closer to those of the United States despite the low GSDP. Adult literacy rate, life expectancy, infant mortality rate and birth rate could be considered reliable measures of the impact of social and economic development, while a high-level per-capita income can hide gross inequalities (Franke and Chasin, 1989). With an annual per-capita income of US$438 (2000–2001), Kerala has achieved a sex ratio of 1,058 females per 1,000 males (2001), an adult literacy rate of 91% (2000–2001), a life expectancy of 73.3 years (1999), an infant mortality rate of 14 per 1,000 births (1998) and a birth rate of 18.2 per 1,000 population. At the national level, with an annual per-capita income of US$343, the indicators are as follows: a sex ratio of 933 females per 1000 males, an adult literacy rate of 65.38%, life expectancy of 61.1 years, infant mortality of 70 per 1,000 births, and birth rate of 26.4 per 1,000 population. Kerala ranks ninth among the Indian states for per-capita income, but first for all the other indicators. It also ranks first in the Human Development Index (0.64 as compared with 0.47 for the country as a whole in 2000–2001).[8]

Agarwal (1997) worked out a composite index for assessing the vulnerability of various states in India to gender, environment and poverty variables – the Gender Environment Poverty (Vulnerability) Index. The variables used were sex ratio, rural female literacy rate, total rural fertility rates, annual rainfall, percentage of forest area and percentage of rural non-poor. Kerala showed the lowest vulnerability index in 1971(0.34) and 1991(0.28). Punjab, the state with the highest per-capita income, had a vulnerability index of 0.69 in 1971 and 0.63 in 1991. The figures for India showed an increase from 0.64 in 1971 to 0.67 in 1991. These figures highlight the fact that Kerala's redistributive policies and social-sector investments have yielded remarkable results with regard to women, the environment and poverty.[9]

A social democratisation process

The vision for post-colonial India was reflected in the constitution – democratic secularism, political pluralism and a federal polity that ensured a certain extent of autonomy to the states. Further, a state-led mixed economy model with Central Plans (Five-Year Plans) was envisaged by the national leadership of the Congress Party. The constitution and the broad national development vision provided a favourable environment for political mobilisation of people and institutional reforms in India. The leaders of the Communist Party of India (CPI) saw the opportunities for radical distributive reforms in this environment. It was in Kerala where they got their first opportunity to utilise the provisions of the country's constitution to institutionalise a series of reforms. In 1957, the year when the Communist Party was elected by the people of Kerala to form the government, the politburo of the CPI declared that the parliament and the state legislatures had become the most important forums for 'fighting for the cause of the people and the country' (Sathyamurthy, 1982: 6).[10] When it became the ruling party in Kerala in 1957, the party already had years of experience in mobilising and organising workers and peasants and agitating for democratic reforms, which included workers' rights and land reforms. The Communists used the opportunity they had as the ruling party to legislate for the basic reforms they had been fighting for. Thus began a process of institutional change aimed at greater equity and social security, a process that can be more aptly described as the social democratisation of the state of Kerala. However, this process was subject to subversion and interruption during the periods when the Communist Party was not the ruling party in Kerala. The Communists of Kerala could be said to have carried out social democratisation, which, while institutionalising some fundamental reforms in areas such as workers' rights, ownership of agricultural land, healthcare and education, moved spasmodically over time in the parliamentary democracy that is India.

Adivasis in the Kerala model of development

In this book we examine the development dilemmas of the indigenous people (*adivasis*) of Kerala. The goal in doing so is, first and foremost, to draw attention to the fact that the political economic processes that create wealth simultaneously produce poverty and deprivation. That the underdevelopment and marginality of the *adivasis* is not an accident, but rather a product of the historical trajectory of development, receives little attention in debates on *adivasi* development in general, or in the debates on the *adivasi* land question. Drawing on a wide range of theoretical and conceptual tools, this book addresses *adivasi* development in relation to the general development experience of Kerala, the new challenges posed by neoliberalism and decentralisation, the historical processes of the alienation of these communities from their resources and means of production and the ongoing struggles to reclaim rights to land. In the same vein, we critically examine the Forest Rights Act of 2006 and the National Rural Employment Guarantee Programme and their effects on the dynamics of the indigeneity–class intersection.

Kerala's unique development experience, as discussed earlier, is characterised by high levels of social development at relatively low levels of economic growth. Our interest in the present work was triggered by the question of why the indigenous people as a group is disproportionately lagging behind in socio-economic development as compared to the rest of the Kerala society. Was the Kerala model helpful at all in addressing their development question? If so, in what way? If not, why? If it was helpful in some respects, were there some conceptual and policy fault lines in the model that prevented the *adivasis* from taking full advantage as compared to other groups such as the oppressed castes? Why and how are the conditions of underdevelopment of the *adivasis* reproduced? Given this situation, what are the impacts of the current neoliberal policies and the shift from state-led to market-led decentralisation on the prospects of *adivasi* development? In the last three decades, the *adivasi* land question has been much debated in Kerala; reclaiming land rights was the issue around which *adivasi* politics was articulated. The issue of land rights is central to *adivasi* development. The question then arises as to how they came to lose control over the vast land and forest resources they controlled. What were the historical-institutional-political processes through which resources and the means of production were alienated from these communities? The government of Kerala enacted a law in 1975 to restore the alienated land to the *adivasis*. Why was the law not implemented? Were the provisions of the law adequate to address the land question of the different *adivasi* groups? How are the *adivasis* responding to the denial of justice? How are the current struggles for rights to land politically articulated by the *adivasis* and contested by the settlers? How is the state responding to the indigenous land question?

We believe that the Kerala model of development has made substantial contributions to equity and social justice, including the rights and welfare of the exploited, oppressed and marginalised classes and social groups. This model of development was, however, dominated by a rather narrow class discourse, which had adverse consequences for addressing the specific development issues of the indigenous communities, as most policies were predominantly informed by this discourse. The historical-material location of the indigenous people at the intersection of class and indigeneity, it would seem, was not given due regard in the Kerala model. This book seeks to problematise the development/marginalisation of the indigenous people (*adivasis*) of Kerala within a broad political economy perspective. Simultaneous production of wealth and underdevelopment is an inherent nature of capitalist development, particularly so in societies characterised by historical inequalities and institutionalised hierarchies of power and access to resources. As observed by James Ferguson:

> [D]isconnection and abjection... occur within capitalism, not outside it. They refer to processes through which global capitalism constitutes its categories of social and geographical membership and privilege by constructing and maintaining a category of absolute non-membership: a holding tank for those turned away at the 'development' door...
>
> (Ferguson, 1999: 242)

This book deals with the *adivasis* – communities that are subject to alienation from their means of production, abjection, pauperisation and proletarianisation at the intersection of indigeneity and class. While the empirical study was conducted at the local level with specific *adivasi* communities, its analytical connections to the larger political economic processes make it of general relevance to social groups that are located at similar intersections within the regional, national and global political economy.

Entering Wayanad: The fieldwork

Wayanad district of northern Kerala was selected for fieldwork, as we deemed it to be an appropriate location for the purpose of our research due to various historical contingencies. This district has the largest indigenous population in Kerala (17% of the total population of the district), and it was under British colonial rule from 1805 to 1947. The intensity of in-migration of planters and peasants to this district had been one of the highest in Kerala.[11] There are six different *adivasi* communities in Wayanad – Kurumar, Kurichiyar, Paniyar, Adiyar, Kattunaicker and Oorali. These communities had historically different relations to land and forests. Kurumar and Kurichiyar were traditionally agriculturists, Paniyar and Adiyar were agrestic slaves and bonded labourers, Kattunaicker were hunters and gatherers and Uralis were artisans. Paniyar constitute the largest *adivasi* community in Wayanad (45%), followed by Kurumar (20%), Kurichiyar (17%) and Kattunaicker (11%).[12] Adiyar and *Uralis* constitute the remaining 7%. For this study we chose three communities, Kurumar, Paniyar and Kattunaicker, who have had historically different relations to land and forests, as this would allow us to trace the different trajectories of development of the *adivasis* and connect these to the wider processes of transition.

Irulam Village, which is part of Poothady *Panchayat*, was selected for detailed field investigation. A 'village' in Kerala does not mean a cluster of settlements; it is the lowest-level unit of revenue administration. *Panchayat* is the local self-government unit, and it is also the lowest-level planning and development unit. A *panchayat* may include one or more entire revenue villages or comprise parts of two or three revenue villages. Poothady *Panchayat* comprises the whole of Irulam Village, Poothady Village and a small part of Nadavayal Village. The main reason for selecting Irulam was that all three *adivasi* communities – Kurumar, Paniyar

12 *Indigeneity in transition*

and Kattunaicker – whom we intended to focus on in this study, live in substantial numbers in this village. This is also a village with a considerable number of unsettled land disputes between *adivasis* and settlers. The village lies in the north-central part of Wayanad district. It has a total geographic area of 4,925 hectares, classified into forest land (38%),[13] garden land (55%) and wetland (7%). Forest land is further classified into natural forest (25%), teak plantation (57%) and coffee plantation (18%).[14] The total population of the village is 18,822, of which *adivasis* constitute 15.05%.[15]

We adopted a case study approach for gathering the data required for the study. This involves a combination of methods, including in-depth interviews with key resource persons, focus group discussions, invoking collective memory through group discussions and oral histories. Secondary data sources, internal (within the communities) and external (outside the communities) narratives are also employed.[16] Our method was unambiguously eclectic, as it allowed us the necessary flexibility to understand the complex synchronic and diachronic processes. Primary data collection involved several field visits at different times between August 1998 and December 2003. The data was updated through field visits in January 2006, February 2010, December 2012, July 2013 and December 2013. We also drew on our close knowledge of Kerala society and its socio-economic changes since the advent of the Kerala model.

An overview of the chapters

This book has eight chapters, including the introduction. Chapter 2 looks into the pre-colonial origins of the processes of marginalisation of Wayanad's three indigenous communities, namely Kurumar, who have traditionally been agriculturalists; Paniyar, who had been agrestic slaves and bonded labourers; and Kattunaicker, the traditional hunters and gatherers. It provides an account of the early phases of the indigeneity–class intersection in processual terms. The indigenous people of Wayanad were being subjected to external interventions that changed the existing property relations and the social arrangements between the three communities, while incorporating them into new hierarchies of power and authority as tenants, workers and agrestic slaves and bonded labourers. These processes created the historical socio-economic setting for the onset of pauperisation and proletarianisation in more modern times. Chapter 3 continues the historical analysis of land dynamics into the colonial and post-colonial periods by focusing on land policies and governance structures and practices. It lays bare the prime motive of the colonial policy to take fuller control over land resources and their utilisation in order to raise revenue and promote commercial plantations while at the same time imposing a more effective administrative system. It shows how the colonial rulers created a local ally in the form of a class of upper-caste land owners whose interests were closely linked to theirs, while turning the indigenous people into insecure tenants who had to pay their rent to the newly created landlords, and taxes in cash to the colonial state. The chapter provides a detailed empirical analysis of the factors that contributed to the combined processes of pauperisation and proletarianisation, both during the colonial period and after, while illuminating the point that the class-indigeneity intersection involves a variety of transitional social locations, with pauperisation being the dominant tendency. The analysis raises questions regarding the inclusivity of the Kerala model of development, which are addressed in Chapter 4.

Chapter 4 takes a critical look at the Kerala model of development and analyses how the workings of the model, in conjunction with forces external to it, have impacted the development of these communities. The radical policies initiated by the leftist government in 1957, which became the defining characteristics of Kerala's development, led to high levels of social development at relatively low levels of economic growth. The question we address in this chapter is how this development process dealt with the *adivasi* question. With regard to the general development strategy of the state, Kerala took advantage of the autonomy it enjoyed as a state in a federal polity and attempted a departure from the mainstream growth-led development path to a predominantly distribution-based development. However, with regard to the *adivasis*, Kerala had to follow the guidelines of the federal government at the centre, which were not so conducive to their development for various reasons. It would also seem that Kerala's Left policymakers were influenced by the notion that the *adivasis* were a 'frozen class', which might have prevented them from more fully comprehending the particularities of the *adivasi* question. Our analysis shows that the *adivasis* have made both economic and social gains, albeit to a limited extent, through the workings of the Kerala model, particularly in education and access to land. Our contention is that although they are still an 'outlier' category, they have not been excluded from the development approach followed by the Kerala model. The chapter sheds light on the forces that precipitated the setback of the Kerala model and its consequences for the *adivasis*. We have highlighted the case of land reforms and how the attempts to expropriate surplus land to be distributed to the *adivasis* were thwarted, despite the best efforts of the protagonists. The *adivasis* of Kerala are now trapped in a triangle – the Kerala model of development, neoliberal policies and decentralised planning. While the development that unfolded through the Kerala model helped the integration process to a considerable extent, the workings of the liberalisation and structural adjustment programmes have shown strong exclusionary tendencies.

The impact of decentralised planning and neoliberalism on the conditions of the indigenous people is the subject of Chapter 5. We critically examine the emerging trends in decentralisation and neoliberal policies and their consequences for indigenous communities in Kerala. The decentralised planning implemented by the leftist government in 1996, through the People's Planning Campaign (PPC), was an attempt to make the development process more inclusive of the marginal groups, such as indigenous communities, and to contain the 'new social exclusion' that had started setting in. We look at the means and processes by which the PPC had envisaged and institutionalised the inclusion of the indigenous communities. In the vision of decentralisation followed by the leftists, the state had a direct role in empowering the people at the grassroots level. The negative effects of liberalisation, particularly in the agricultural sector, have contributed to further marginalisation of the *adivasis*. The amended decentralisation introduced by the Congress government in 2001 resulted in a decreased role and space for the state bureaucracy in mobilising people for planning and implementing projects at the local level. At the same time, the bureaucracy intervened in ways that undermined the powers of the local bodies. We argue that shifts in political power and the change of government in 2001 led to an environment that was more favourable to the entrepreneurial class and less helpful to the marginalised in general and the *adivasis* in particular. The chapter shows how, by making certain amendments to the radical provisions of the original decentralised planning, the Congress coalition government has, to a large extent, reversed the control over resources and decision-making powers that were extended to the local bodies by the Left coalition government, thus undermining the transparency, accountability and improved governance fostered by the PPC. These changes have also reduced the space for indigenous people's participation and increased the power of the bureaucracy. Such measures have adversely affected the indigenous people's agency and their chances of defining their own development priorities. The *adivasis* are now caught in the dynamics of Kerala's politics and the larger neoliberal politics.

Chapter 6 examines the Land Restitution Law of 1975 and the narratives of settlers and their fight to retain the land they had acquired and developed. It shows that the Land Restitution Law of 1975 was flawed in that, even if implemented, it would have benefitted only a minority of *adivasis* who had historically owned land and who could provide proof of the same. However, the implementation of this law was contested by the organised power of the settlers. We discuss the powerful narratives of the settlers and the arguments for their hard-earned rights in land, which they defend at any cost. This led to the enactment of a series of legislations, which could be interpreted as being more sensitive to the differential locations of the *adivasis* in the indigeneity–class intersection. However, these interventions generated their own contradictions which we address in Chapter 7.

Chapter 7 deals with the land struggles of *adivasis* in the changing political contexts in Wayanad and Kerala in the last three decades. The identities came to be reconstituted and articulated as *adivasis* encompassing the different communities, while at the same time projecting their specific identities as Kurumar, Paniyar, Kattunaicker and so on. These articulations, however, are closely interlinked with their historical-material conditions of existence. The chapter highlights the continuing resistance of the indigenous people to pauperisation and proletarianisation and their demand for land as the solution. The *adivasis*' demand for redistribution of state plantation land posed an obstacle to forging alliances with non-*adivasi* sections of plantation workers' unions. While this was an instance of conflict of interest between the two subordinated groups, there have been other instances of solidarity and collective action across the *adivasi*/non-*adivasi* divide. In the Muthanga struggle, the *adivasis* were projecting an image of their future based on individual land ownership, along with access to opportunities for human development and upward social mobility. The struggle was indeed not to reinvent a past, but to secure the material basis and human freedoms for a better future. The legislative and policy interventions of the state and the sustained struggles and aspirations of the *adivasis* continuously impact the dynamics of the indigeneity–class intersection.

The final chapter provides an update of the recent developments concerning *adivasi* land issues in Wayanad and reflects on the broader problems of the indigeneity–class intersection. We revisit the *adivasis'* demand for land in the context of the Forest Rights Act of 2006 of the government of India and its implementation, and we comment on the recent land struggles. We discuss the National Rural Employment Guarantee Act (NREGA) and the Kerala model in the context of neoliberalisation and their implications for indigeneity and its transition. We reiterate our argument that, given the material deprivation and inability to be competitive in the labour market, the *adivasis* would fall back on land as the central demand for their socio-economic advancement, as shown by the widespread land occupation struggles in Wayanad and other *adivasi* areas in Kerala. At the same time, there are compelling objective reasons for them to make common cause with other subordinate groups, such as the working class, whose demands include higher wages, better working conditions, freedoms and opportunities for human development and social mobility.

Notes

1 We are adapting a theoretical insight developed by Shanmugaratnam in a study of the impact of the colonial plantation economy on the peasantry in Sri Lanka.
2 We use the term 'integration' in the sense of socio-economic and political inclusion. We are aware that, in the Indian context, integration of *adivasis* can be misrepresented as conversion and assimilation through Hinduisation or Christianisation. This point has been made by other writers, including Singh (1985) and Heredia (2002). The 'tribal question' was much debated in the post-independence period. Although some authors and commentators argued for the assimilation of *adivasis* into the Hindu caste structure (see, for example, Bailey, 1961; Srinivas, 1966; Ghurye, 1963) and assimilation by de-tribalisation (Chattopadhya, 1972), others proposed integration of the *adivasis* into the socio-economic and political mainstream without denying them the freedom to maintain their ethnic identity and cultural autonomy (Goodland, 1982; Singh, 1985). As pointed out by Prasad (2004), it was imperative for the newly independent India to create an image that projected cultural pluralism. Though integration in this sense had been the official policy of the Indian Government, varying degrees and forms of assimilation have occurred in many regions of India. In Kerala, integration was clearly the approach to the 'tribal question'; there is no evidence of assimilationist tendencies at policy levels. It may also be noted that identity was not a central concern of development and change in Kerala in the 1950s and 1960s when the Kerala model took shape. Focusing primarily on issues of equity and social security, the political leadership did not seem to be in a position to anticipate the later emergence of identity politics in the *adivasi* struggles. The political articulation of indigenous peoples' identities is discussed in considerable detail in Kjosavik (2004).
3 Article 342 states that '[t]he President may with respect to any State or Union territory, and where it is a State, after consultation with the Governor thereof, by public notification, specify the tribes or tribal communities or parts of or groups within tribes or tribal communities which shall for the purposes of this Constitution be deemed to be Scheduled Tribes in relation to that State or Union territory, as the case may be'.
4 www.tribal.nic.in/Content/DefinitionpRrofiles.aspx. Accessed 16 January 2014.
5 See, for example, Kunhaman (1982) and Sivanandan (1989). While analysing the fishing community as an 'outlier' vis-à-vis the 'central tendency' of the Kerala model,

16 *Indigeneity in transition*

    Kurien (1995) mentions in passing that the tribal communities are in a similar predicament. Franke (1992, 1993a, 1993b) conducted a village study on the impact of the Kerala model of development, but the village does not have an indigenous population. See Ravi Raman (2010) for a critique of some aspects of the Kerala model.
6. See Nossiter (1982) for a treatise on the Communist movement in Kerala, and Nossiter (1988) for a study of Marxist state governments in India.
7. Similar to gross domestic product (GDP) of a nation-state.
8. Source: Economic Survey (various years), Government of India; Statistics for Planning (various years), Government of Kerala.
9. Though the position of Kerala women is far better than that of their counterparts in the other regions of India, gender inequalities persist in the socio-economic and political spheres (see Jeffrey, 1992; Jose and Shanmugaratnam, 1999; Devika and Kodoth, 2001).
10. In 1964 the Communist Party of India went through a split under the impact of the Sino-Soviet split. The pro-Moscow CPI and the Communist Party of India (Marxist) – the CPI(M) – which had an independent international outlook were the major factions that emerged. CPI(M) has been the major Communist Party in Kerala since then and has continued to actively pursue a reformist approach. Some radical groups later left the party to form the Communist Party of India (Marxist-Leninist) – the CPI(ML) – which advocates the ideology of peasant insurgency. However, this is a marginal faction in Kerala.
11. Of the total population of Wayanad in 1981, 38.67% were in-migrants (Census of India 1981, Migration Tables, Kerala).
12. Source: Records of the District Planning Office, Sulthan Bathery.
13. In this case, forest land means land under the ownership of the Forest Department.
14. Source: Records of the Village Office, Irulam.
15. Source: Records of the Village Office, Irulam.
16. See also, Gullestad (1996) and Chamberlayne *et al* (2000).

References

Agarwal, B., 1997, 'Gender, Environment, and Poverty Interlinks: Regional Variations and Temporal Shifts in Rural India, 1971–91', *World Development*, 25(1): 23–52.

Bailey, F. G., 1961, '"Tribe" and "Caste" in India', *Contributions to Indian Sociology*, vol. 5, pp. 7–19.

Bates, C., 1995, '"Lost Innocents and the Loss of Innocence": Interpreting *Adivasi* Movements in South Asia', in Barnes, R. H., Gray, A., and Kingsbury, B. (eds.), *Indigenous Peoples of Asia*. Michigan: The Association for Asian Studies, University of Michigan: 103–119.

Béteille, A., 1998, 'The Idea of Indigenous People'. *Current Anthropology*, 39(2): 187–191.

CDS, 1977, *Poverty, Unemployment and Development Policy: A Case Study of Selected Issues with Reference to Kerala*, Bombay: Orient Longman.

Chattopadhya, G, 1972, 'The Problem of Tribal Integration to Urban Industrial Society: A Theoretical Approach', in Singh, K. S. (ed.), *The Tribal Situation in India*, Shimla: Indian Institute of Advanced Studies: 486–493.

Chamberlayne, P., Bornat, J. and Wengraf, T., 2000, *The Turn to Biographical Methods in Social Science – Comparative Issues and Examples*. New York: Routledge.

Collins, P. H., 1998a, *Fighting Words: Black Women and the Search for Justice*. Minneapolis: University of Minnesota Press.

Collins, P. H., 1998b, 'Intersections of Race, Class, Gender, and Nation: Some Implications for Black Family Studies', *Journal of Comparative Family Studies*, 29(1): 27–36.

Crenshaw, K. W., 1991, 'Mapping the Margins: Intersectionality, Identity, Politics, and Violence against Women of Colour', *Stanford Law Review*, 43(6): 1241–1299.

Devika, J. and Kodoth, P., 2001, 'Sexual Violence and Predicament of Feminist Politics in Kerala', *Economic and Political Weekly*, 36(33): 3170–3177.

Franke, R. W., 1992, 'Land Reform Versus Inequality in Nadur Village, Kerala', *Journal of Anthropological Research*, 48(2): 81–116.

Franke, R. W., 1993a, *Life Is a Little Better: Redistribution as a Development Strategy in Nadur Village, Kerala*. Boulder: Westview Press.

Franke, R. W., 1993b, 'Feeding Programmes and Food Intake in a Kerala Village', *Economic and Political Weekly*, 27(8–9): 355–360.

Franke, R. W. and Chasin, B. H., 1989, *Kerala: Development Through Radical Reform*. San Francisco: The Institute for Food and Development Policy.

Ferguson, J., 1999, *Expectations of Modernity: Myths and Meanings of Urban Life on the Zambian Copper Belt*. Berkeley: University of California Press.

Ghurye, G. S., 1963, *The Scheduled Tribes*. Bombay: Popular Prakashan.

Goodland, R., 1982, *Tribal Peoples and Economic Development: Human Ecologic Considerations*. Washington: The World Bank.

Gray, A., 1997, 'Who Are Indigenous People?', in Büchi, S., Erni, C, Jurt, L. and Rüegg, C. (eds.), *Indigenous Peoples, Environment and Development*. Copenhagen: IWGIA: 15–18.

Gullestad, M., 1996, *Everyday Life Philosophers – Modernity, Morality, and Autobiography in Norway*. Oslo: Scandinavian University Press.

Harvey, D., 2005, *A Brief History of Neoliberalism*. New York: Oxford University Press.

Heredia, R. C., 2002, 'Interrogating Integration: The Counter-Cultural Tribal Other', *Economic and Political Weekly*, 37 (52): 5174–5178.

ILO (International Labour Organisation), 1957, Indigenous and Tribal Populations Convention, 1957 (No. 107) Convention Concerning the Protection and Integration of Indigenous and Other Tribal and Semi-Tribal Populations in Independent Countries. Retrieved from www.ilo.org/dyn/normlex/en/f?p=NORMLEXPUB:12100:0::NO::P12100_INSTRUMENT_ID:312252 (accessed 2/2/14).

ILO (International Labour Organisation), 1989, C169 Indigenous and Tribal Peoples Convention, 1989. Retrieved from www.ilo.org/wcmsp5/groups/public/—-ed_norm/—-normes/documents/publication/wcms_100897.pdf (accessed 2/2/14).

Jeffrey, R., 1992, *Politics, Women and Well-Being. How Kerala Became 'a Model'*. London: Macmillan.

Jose, D. and Shanmugaratnam, N., 1999, 'The Invisible Work Force: Women in the Traditional Farming Systems of Kerala, Southern India. Paper presented at the Seventh International Interdisciplinary Congress on Women, June 20–26, University of Tromso, Norway. Retrieved from www.skk.uit.no/WW99/papers/Jose_Darley.pdf (3/1/04).

Karlsson, B. G, 2006, 'Anthropology and the "Indigenous Slot": Claims to and Debates About Indigenous Peoples' Status In India', in Karlsson, B. G. and Subba, T. B. (eds.), *Indigeneity in India*. London: Kegan Paul: 52–73.

Karlsson, B. G. and Subba, T. B., ed., 2006, *Indigeneity in India*. London: Kegan Paul.

Kingsbury, B., 1998, '"Indigenous Peoples" in International Law: A Constructivist Approach to the Asian Controversy', *American Journal of International Law*, 92 (4): 414–457.

Kjosavik, D. J., 2004, 'Contested Frontiers: Re-imagining *Adivasi* Land Rights and Identities in Highland Kerala, South India', Paper presented at the XI World Congress of Rural Sociology – Globalisation, Risks and Resistance, 25-30 July, Trondheim, Norway.

Kjosavik, D. J., 2005, *In the Intersection of Class and Indigeneity: The Political Economy of Indigenous People's Development in Kerala*, India, PhD Thesis, Aas, Norway:

Department of International Environment and Development Studies, Norwegian University of Life Sciences.

Kjosavik, D. J., 2011, 'Standpoints and Intersections: Towards an Indigenist Epistemology', in Rycroft, D. and Dasgupta, S. (eds.), *The Politics of Belonging in India: Becoming Adivasi*. London: Routledge: 119–135.

Kunhaman, M., 1982, *The Tribal Economy of Kerala: An Intra-Regional Analysis*. M. Phil. dissertation. Trivandrum: Centre for Development Studies.

Kurien, J. 1995, 'The Kerala Model: Its Central Tendency and the Outlier', *Social Scientist*, 23(1–3): 70–90.

Nossiter, T. J., 1982, *Communism in Kerala: A Study in Political Adaptation*. Delhi: Oxford University Press.

Nossiter, T. J., 1988, *Marxist State Governments in India*. London: Pinter Publishers.

Prasad, A., 2004, *Environmentalism and the Left: Contemporary Debates and Future Agendas in Tribal Areas*. New Delhi: LeftWord.

Ravi Raman, K., 2010, ed., *Development, Democracy and the State: Critiquing the Kerala Model of Development*. London: Routledge.

Sathyamurthy, T. V., 1982, *Centre-State Relations in India With Special Reference to Kerala (1947–77)*. DERAP Working Paper No. 264, Bergen: Christian Michelsen Institute.

Shanmugaratnam, N., 1985, 'Colonial Agrarian Changes and Underdevelopment', in Abeysekera, C. (ed.), *Capital and Peasant Production: Studies in Continuity and Discontinuity in Agrarian Structures in Sri Lanka*. Colombo: Social Scientists' Association: 1–19.

Singh, K. S., 1985, ed., Tribal Society in India: An Anthropo-Historical Perspective. New Delhi: Manohar.

Sivanandan, P., 1989, *Caste and Economic Opportunity – A Study of the Effect of Educational Development and Land Reforms on the Employment and Income Earning Opportunities of the Scheduled Castes and Scheduled Tribes in Kerala*. Ph.D. thesis, Trivandrum: Centre for Development Studies.

Srinivas, M. N., 1966, *Social Change in Modern India*. Berkeley: University of California Press.

Tauli-Corpuz, V., 1997, 'Three Years After Rio', in Büchi, S., Erni, C, Jurt, L. and Rüegg, C. (eds.), *Indigenous Peoples, Environment and Development*. Copenhagen: IWGIA: 39-50.

United Nations, 1975, *Poverty, Unemployment and Development Policy: A Case Study of Selected Issues with Reference to Kerala*. New York: United Nations.

UN, 2007, Declaration on the Rights of Indigenous Peoples. Retrieved from www.un.org/esa/socdev/unpfii/documents/DRIPS_en.pdf (accessed 1/5/14).

UN, 2009, *State of the World's Indigenous Peoples*. New York: United Nations.

World Commission on Dams (WCD), 2000, *Dams and Development: A New Framework for Decision-making*. The Report of the World Commission on Dams. Retrieved from www.internationalrivers.org/files/attached-files/world_commission_on_dams_final_report.pdf (accessed 1/5/14).

2 Property rights transitions and alienation of indigenous people's (*adivasis'*) land

Pre-colonial period

Introduction

Property rights could be described as the set of economic and social relations that define the position of each individual with respect to the utilisation of a resource (Furubotn and Pejovich, 1972). Changes in property rights to land and related resources such as forests and water have universally had adverse effects on indigenous people's livelihoods, which are highly dependent on these resources and the ecosystems to which they belong. The historical processes behind these changes have their political, economic and cultural specificities. A deep understanding of transitions in property rights in the traditional habitations of indigenous communities is crucial in capturing these specificities and the socio-economic consequences of the changes.

Institutions and laws are historically constituted and reconstituted. External and internal factors may cause changes in institutions and institutional arrangements. These changes are often gradual, but occasionally radical and abrupt, as in the case of nationalisation, radical redistribution or large-scale privatisation. The outcome, however, is a function of the interplay of the power relations between individuals within as well as outside the community. Such power relations are often mediated through the state. Situations that precipitate unequal distribution of rights and entitlements,[1] as well as historical dispossession and marginalisation, are characterised by increasing conflicts of an economic, social and political nature. Such a situation currently exists in highland Kerala, where conflicts over natural resources occur among unequal contenders – the indigenous communities[2], the settler communities[3] and the state.[4]

Highland Kerala has been the abode of several indigenous communities (*adivasis*) since time immemorial.[5] The livelihoods of the indigenous peoples have been predominantly land and forest based, and they relate to land and forests in specific ways. It could be presumed that these communities have been largely self-sustaining, and their economy was embedded in social relationships meant to ensure security for all members of the community.[6] The socio-economic security of the individual was intimately bound to the collective security of the community. Later, various types of interventions into these societies ensued, starting with the conquest of their land by the neighbouring kingdoms, followed by in-migrations from these regions, British policies regarding land and forests, establishment of large plantations by the British, the colonisation programmes by the government of Kerala, large-scale peasant in-migration to the highlands and, of late, a developmental state. All these resulted in the opening up of the indigenous peoples' economy and its uneven integration into the larger market economy. Their resource base and livelihood systems underwent drastic changes, and their property rights regimes, including ownership and control over resources, transformed over time and space. These processes have had serious socio-economic consequences for the indigenous communities, particularly with regard to property rights in land and forest resources and, consequently, their livelihoods. In this chapter we explore the evolution of property rights in land and forests in highland Kerala, with special reference to the indigenous peoples' access to and control over resources. This and the next chapter trace the historical settings of the transition of indigeneity in pre-colonial and colonial times.

We are aware that 'evolution' is a loaded term that could imply a change to superior forms or formations, which is rather misleading.[7] The term, however, can be used fruitfully to denote institutional change as a cumulatively unfolding process that occurs over a long period of time. This change either can be a gradual process or it can occur in the form of 'punctuated equilibria', an idea put forward by biologists like Eldredge and Gould (1972, 1977). The Old Institutionalism and the Alternative Institutionalist School stress the evolutionary nature of institutions in this sense (see Veblen, 1899, 1934; Hodgson, 1988, 1991,1993; Mokyr, 1990, 1991). Institutionalism's idea of evolution is more like 'punctuated equilibria', where relative stability may arise from sufficient compatibility between different levels of the system; however, cumulative disturbances at one or more levels or exogenous shocks may lead to a breakdown of the system and lead to developments down a different path. We conceptualise the evolution of property rights institutions in highland Kerala in this sense. At the same time, we may clarify that our conceptualisation is different from the 'evolutionary theory of land rights', where institutional change is posited as spontaneous and linear, necessarily from common property regime to individualised tenure, the driving force being relative change in factor prices.[8]

The indigenous communities of Wayanad are a highly heterogeneous group, stratified socio-economically with regard to initial endowments, entitlements and capabilities. This has implications for the direction of transition of each group. These initial positions, essentially determined by the way in which they related to land historically, have had significant influence on the trajectories of change experienced by these communities. In this chapter we explore the processes of transition of property rights in land and forests in Wayanad. We identify the external forces and institutions that intervened at each historical point and analyse how these impacted the further evolution of property rights of indigenous peoples.

We employ a broad historical-institutionalist framework to situate the study. We selected three communities who have had historically different relationships with land and forests for detailed analysis to capture the dynamics of change and continuities. They are the Kurumar, who had been traditionally agriculturists; the

Paniyar, who had been agrestic slaves (at least from the late middle ages); and the Kattunaicker, who are traditionally hunters and gatherers.

The political economy of an early social formation

'All beginnings contain an element of recollection. This is particularly so when a social group makes a concerted effort to begin with a wholly new start' (Connerton, 1989: 6).

Recorded history of Wayanad and its early population does not exist. However, based on archaeological evidence, historians believe that a relatively advanced culture existed in Wayanad, at least by the neolithic age, and that the indigenous peoples were the inhabitants of this region during that period. Plough agriculture with surplus production prevailed in Wayanad at least by the megalithic age, between 400 BC and AD 400. (Raghava Warriar, 1995). Narayanan (1995) infers that the indigenous people are the original inhabitants of Wayanad and the first in-migration to this region might have occurred in pre-historic times. The Edakkal rock engravings[9] in Wayanad can be dated back to the first millennium, as it shows both neolithic and megalithic representations; despite their different periods of origin, the engravings are organically woven into a single entity representing a continuity embedded in the changing culture, a continuity into the iron-using culture (Gurukkal, 1995). Anthropologists have presumed that the Australoid groups that lived in the region prior to the arrival of the Dravidians and the Aryans were responsible for the Edakkal rock engravings. The indigenous community Kurumar is believed to be the descendants of the Veda kings, who were preceded by the Kudumbiya dynasty mentioned in the rock engravings (Johnny, 1995, 2001). The myths, stories, places of worship and names of places that still exist in Wayanad point to it.[10]

The Edakkal rock engravings indicate the existence of a stratified society (Raghava Warriar, 1995). Nothing much is known about the socio-economic system that prevailed during the period. However, societies remember through collective memory or social memory that is represented in commemorative ceremonies and bodily practices, such as the performance of rituals (Connerton, 1989).[11] Cultural traditions can be either inscribed or performative. They constitute representations of the past, and are often explicable through hermeneutics. However, hermeneutics has chosen inscriptions as its privileged subject, though any object or practice capable of bearing a meaning can be subject to interpretive activity (Connerton, 1989). The practice of hermeneutics has thus effectively precluded the histories of subordinated communities whose representations of the past are largely in non-inscribed forms. The practitioners of 'professional' history, in a similar vein, tend to give primacy to 'factual evidence' in the form of artefacts or inscriptions in their quest for historical 'truth'. Therefore, societies with non-inscribed representations of the past had been relegated to 'historyless' societies. The statement by Langlois and Seignobos (1898: 17, quoted in Thompson, 1978: 47) is telling: 'The historian works with documents. . . . There is no substitute for documents: no documents, no history'. This 'historylessness', however, should be distinguished from Marx and

Engels' conceptualisation of 'non-historic nations' as nations or peoples who do not make their own histories through struggles against their oppressors.[12]

We have tried to reconstruct the socio-economic system based on myths, stories, folklore and oral narratives passed down from generation to generation, the rituals and ceremonies which were practised until the recent past and remnants of which still remain and hold symbolic meanings, as well as discussions with elders of the communities. All these form part of their self- interpretation and identity. It is often difficult to say where myth ends and history begins.

> Historians have labelled as 'myth' what seem unrealistic ways of representing the past, but it can sometimes be shown that mythic structures encode history, that is they register actual happenings or significant changes. 'Realism', on the other hand, is an equally culture-bound judgment of likelihood.
> (Tonkin, 1992: 8)

In Collingwood's idea of history as a re-enactment of past experience, it is the historian who has to re-enact the past in his or her mind by looking at the documents or relics (Collingwood, 1994). Given the objectivity claims of professional history, such an idea of history is problematic, as the historian's act of re-enacting is not a neutral process but informed by his or her ideology, values and culture. Thompson (1978), while questioning the objectivity claims of professional history, observes that most historians make implicit or explicit judgements, and rightly so, as the social purpose of history warrants an understanding of the past that relates to the present, either directly or indirectly. However, he points out that as most existing records reflect the standpoint of authority, the judgement of history has often vindicated the wisdom of the powerful. Marx's observations on the history of India are revealing: 'Indian society has no history at all, *at least no known history*. What we call its history, is but the history of the successive intruders who founded their empires' (Marx, 1853, authors' emphasis).

> Oral history by contrast makes a much fairer trial possible: witnesses can now also be called from under-classes, the unprivileged, and the defeated. It provides a more realistic and fair reconstruction of the past, a challenge to the established account. In so doing, oral history has radical implications for the social message of history as a whole.
> (Thompson, 1978: 5)

Oral history thus allows for a multiplicity of standpoints to be re-created, which is important for getting near to a reality that is complex and many sided. This method had been widely recognised and employed in the writing of history until the eighteenth century. It was the emergence of the documentary tradition in the nineteenth century as the mark of professional history that discredited the oral traditions. This, in turn, has its roots in the 'negative scepticism' of the eighteenth-century Enlightenment and the 'archival dreams of the Romantics' (Thompson, 1978: 44). Thompson gives an illuminating account of the rise of 'professional' history, how its claims for 'scientism' and eagerness to imitate natural sciences and, later, the neopositivist hostility to traditional history resulted in the neglect of qualitative sources in general and discreditation of oral history as a historical method. For example, Robertson (1759: 5–11) rejects the entire oral tradition of early Scottish history as

> ... the fabulous tale of ... ignorant Chroniclers .... Everything beyond that short period to which well attested annals reach, is obscure ... the region of pure fable and conjecture and ought to be totally neglected.

Thompson (1978: 90) argues that '[w]hile historians study the actors of history from a distance ... Oral evidence, by transforming the 'objects' of study into 'subjects', makes for a history which is not just richer, more vivid and heart-rending, but *truer*' (original emphasis).

For Tonkin (1992), the word 'history' stands both for 'the past', that is, history-as-lived and 'representation of pastness', that is, history-as-recorded. Tonkin argues that it is often easy to slip from one meaning to another because of the different ways that the past lives in the present. Representations of pastness can take written or oral forms, and they are purposeful social actions that act as a guide to the future. Our purpose here is to reconstruct history as a representation of the past, with the intention of narrating the processes of marginalisation of indigenous communities as a people.

In pre-literate societies, oral tradition was a major form of handing down history. Most of these societies had a considerable range of oral evidence and had reliable systems of handing them down from generation to generation with a minimum of distortion (Tonkin, 1992). Practices such as group testimony on ritual occasions, disputations, schools for teaching traditional lore and recitations on taking office were some of the ways in which this was ensured. Such practices were and are still prevalent among the indigenous communities of Wayanad as well. The genre of *Aivu* of the Kurumar represents the way in which the daily life of Kuruma society was ordered ideologically and functionally within their members and with regard to their relationship with members of other indigenous communities. The chief of the sub-lineage (*moopan*) is responsible for organising the social, economic, political and spiritual life of the community and its members according to the rules laid down in the *Aivu*. He is also responsible for handing down the *Aivu* to his successor. The *Penappattu* of the Paniyar represents the history of their people starting from the early forefathers, and this is recited by a specially trained person (*aattali*) at the death of a member of their community and repeated on the anniversary of the death for three consecutive years.[13] The *aattali* has to sit continuously for 24 hours with great concentration and recite the genealogies, the events surrounding each generation of his forefathers and their philosophical interpretations.

We have employed the genre of the *Aivu*, the political-economic and social-spiritual code of conduct of the Kurumar, passed down from generation to generation, as the major source to reconstruct the socio-economic system of the period. The narrative may not be neutral, as is the case with genre in general, and it may put forward moral and other arguments (Tonkin, 1992). This could be true in the case of *Aivu* as well, especially when it comes to relationships with other communities. Porter (1981) argues that narrative history is a proper form of interpretation; it is a means of proposing plausible connections, which is different from the scientific-experimental method, and for which the truth criteria proposed by some philosophers of history, may be irrelevant. '[A] narrative represents a complex reconstruction of the past by the historian, which the reader is expected to use as a template for her or his own reconstruction' (Porter, 1981: 48). This view can be usefully extended to oral narratives of pre-literate societies; in the present case, the narrator/historian is the Kuruma community and we (the authors) are the readers who use it as a 'template' for our reconstruction of the past. In this way, the narrative account provided by us is a meta-narrative. The narrator makes a 'synoptic judgement' based on her or his pre-narrative comprehension of past events, meaning narration involves dynamic reflection in the synthesis of the historical process (Mink, 1966).[14] Our understanding is that this 'synoptic judgement' occurs as much in oral narratives as in the historian's recorded narrative. We are aware that 'synoptic judgements' are inherent in the indigenous community's narrative as well as our meta-narrative. We proceed with this comprehension.

The narrative of the *Aivu* claims that Kurumar are the first inhabitants of Wayanad. The fact that the other indigenous communities address them with terms that indicate their earliness in the region may be taken as evidence of this. For example, the Kattunaicker address them as 'Pethiyar', meaning 'those who arrived before us'; the Paniyar address them as 'Nannaru', meaning 'lords of the country'; and the Uralis address them as 'Pithalar', meaning 'fore-fathers'.[15] During this period *adivasi* self-rule prevailed. The socio-economic, administrative, cultural and spiritual realms were inextricably interwoven. During our fieldwork in Poothady Village, Wayanad district, we observed that many of the place names in the village are the family names of Kuruma sub-lineages. During discussions with the chiefs of such sub-lineages, we came to understand that the entire land in the place named after the sub-lineage was under their control in the past.

Later, the Uralis arrived in Wayanad, followed by the Kattunaicker and Paniyar, as narrated in the *Aivu*. The Uralis were good at artisanal work, and therefore they were granted the right to collect raw materials from the forest for their work. However, they had the duty to provide the Kurumar with bamboo for making bows and arrows, the chief weapon of the Kurumar. Earthen pots, wooden plates and spoons, iron implements, ovens and similar household utensils had to be supplied to the Kurumar in exchange for food and cereals. The Kattunaicker were a fearless people and were experts in handling wild animals, and therefore they were given control over the wildlife. The Paniyar were good at working the wetlands and were given control over the paddy lands. Initially, the Kurumar were engaged only in shifting (swidden) cultivation of the uplands. Though the Kurumar observed 'pollution' with the other tribes, they included them and accepted their rights in agricultural activities, hunting, festivals and other rituals. Thus, an interpretation of the *Aivu* would reveal the existence of a stratified social organisation during the early period.

As narrated in the *Aivu*, the Kurumar, the land-owning community, occupied the highest social position as compared to the other communities. It would seem that division of labour and socio-economic stratification among the indigenous communities of Wayanad date back to the early period. The co-existence of different socio-economic categories is revealed by archaeological evidence (Raghava Warriar, 1995). However, the factors leading to the origin of this division of labour is a moot point. Was it due to the differences in skills possessed by each community, or did each community develop specific skills to suit the resources accessible to them? Or were they forced to develop skills to produce the outputs demanded by the dominant community? These questions are beyond the scope of this chapter.

Property rights among indigenous communities

It can be assumed that the indigenous communities (*adivasis*) subscribed to the notion that land and forests were the common wealth of the community, that is, 'common property'. Here the term 'common property' is used to refer to 'those objects and rights jointly possessed by some restricted group within a given society, to the exclusion of the other members of this society' (Herskovits, 1965: 324). As narrated in the *Aivu*, though land was collectively 'owned' by the community, the ultimate right was vested with the chief (*moopan*) of the community in the form of a trust. The chief exercised his right to grant plots for cultivation to the community members. The community's ownership right was also symbolically exercised by the chief by giving permission to other communities, like the Paniyar or Kattunaicker, to cultivate certain fields or to establish their settlements in a designated location. Individual families had the right to appropriate the land and utilise the fertility of the soil to grow crops, but the land was then returned to the 'common pool' after each cycle of use. All families in the community had the right to cultivate a plot of land. However, the appropriation and use of land by individuals was governed by a set of rules and norms, a code of conduct. The cultivating family had the right to keep the produce from their plot, though a nominal gift was given to the chief as a token of the services provided by him, and a fraction of the produce had to be contributed to the common pool for festivals, rituals and ceremonies. Each Kuruma family had to strictly follow all the rituals laid out in the *Aivu* with regard to land clearing, sowing, weeding, harvesting and other cultivation operations. The land was held in trust by the chief for the use of the community members and re-allotted to them for each cycle of use. Individual families did not have any claim to a plot of land on the basis of previous use. This meant that a family's right to a particular plot of land was limited to a cropping season, after which the right to the plot reverted to the community. The fields were then left fallow until they were allotted anew for cultivation after a time lag. The new allotments were independent of the earlier allotments. The Kurumar followed patrilineal inheritance and a patrilocal residence system. All the male members of the patrilineage inherited the right to cultivate a plot in the land held by the sublineage. Women did not have independent land rights. Married women's access to land was mediated through the husband, and unmarried women's access was mediated through the father. No community member was excluded from having access to the community's lands.[16] Marx and Engels (1976) identify this form of property rights as 'kin-corporate' property. Membership of the group determines residence and access to land for cultivation.[17]

The notion that the Kurumar were the 'owners' of the lands and forests in Wayanad is also derived from the *Aivu*. Accordingly, the Paniyar were assumed to have no 'ownership' rights in land or forests. They were given permission by the Kuruma chief to build their settlement in a specific area and cultivate the wetlands. After a few seasons, they moved to another locality with the permission of the Kuruma chief and cultivated another patch of wetland. According to the narrative of *Penappattu*, the genre of the Paniyar, the Creator distributed all the land on earth to different communities and no land was left for the Paniyar. However, on the recommendation of one of the gods (*Kalimalathampuran*), the Paniyar were given ownership of a handful of soil, along with the advice that they should earn their livelihood by working in paddy lands. The Paniyar believe that this is the fistful of soil the relatives throw into the grave when a person dies. The *Penappattu* also stipulates that a Paniyan should follow the footsteps of his or her forefathers to attain peace of the soul after death. It follows from the *Penappattu* that the members of the community should not aspire to ownership of land. The Kattunaicker were assumed to have no 'ownership' rights as well, following the *Aivu*. They were a nomadic people.

The forests were also considered the collective property of the Kuruma community, held in trust and managed by the chief for the benefit of the community. The forests were divided into territories, and each sub-lineage had control over a specific territory. This territoriality was strictly observed by the community members. They had access to the forests for hunting, grazing cattle, gathering food and fuelwood and collecting building materials. However, all these activities were strictly regulated by the rules laid down in the *Aivu*: who should go for collection (men, women or children), how many should go, which roots and tubers to collect, the method of collection, how many bundles of fuelwood to take, the type of wood to take (species, deadwood or live wood), size of the wood and so on. The rules for hunting pertained to the type and number of animals to be hunted, the age and size of the animal, frequency of hunting, weapons to be used for specific hunting expeditions, who the members of a specific hunting group would be, which section of the forest would be hunted, how to share the catch, and other aspects. Some territories were specifically demarcated for use of the Kattunaicker by the Kuruma chief. However, they, too, had to follow the rules of the *Aivu*. The Kattunaicker were given permission to collect honey, herbs and other forest products. The Kattunaicker were a nomadic people, and as and when they came to a specific area, they asked permission from the Kuruma chief of that area to build their settlement and use the forests, which was always granted. An occasional gift, mainly in the form of honey, was given to the chief by the Kattunaicker.

The Paniyar's access to forests was mainly limited to food gathering. They were given permission by the Kuruma chief of the area. Thus, the 'ownership' of the Kuruma community over tracts of land and forests was expressed by 'granting permission' to other communities and exercising some sort of stewardship over the resources. As a general rule, 'permission' was granted to other communities. It would seem that the word 'own' or 'ownership' was used by these communities not to mean 'exclusive' right, but to mean a 'trusteeship' in regulating the use of resources. The value of 'inclusion' was a basic organising principle in the property arrangements of these communities so as to enable all members of the community, and even other communities, to have the opportunity to meet their basic necessities.[18] Inequalities in such societies may be in rank and power, not in wealth. Polanyi (1968) argues that the productive system in early societies was usually arranged in such a fashion as not to threaten any individual with starvation:

> His place at the camp fire, his share in the common resources, was secure to him, whatever part he happened to have played in the hunt, pasture, tillage, or gardening . . . In effect, the individual is not in danger of starving unless the community as a whole is in a like predicament.
> (Polanyi, 1968: 65–66)

The beginnings of exclusion

Early in-migrations (AD 500–1400)

Outsiders had contact with Wayanad at least from the early Middle Ages. This is evident from the ancient Tamil songs which refer to the hills of Wayanad where spices like pepper, ginger and cardamom were grown; the paths winding down the hills of Wayanad; the stacking of bags of pepper brought from the hills in Kodungallur Harbour and so on (Raghava Warrier, 1995). By the high Middle Ages, a temple-based economic system developed in at least a few places in Wayanad – Thirunelli, Thrissileri and Ambalavayal – which shows the extension of Chera rule to Wayanad.[19] The Wayanadan Chetty community is believed to have arrived some time during this period. The Jains (known locally as Gownders) also arrived starting in the eighth century, and their inflow continued until the fourteenth century (Johnny, 2001).

The history of the indigenous people during this period has not been recorded or speculated on by historians. Therefore, we hazard a plausible construction of the past based on oral histories and the present geographical distribution of the various communities in the region. The development of the temple-based economy led to the loss of access to some land by the Kurumar as large areas were brought under the control of the temples. The Paniyar were largely co-opted as workers and then reduced to slaves in the paddy lands for the production of rice. The Kattunaicker withdrew farther into the forests. The Gownders and Chettys cleared forestlands with the help of Paniyar and Kurumar and started settled agriculture. They established exclusive rights on the lands they cultivated, thereby excluding the indigenous communities from vast areas.

Changes in the material processes of production occurred among the Kurumar as well. Following the example of the Gownders and Chettys, some sections of the Kuruma community started settled agriculture to a limited extent, but still continued with the shifting cultivation practice. However, the ownership of land remained with the community, and they were bound by the rules and norms of the *Aivu* with regard to access and use rights, the rituals related to agricultural activities and so on. At this point in time, the Kurumar cultivated their own land, the Paniyar were reduced to agrestic slaves of Chettys and Gownders and the Kattunaicker mostly withdrew into the forests or worked as cattle herders for the Chettys and Kurumar. Thus, the early relation of the three indigenous communities to land is a major factor that predetermined the later socio-economic transformation of these communities and their current status vis-à-vis land. The collective ownership rights in forests by the Kurumar remained unchanged, though the area accessible to them and other indigenous communities decreased considerably. Their access and use rights remained in the communal realm with the attendant rules and regulations. However, the resources of the same forests were used freely by the Gownders and Chettys without any special regulations.

The landlord-chieftain regime (1400–1766)

It is believed that Wayanad came under the rule of the Kottayam and Kurumbranad regimes in the late Middle Ages, that is, in the late fourteenth or early fifteenth century[20] (Johnny, 2001). However, the written history after the arrival of the British completely neglected the oral stories told by the indigenous communities, especially the Kurumar. The written history focuses only on the conquerors of Wayanad. For example, the history written by the then-deputy collector of Wayanad, Rao Bahadur C. Gopalan Nair, in AD 1810,[21] as per the orders of the Malabar collector R.B. Wood, is the history of the upper-caste conquerors and neglects the native inhabitants and their political history. The oral history passed down through generations of the Kuruma community is apparently more reliable than the written history, based on the evidence that still exists in Wayanad (Johnny, 2001). According to the oral tradition, the Veda king (the descendant of the Kudumbiya dynasty and the king of the Kurumar) was defeated by treachery on the part of the Kottayam and Kurumbranad kings and Wayanad came under their rule.[22] The oppression of the indigenous communities started during this period. This history is relegated to the realm of myth by the history writers of the colonial period. In any case, in the colonial period,

> ... documents were written solely from the administrative point of view, and to justify or recommend a certain practical course of present action; and it is often forgotten that our earlier Indian worthies were great masters of administration, but this did not necessarily imply that they had a special knowledge of historical details or an aptitude for land tenure investigations.
> (Baden-Powell, 1972: 33)

During this period, sixty-four Nair/Nambiar families were settled in Wayanad by the king, together with different caste groups of people to do various jobs.[23]

Wayanad was divided into ten divisions (*nadu* or *desam*) for administrative purposes and a division head, or *desavazhi*, who had powers in both civil and criminal adjudications, ruled each *desam*. Under the *desavazhi* there were landlords (*janmis*) who controlled and managed the land. The *desavazhis* were also the overlords of the land. A complex version of the feudal regime, called the landlord-chieftain system, that prevailed elsewhere in Kerala originated in Wayanad during this period. The land relationships in this regime were regulated by status rather than contract, and therefore, this regime was also known as 'the reign of King custom'.[24] Though the upper-caste Hindus became the masters of the society during this period and assumed nominally all the important rights connected with land, they did not assert their rights in such a way as to infringe on the rights of inferior tenure holders. The inferior tenure holders were required to pay only nominal dues in the form of products from the farmland, or in the form of services, as a token of allegiance to their superior rights holders. Therefore, the cultivators, although they lost ownership rights to the land, did not experience the full significance of the change until the arrival of the British (Varghese, 1970). The tenure systems that existed during this period were complex.[25] The king (*raja*) had only limited prerogatives under this system; he could neither exact revenue from the tenants nor exercise any direct authority (Menon, 1962). This is evident from Major Walker's statement in 1801 in his *Report on the Land Tenures of Malabar*:

> There seems to have been no regular tax anterior to the Mahommedan invasion. The Rajas were supported by the produce of their own lands and by certain fugitive forfeits or immunities which were more singular than advantages. In cases of public necessity, they might have recourse to the voluntary or constrained assistance of their subjects; but their power was very limited.
> (Quoted in Innes 1951: 307)

According to William Thackeray's report in 1807:

> There is no proof that any land-tax existed in Malabar before Hyder's invasion. The proprietors were bound to render military service and were liable to contribute 2 per cent in case of invasion. The pagodas and Rajas had lands of their own; the Rajas had other sources of revenue.[26]

The British, however, to suit their purposes interpreted the customary practices in terms of contractual arrangements. This had an irreversible effect on the further unfolding of land rights in Malabar, including for Wayanad in general and for the indigenous communities in particular.

Drastic changes occurred in the land rights of indigenous communities during this period (Table 2.1). The land on which the indigenous people held undisputed rights now came under the control of landlords. The Kurumar were reduced to the status of tenants. However, the payment of rent was limited to giving occasional gifts of agricultural produce during festivals and other occasions. They in turn received tobacco, clothes, food materials and so on from the landlords. The Paniyar were

30 *Property rights and alienation of land*

Table 2.1 Property rights in Wayanad during the Kottayam–Kurumbranad regime

Communities	Ownership rights	Access to rights/Use rights/Relation to land	Exchange rights
Kurumar	Nil	Tenants	Chief (exchange limited to community members)
Paniyar	Nil	Agrestic slaves	Nil
Kattunaicker	Nil	Nil	Nil
Gownders	Nil	Tenants	Individual tenant to other tenants
Chettys	Nil	Tenants	Individual tenant to other tenants
Nairs/Nambiars	Individual	Landlord	Individual right to customary share of produce was exchanged

reduced to being the agrestic slaves of landlords. The Kattunaicker were pushed farther into the forests, and some of them were employed as cow and goat herders for the landlords. Under the regime, the Gownders and Chettys also became tenants. However, the system operated on the basis of custom rather than contract.

The major change during this period was that there was a negative shift in the nature of property rights of the Kurumar from community ownership to tenancy status. However, within the community there was little difference in their organisation of production and distribution. Allotment of land for cultivation was still made by the *moopan*, and the belief systems regarding land and the rituals related to cultivation operations and distribution still remained the same. The Kurumar lost their collective ownership rights in the forests, and the forests came under the control of Nairs and Nambiars. However, with regard to access/use rights of the Kurumar, Paniyar and Kattunaicker, the status quo was more or less retained, although there was a reduction in the area accessible.

Thus we can see a phenomenal shift in the ownership rights of both agricultural and forestlands. In one sweep the owners were transformed into tenants on their own land and ownership rights in forests were withdrawn from them. However, the notion of 'ownership' in the modern sense of the term was external to them; shifts in ownership occurred around them and in their ownership rights without a realisation of what it signified. The landlord–chieftain regime continued until the mid-eighteenth century when Wayanad was invaded by the Mysore sultans.

Continuing exclusion: The Mysore regime (1766–1792)

The conquest of Wayanad by the Mysore sultans had a significant impact on the property rights of the indigenous communities. The major motive of the Mysore regime in terms of land was the extraction of large revenues from the lands; therefore they made 'settlements' with the *Moplahs* (Muslims) and other lower-caste peasants, who were the real cultivators, at the expense of the landlords

(Varghese, 1970). They introduced a comprehensive land-revenue assessment, according to which six-twentieth of the produce was to go to the state, eleven-twentieth to the cultivators and three-twentieth to the landlords.[27] During this period, there was a thorough shake-up of the Malabar community that was until then functioning within a customary framework. This resulted in chaos and confusion, which the British later used to interpret for their convenience the rights and interests connected with land when they conquered the rest of Malabar in 1792 and Wayanad in 1805 (Varghese, 1970). The higher castes began asserting their land rights during this period in order to emphasise their superior status, and began using the term *janmam*, meaning *water-contact-birthright* (*Nir-atti-peru*) (Menon, 1962, Logan, 2001). Baden-Powell (1892) identifies this period as the point at which the *janmis* began to claim definite soil rights. William Logan, however, reports that though the word *janmam* began to be used by the middle of the eighteenth century by the Namboothiri Brahmans (the upper caste of Kerala), the use of the term was rare and it did not become more widespread until the end of the eighteenth century when the strong Nair families started using the term *janmam* on their family property; the British later interpreted the word to mean free-hold, the Roman legal concept of dominium in the soil (Logan, 1951). As noted earlier, the Mysore rulers had settled the land with the lower castes and the Muslims; the upper castes' attempts to assert the *janmam* claims could be seen as a response to this phenomenon.

The upheavals during this period thus engendered grave consequences for the indigenous communities with regard to access to land and forests, particularly the Kurumar and Kattunaicker. Although in-migration of the Muslim population to Wayanad had started as early as the sixteenth century (Johnny, 2001), it accelerated during the Mysore regime. During this period, they came mostly as timber traders and contractors, and acquired large extents of land from the landlords, further depriving the indigenous people of land and forest resources.

The forests were treated as de facto private property of the landlords. Timber trade in Wayanad started during this period, and timber extraction was directly conducted by the state. Tippu Sultan paid an allowance of two fanas per tree to the landlords, whom he considered the proprietors.[28] Large extents of forests were also mortgaged by the landlords to certain Mappilah merchants, who then exercised the rights of the original proprietors.[29] This impinged on the access to and control over both agricultural and forestlands by the indigenous communities. The forest-dependent community of Kattunaicker was forced to further retreat into the forests. However, the indigenous people still followed the rules of the *Aivu* in using forest resources, although accessible areas were considerably reduced and forests were owned by the landlords and operated by the state.

Conclusion

In this chapter we have provided an overview of the historical origins of the processes of marginalisation of Wayanad's indigenous communities (*adivasis*). It helps to understand the early phases of the intersection in processual terms. The indigenous people of Wayanad were subjected to external interventions that changed the existing property relations and the social arrangements between the three communities, while incorporating them into new hierarchies of power and authority as tenants, workers and agrestic slaves. These processes created the historical socio-economic setting for the onset of pauperisation and proletarianisation in more modern times.

Notes

1. See Sen (1988, 1992, 1993, 1999) for the meaning of this concept; see Gore (1993) and Osmani (1995) for elaborations. Shanmugaratnam (2001) has added access to common property resources and social capital as components of the endowment set and has also broadened the scope of the entitlement set.
2. The indigenous communities are included in the Constitution of India as Scheduled Tribes for the purpose of affirmative action policies. They identify themselves as *adivasi*, meaning original inhabitants or indigenous peoples. See Ray (1973), Pathy (1992a, 1992b), Roy Burman (1992), Betteille (1986, 1998), Xaxa (1999) and AICFAIP (2001) for discussions on the tribal communities of India as indigenous peoples.
3. The settler communities are largely composed of small peasant groups and large plantation owners who migrated to the highlands.
4. The state is the owner of all the forestlands and forest resources.
5. As per Section 342 of the Indian Constitution, there are thirty-five indigenous communities in Kerala.
6. This theme is borrowed from Polanyi (1968).
7. In fact, Darwin himself did not use the term 'evolution' in the first edition of *On the Origin of Species* in 1859 precisely for this reason. Rather, he speaks of 'descent with modification'.
8. See Platteau (1996) for an exposition of 'evolutionary theory of land rights' and its critiques.
9. The engravings were accidentally discovered in 1890 by F. Faucett, the then-superintendent of police of Malabar, of which Wayanad was a part.
10. This interpretation is, however, refuted by Gopi (2002), who argues that the king who was appointed by the Pallava dynasty (a major South Indian dynasty) to rule the land of Kurumbar (Kurumar) adopted the name Kudumbiyathiri, and it is this Kudumbiyathiri that is mentioned in the Edakkal rock engravings. However, both interpretations point out that the Kurumar were inhabiting Wayanad from very early times.
11. See also Shils (1981) and Hobsbawm and Ranger (1983) for the idea of social memory as enacted through traditions.
12. See Marx and Engels (1975).
13. See Raju (1995) and Raju (1999) for detailed accounts of *aivu* and *Penappattu*, respectively.
14. See also Elton (1967).
15. The translations are approximate, as it is not possible to give an exact translation.
16. However, strict social sanctions prevailed, and if a community member broke the rules of the *aivu*, he or she could be ex-communicated and denied access to land for cultivation or even denied the right to reside in the settlement.
17. See also Kelkar and Nathan (1991).
18. This is in contrast to modern property rights where the right to 'exclusion' is a defining character.
19. This is evident from the *Thirunelli Chepped* which is believed to have been written around AD 1000. See Raghava Warrior (1995).
20. Kottayam and Kurumbranad were two neighbouring kingdoms of Wayanad. The date of conquest of Wayanad, however, is controversial. According to Gopi (2002), this must have happened at least in the thirteenth century.
21. Wayanad came under British rule in 1805.

22 See Johnny (2001) for a detailed narration of this story.
23 This section is based on discussions with the last Poothady Adhikari (village officer), the descendant of the Nambiar family who was the ruler of Poothady *desam* settled by the Kottayam king.
24 Logan, W., 1882, *Malabar Special Commissioner's Report on Malabar Land Tenures*, Vol. 2, Appendix 1, Chapter 1, Madras (quoted in Varghese 1970).
25 Francis Buchanan, who travelled through Malabar in 1800–1801, gives a detailed description of the complex land tenure systems that prevailed in Malabar in his *Journey through Mysore, Malabar and Canara*. See (Innes 1951).
26 Mr. Thackeray's report to the Board of Revenue, dated 4 August 1807 (quoted in Innes, 1951: 307–308).
27 George Shore, *Minutes of the Governor-General and Supplementary Reports of the Joint Commissioners of the Province of Malabar in the years 1792–93* (cited in Varghese 1970).
28 Report of the Joint Commission, 1792–1793, para 445 and 446 (quoted in Kunhikrishnan 1987).
29 ibid., para 445.

References

AICFAIP, 2001, *Voices of the Adivasis/Indigenous Peoples of India*. New Delhi: All India Coordinating Forum of the Adivasis/Indigenous Peoples.
Baden-Powell, B. H., 1892, *Land Systems of British India, Vol. 3*. Oxford: The Clarendon Press, 1892.
Baden-Powell, B. H., 1972, *The Indian Village Community*. Delhi: Cosmo Publications.
Betteille, A., 1986, 'The Concept of Tribe with Special Reference to India', *European Journal of Sociology*, XXVII: 297–318.
Betteille, A., 1998, 'The Idea of Indigenous People', *Current Anthropology*, 39(2): 187–191.
Collingwood, R. G., 1994, *The Idea of History*. Oxford: Oxford University Press.
Connerton, Paul, 1989, *How Societies Remember*. Cambridge: Cambridge University Press.
Eldredge, N., and Gould, S. J., 1972, 'Punctuated Equilibria: An Alternative to Phyletic Gradualism', in Schopf, T. J. M. (ed.), *Models in Paleobiology*. San Francisco: Freeman, Cooper and Co.: 82–115.
Eldredge, N. and Gould, S. J., 1977, 'Punctuated Equilibria: The Tempo and Mode of Evolution Reconsidered', *Paleobiology*, (3): 115–151.
Elton, G. R., 1967, *The Practice of History*. New York: Crowell.
Furubotn, E. G. and Pejovich, S., 1972, 'Property Rights and Economic Theory: A Survey of Recent Literature', *Journal of Economic Literature*, 10(4): 1137–1161.
Gopi, M., 2002, *The Unknown Wayanad (History)*. Kalpetta: Sahya Publications.
Gore, C., 1993, 'Entitlement Relations and "Unruly" Social Practices: A Comment on the Work of Amartya Sen', *The Journal of Development Studies*, 29(3): 429–460.
Gurukkal, R., 1995, 'The Edakkal Rock Engravings: Morphology and Meanings', in Johny, K. P. (ed.), *Discover Wayanad – The Green Paradise*. Kalpetta: District Tourism Promotion Council, Wayanad: 28–32.
Herskovits, M. J., 1965, *Economic Anthropology: The Economic Life of Primitive Peoples*. New York: W. W. Norton.
Hobsbawm, E. and Ranger, T., 1983, *The Invention of Tradition*. Cambridge: Cambridge University Press.
Hodgson, G. M., 1988, *Economics and Institutions: A Manifesto for a Modern Institutional Economics*. Cambridge: Polity Press.

Hodgson, G. M., 1991, 'Economic Evolution: Intervention Contra Pangloss', *Journal of Economic Issues*, 25(2): 519–533.

Hodgson, G. M., 1993, 'Institutional Economics: Surveying the "Old" and the "New"', *Metroeconomica*, 44(1): 1–28.

Innes, C. A., 1951, *Madras District Gazetteers: Malabar*. Madras: Government Press.

Johnny, O. K., 1995, 'Wayanad: A Preface', in Johny, K. P. (ed.), *Discover Wayanad – The Green Paradise*. Kalpetta: District Tourism Promotion Council, Wayanad: 71–73.

Johnny, O. K., 2001, *Wayanad Records – A Regional History*. Calicut: Pappiyon.

Kelkar, G. and Nathan, D., 1991, *Gender and Tribe: Women, Land and Forests in Jharkhand*. New Delhi: Kali for Women.

Kunhikrishnan, K. V., 1987, *The British Indian Forestry: Malabar Experience*. M. Phil. dissertation, Calicut: University of Calicut.

Langlois, C. V. and Seignobos, C., 1898, *Introduction to the Study of History*. London: Duckworth & Co.

Logan, W., 1951, *Malabar, Vol. 1*. Madras: Government Press.

Logan, W., 2001, *Malabar Manual*. New Delhi: Asian Educational Services.

Marx, K., 1853, 'The British Rule in India'. *New York Daily Tribune*, June 10.

Marx, K. and Engels, F., 1975, *Karl Marx and Frederick Engels, Collected Works*. London: Lawrence and Wishart.

Marx, K. and Engels, F., 1976, 'The German Ideology', in *Collected Works*, Vol. 5. Moscow: Progress Publishers.

Menon, S. A., 1962, *Kerala District Gazetteers: Kozhikode*. Trivandrum: Government of Kerala.

Mink, L., 1966, 'The Autonomy of Historical Understanding', in Dray, W. (ed.), *Philosophical Analysis and History*. New York: Harper and Row: 178–179.

Mokyr, J., 1990, *The Lever of Riches: Technological Creativity and Economic Progress*. Oxford: Oxford University Press.

Mokyr, J., 1991, 'Evolutionary Biology, Technical Change, and Economic History', *Bulletin of Economic Research*, 43(2): 127–149.

Narayanan, M. G. S., 1995, 'History of Wayanad', in Johny, K. P. (ed.), *Discover Wayanad – The Green Paradise*. Kalpetta: District Tourism Promotion Council, Wayanad: 65–67.

Osmani, S., 1995, 'The Entitlement Approach to Famine: An Assessment', in Basu, K., Patnaik, P. and Suzumura, K. (eds.), *Choice, Welfare and Development: A Festschrift in Honour of Amartya K. Sen*. Oxford: Clarendon Press: 253–294.

Pathy, J., 1992a, 'What Is Tribe? What Is Indigenous? Turn the Tables Toward the Metaphor of Social Justice', *Samta* 1: 6–12.

Pathy, J., 1992b, 'The Idea of a Tribe and the Indian Scene', in Chaudhuri, B. (ed.), *Tribal Transformation in India, Vol. 3*. New Delhi: Inter-India Publications: 43–54.

Platteau, J. P., 1996, 'The Evolutionary Theory of Land Rights as Applied to Sub-Saharan Africa: A Critical Assessment', *Development and Change*, 27(1): 29–86.

Polanyi, K., 1968, *Primitive, Archaic and Modern Economies, Essays of Karl Polanyi*, Dalton, G. (ed.). New York, Anchor Books.

Porter, D. H., 1981, *The Emergence of the Past: A Theory of Historical Explanation*. Chicago: The University of Chicago Press.

Raghava Warriar, M. R., 1995, 'Wayanad in the Middle Ages', in Johny, K. P. (ed.), *Discover Wayanad – The Green Paradise*. Kalpetta: District Tourism Promotion Council, Wayanad: 68–69.

Raju, E. T., 1995, *Aivu*. Sulthan Bathery: FEDINA-HILDA.

Raju, E. T., 1999, *Penappattile Chettadiyar*. Sulthan Bathery: FEDINA Publications.

Ray, N., 1973, *Nationalism in India*. Aligarh: Aligarh Muslim University.

Robertson, W., 1759, *History of Scotland During the Reigns of Queen Mary and of King James VI Till His Accession to the Crown of England*. London: A. Millar in the Strand.

Roy Burman, B. K., 1992, 'Historical Processes in Respect of Communal Land System and Poverty Alleviation Among Tribals', in Budhadeb Chaudhuri (ed.), *Tribal Transformation in India, Vol. 1, Economy and Agrarian Issues*. New Delhi: Inter-India Publications: 131–161.

Sen, A., 1988, 'The Concept of Development', in Chenery, H. B. and Srinivasan, T. N. (eds.), *Handbook of Development Economics, Vol. 1*. Amsterdam: North Holland: 10–26.

Sen, A., 1992, *Inequality Re-examined*. Oxford: Clarendon Press.

Sen, A., 1993, 'Capability and Well-being', in Nussbaum, M. and Sen, A. (eds.), *The Quality of Life*. Oxford: Clarendon Press: 30–53.

Sen, A., 1999, *Development as Freedom*. London: Oxford University Press.

Shanmugaratnam, N., 2001, 'On the Meaning of Development: An Exploration of the Capability Approach', *Forum for Development Studies*, No. 2–2001: 263–288.

Shils, E., 1981, *Tradition*. London: Faber and Faber.

Shore, G., 1793, *Minutes of the Governor-General and Supplementary Reports of the Joint Commissioners of the Province of Malabar in the Years 1792–93*, cited in Varghese, T. C., 1970, *Agrarian Change and Economic Consequences: Land Tenures in Kerala 1850–1960*. Bangalore: Allied Publishers Private Limited.

Thompson, P., 1978, *The Voice of the Past: Oral History*. Oxford: Oxford University Press.

Tonkin, E., 1992, *Narrating Our Pasts: The Social Construction of Oral History*. Cambridge: Cambridge University Press.

Varghese, T. C., 1970, *Agrarian Change and Economic Consequences: Land Tenures in Kerala 1850–1960*. Bangalore: Allied Publishers Private Limited.

Veblen, T. B., 1899, *The Theory of the Leisure Class: An Economic Study of Institutions*. New York: Macmillan.

Veblen, T. B., 1934, *Essays on Our Changing Order*. New York: The Viking Press.

Xaxa, V., 1999, 'Tribes as Indigenous People of India', *Economic and Political Weekly*, 34(51): 3589–3595.

3 Pauperisation and proletarianisation of *adivasis*
Colonial and post-colonial property relations

Introduction

After a protracted war, Malabar was ceded to the East India Company by Tippu Sultan in 1792. The ceded territory included Coorg, Cochin State and the district of Malabar, excluding Wayanad. Pazhassi Rajah of Kottayam, who was the heir to Wayanad, entered into a war with the British. In this war, along with the Nairs, the indigenous communities like the Kurichiyar, Kurumar and Paniyar fought against the British. However, Pazhassi Rajah was defeated and the British took complete control of Wayanad in 1805. This chapter continues to unravel the processes of transition of indigenous people's rights in land and forests during the colonial and post-independence periods.

The colonial period 1805–1947

The pre-settler period (1805–1930)

Creation of private property rights in agricultural land

The British land policy in Malabar was motivated by two main considerations: to extract a large share of the agricultural produce as land revenue, and to create and recognise a few superior rights-holders on the land, who would then act as British agents in the region (Varghese, 1970). The British identified and interpreted three types of rights-holders in land: (1) *janmis*, or freeholders who held their lands either by purchase or by inheritance; (2) *kanamkars*, or mortgagees, to whom actual delivery of the land appeared to be made, although the money taken upon it was not at all proportionate to the value of the land; and (3) *verumpattamkars*, who were tenants-at-will.[1] The tenure system described by Farmer (1793) included the *jelm-kars* (*janmis*, or landlords) and *kanoom-kaars* (*kanamkars*, or tenants).

> The farmer, called Kanook-kaar, deposited with the landlord a certain sum to remain with him as a pledge for the due payment of the stipulated rent; on this sum an interest was allowed to the Kanoom-kar or farmer, who might perhaps frequently be obliged to borrow the money on other pledges; after deducting

the amount of this interest from the *pattom* or rent agreed on, the difference was paid to the Jelm-kaar or landlord.[2]

Walker (1801) interpreted that

> ... [t]he jenma-karan possesses entire right to the soil and no earthly authority can with justice deprive him of it. But his right is confined to the property, and he possesses neither judicial nor political authority ... In no country in the world is the nature of this species of property better understood than in Malabar, nor its rights more tenaciously maintained. It is probable that the possession of janmam land was originally unalienable and confined to one or two castes ... It is obvious from the tenor of the deeds that considerable provision has been made in Malabar for the security of landed property ... In all the stages of conveyance, the most watchful jealousy is observed, to prevent the possession being loaded with additional engagements, and to save it from total alienation ... In the inferior tenures, which only convey a temporary possession, there appears an equal attention to the interests of the proprietor and of the tenant ... Few or none of these tenures are simple. They unite almost in every case the consideration of mortgage and rent ... another proof of the great antiquity of these institutions.[3]

Later accounts by William Thackeray and Thomas Warden follow along similar lines. For instance, Thackeray (1807) reported:

> ... [a]lmost the whole of the land in Malabar, cultivated and uncultivated, is private property and held by jenmam right, which conveys full absolute property in the soil. We find the land occupied by a set of men, who have had possession, time out of mind; we find that they have enjoyed a landlord's rent, that they have pledged it for large sums, which they borrowed on the security of the land, and that it has been taken as good security, so that at this day, a very large sum is due to creditors to whom the land is mortgaged ... The deeds which serve to record these transactions are drawn out in a peculiar character, which may be termed the black letter of Malabar.[4]

Warden (1815) held the opinion that

> ... [t]he *jenm* right of Malabar vests in the holder an absolute property in the soil. *Kanamkar* is a mortgage, or one who has land pledged to him in security for the interest of money advanced to the jenmkar, which advance is the kanam that is ever incumbent on the land until it be redeemed ... The peculiarity of the kanam or Malabar mortgage is that it is never foreclosed, but is redeemable after the lapse of any number of years ... There is no such thing as an established division of the produce in shares between jenmkar and tenant.[5]

38 *Pauperisation and proletarianisation*

According to their interpretations, the landlords, or *janmis*, possessed entire rights in the land (*janmam* right, or birth right). The British government in India took the previously mentioned reports as the basic principles on which land revenue was to be settled (Innes, 1951). It would seem that these interpretations were also convenient for them, as they suited the purpose of land revenue extraction. At the same time, the upper castes began to assert *janmam* right in such a way as to facilitate a British interpretation that was in their (upper castes') interest. The objective of creating a powerful landed class to subserve the colonial revenue system was also achieved through these interpretations. During Warden's term as the Collector of Malabar (1804–1816), *janmis* were ascribed the sole ownership of the landed properties of Malabar. This was accepted by the British administrators unconditionally, and steps were taken to legalise their 'assigned' ownership right. The civil courts also accepted the position that the *janmam* of Malabar was absolute private property, the *janmi* the *dominus* or the landlord in the English sense, and then proceeded to define the legal incidents of the various tenancies (Innes, 1951). Thus, the creation of private property rights in this region occurred through the power of the colonial discourses and the legitimisation of the same using the British legal system that was transplanted to India.

The interpretations made by Warden with regard to different land tenures – *kanam* as a mortgage and *verumpattam* as mere tenancy-at-will – did not take into consideration the customary practices that had been in vogue for centuries. The British even recognised all the wastelands in the region as the private property of *janmis*, thus recognising every inch of land in Malabar, including Wayanad, as *janmam* land. According to the British interpretation of property rights, the indigenous agricultural community of Kurumar was enfolded in the category of *verumpattamkars*, tenants-at-will with no security of tenure. Thus, a community who had been exercising unrestricted control over its land historically was reduced to the status of tenants-at-will. The Paniyar remained agrestic slaves, and the Kattunaicker withdrew farther into the forests.

However, when the Nilambur Rajah claimed *janmam* rights over land in Wayanad in the 1830s, Sallivan, the then-Collector of Malabar, argued against it. His argument was that if the Rajah was given *janmam* rights, it could be used against the government, as well as against the ancient occupants (the tribal/indigenous communities) of the region, as it gives the proprietor the right to alienate land in every possible way and to oust all the occupants at will – at least those who do not have a lease from the proprietor. The following statement, however, reveals that his primary interest was not the welfare of the indigenous communities living in those lands, but to safeguard colonial interests:

> From its (Wynad's) temperature and the salubrity of its climate, it is peculiarly adopted for the settlement of Europeans and I need not dwell upon the important consequences that would follow from the planting of [a] European Colony in such a position. The *Jenm* is a right as absolute as can be had in property . . . The consequence, therefore, of a recognition by the Government of this claim of the Raja or of its establishment in a Court, would be not

merely the ousting of the ancient occupants, the Todas, but the prohibition, except with the consent of the Raja of any attempt to turn the land in question to profitable account.

(Sullivan, 1841)[6]

This is one of many instances where the colonial rulers chose to ignore their own rules when they did not subserve their hegemonic interests. Thus, in Wayanad, a new form of property rights called government *janmam* (in contrast to private *janmam*) was created. In 1848 the Pazhassi escheats, that is, the land owned by the late Pazhassi Rajah, was taken over by the colonial government and was declared government *janmam* lands. The cultivators of the government *janmam* lands, mostly indigenous communities such as the Kurumar and Kurichiar, were then forced to pay rent directly to the government, as the government acted as the *janmi*.

Later, some British writers, after careful study of the ground realities, pointed out that the declaration of the entire lands, including waste lands, as *janmam* lands was unwise and was based on the wrong interpretation of the complex customary property rights systems obtained in Malabar.[7] The first serious attempt to question the British interpretation of the *janmam* as dominium was made by William Logan, who was appointed in 1884 as the special commissioner to enquire into the tenancy rights in connection with the peasant unrests. He concluded that the wrong interpretation of *janmam* as freehold by the British courts completely upset the customary land tenure system in Malabar. The commission appointed to examine Logan's report also agreed with his conclusions. They reported that

> ... [a]ll that we maintain is, that at no period had the relations of the janmi and the kudian reached that stage of development, that it was proper to apply to them literally the terms landlord and tenant, and that at all events as regards the bulk of the old Nayar kudians, the ancient custom had never been lost sight of.
>
> (Report on Malabar Land Tenures, 1884: 122)[8]

Logan's report and the commission's observations were, nevertheless, dismissed by Sir Charles Turner, the then-chief justice, who held that the earlier British interpretations of the land tenures were correct.[9]

Until the arrival of the British, there was no systematic land tax system, although the Mysore regime made attempts to collect some tax. The share given to the landlord was also nominal, in the form of gifts and so on. However, in 1806, the rent-tax (*patta-nikuthi*) system was introduced by Warden, the then-Collector of Malabar. According to this system, a part of the produce had to be given to the landlord as rent and a part to the government as tax, and the tax had to be paid in cash. This system came to be popularly known as Warden *pattam* (Warden rent).[10] This was a double burden on the cultivators, with the major cultivators in Wayanad being *adivasi* communities such as the Kurumar and Kurichiar, and others such as the Gownder and Chetty, and a few other Hindu castes. This raised serious protests from the agricultural communities, which resulted in an uprising in 1812 led by the

Kurumar and Kurichiar (Logan, 1951).[11] This is considered one of the first agrarian revolutions in Kerala. It took about six months for the colonial regime to suppress this uprising, with the help of armed forces.

According to a law passed by the British in 1837, British citizens were allowed to purchase land in areas under the East India Company. This led to the large-scale establishment and spread of British plantations in Wayanad (Kurup, 1986). This had adverse consequences for the indigenous communities with regard to access to land and forest resources. On the one hand, they were further driven away from the lands bought by planters for establishing plantations, and at the same time the colonial state restricted the areas available to them (indigenous communities) for grazing as well as shifting cultivation.[12] The first coffee plantation in Wayanad was established in 1840 by Major Gladson. The establishment of the British plantations was the beginning of the capitalist mode of production in Wayanad. In 1841, a metropolitan merchant enterprise called Parry and Company established the 'Wayanad Coffee Plantations' (Brown, 1953). This marked the entry of organised metropolitan capital into the planting sector in southern India (Ravi Raman, 2000). By the mid-1860s 14,613 acres of land were brought under coffee in Wayanad. Tea plantations began to spread in Wayanad starting in 1875, followed by Cinchona trees in 1880. The British abolished slavery in 1843 to release the workers required to work the plantations. The abolition of slavery was aimed at promoting the basic capitalist ideas of free labour and free market (Kurup, 1986). Nevertheless, the law did not succeed much in releasing the workers, as these workers, mostly constituted by the *adivasi* communities Paniyar and Adiyar, were already attached to the *janmis* – Nairs, Nambiars, Gownders and Chettys. Moreover, the working conditions in the British plantations were highly oppressive and exploitative, and those indigenous people who first dared to accept work in the plantations later escaped by running away.[13] Therefore, workers had to be imported from the drought-affected areas of Mysore and Tamil Nadu to work in the Wayanad plantations, and both physical and legal alienation of indigenous people's lands occurred to a great extent during this period.

Conferring exclusive ownership rights in land to the landlords by the colonial state gave them unlimited powers over the inferior tenure holders, and this resulted in a chaotic situation. The *kanamkars* and the *verumpattamkars* lost their security of tenure, and the *janmis* used their political clout to extract higher rents from them. This led to increasing peasant unrest. Sir William Logan's enquiry was a result of this situation, and we have seen that his findings on the customary property rights arrangements were unceremoniously rejected by the colonial state. He came to the conclusion that in ancient days there existed no 'ownership' of land in the modern sense of the term and that the organising of the body politic was by guilds or corporate bodies, which according to him continued until the arrival of the British.[14] As a result of the dual processes of conferring private property rights on the *janmis* and the large-scale spread of British plantations in Wayanad, the indigenous people's 'ownership' and access rights to agricultural lands were largely curtailed.

Survey and settlement

Survey and settlement of Wayanad commenced in 1886 and was completed in 1889. This was deemed necessary for the systematic assessment and collection of revenue. Initially, following the *ryotwari* system of revenue administration, the revenue settlement of Wayanad was done directly with the occupants of the land, the de facto holders, rather than with the *janmis*, the de jure holders. The title document, or *patta*, which was a mere note of the revenue payable, was issued in the name of the actual occupiers and cultivators, whether *janmi* or not, who, by virtue of occupation, paid the tax (Innes, 1951). Thus all the Kuruma sub-lineages got titles issued in the name of the chief.[15] However, subsequently, these settlements were pronounced illegal by the High Court, 'as it was incompatible with janmam right, and unsuited to the country and its peculiar tenures' (Innes, 1951: 357). The court decreed that all settlements in Malabar should be done with the *janmi*.[16] Accordingly, the settlement notification of Wayanad was amended by a proclamation issued in 1893. The land registers in Wayanad were then rewritten in the name of the landlords after making a new *janmam* investigation. Thus the *janmis* became the undisputed landowners and a historical opportunity for future claims in land rights was lost forever with regard to the indigenous peoples. Some holdings in Wayanad were treated as government *janmam* lands, '*puramboke*' lands (lands earmarked for community use), and government reserve forests. For revenue purposes, the land on which the government was free to charge revenue was classified as government '*ryotwari*' lands (revenue lands). There was also another category of land known as minor '*inam*' lands, which was revenue-free land enjoyed by a few institutions and chieftains.

Thus, the land available to the indigenous people for cultivation was reduced considerably.[17] Their access to agricultural land was limited to leasing-in land from *janmis* and government *ryotwari* land. The revenue assessment at the time was in line with the Warden *pattam* of 1806, that is, the rent-tax system. The *adivasis* were forced to pay double revenues for any land occupied by them – rent to *janmi* and tax to the government for private *janmam* lands, and both rent and tax to the government for government *ryotwari* lands. The taxes and the rent to the government had to be paid in cash. Those who paid this were given titles to the government *ryotwari* lands. Thus a miniscule number of indigenous people, especially Kurumar and Kurichyar, obtained titles to the land worked by them. However, as the government share had to be paid in cash, indigenous peoples were placed in a vulnerable situation. They were not well integrated into the market system, and therefore they could not often raise the cash required to pay the government. As a result of the settlement, large tracts of land were brought under the 'occupied' land category and there was a tremendous increase in the assessment. In North Wayanad the occupied area increased by 289% and the assessment was increased by 154%; the corresponding figures for South Wayanad were 226% and 120%, respectively (Innes, 1951). The revenue assessment was quite high compared to the yields obtained, and it was impossible for indigenous people to make regular payments. The result was that they were forced to borrow money from the landlords

(Nairs/Nambiars), Chettys, Gownders or Muslim traders by pledging their land, cattle and other assets, even household utensils, as collateral to pay rent and tax to the government. In most of these cases, they were unable to pay back the debt and thus lost their lands.

There were also a large number of cases where the Kurumar had to pledge their future labour to the landlords, Chettys or Gownders to borrow the money needed to pay taxes and rent to the colonial government.[18] This practice was called *vallippani*, a sort of bonded labour, where the labour of the person, and often that of the whole family, had to be pledged to the landlord or Chetty or Gownder for a year and then renewed every year until the loan was repaid.[19] However, the Kurumar often ended up losing their lands and the cycle of bonded labour turned permanent, from which there was no escape, as they could never earn enough cash to pay back the debt. Thus, the story of the survey and settlement of Wayanad, for the purpose of revenue extraction by the British, is also the story of reducing a land-owning, self-reliant and independent-spirited community to the status of bonded labourers.

Fugitives on their own land

The British authorities made 'occupation' of land rather than 'cultivation' the necessary condition for rent and tax assessment, except in the case of 'fugitive' crops cultivated irregularly on 'unoccupied' dry lands. The rule was that if a family occupied a plot of government *janmam* land continually for three years, then the occupant had to pay tax in cash and obtain title for the plot of land and pay the rent as well. If it was *janmi* land, then they had to pay rent for the cultivating years and tax if cultivated for three consecutive years. The indigenous people in general were unable to pay tax and rent, and therefore they moved to a new plot after cultivating the land for two years.[20] Thus they kept on moving continually from one plot to another every two years, thereby losing the opportunity to obtain titles to land, which had adverse consequences for their future claims on land.

The government was well aware of the fact that the change from 'cultivation' to 'occupation' as the basis for rent and tax assessment would result in abandonment of large tracts of land (Innes, 1951). The idea was that such abandoned lands could then be taken over by the government and sold to individual British planters and plantation companies. The Kuruma sub-lineages claimed the traditional lands they had been holding as their 'occupied' lands, in the case of government *janmam* lands. When it was *janmi* land, they got leases for lands they had been occupying for generations. These lands, however, were traditionally used for shifting cultivation. But according to the new survey and settlement, they were assessed for all these lands even though much of the lands were not cultivated every year. The Kurumar could not raise the money to pay rent and taxes and had to abandon most of these lands.[21] Moreover, in the following three years after settlement, Wayanad experienced a serious attack of rinderpest disease that wiped out large numbers of livestock, and the cropping seasons were especially poor. This ensured the abandonment of large tracts of lands. By 1895–96, 19,420 acres of land had been

Pauperisation and proletarianisation 43

relinquished and 18,826 acres had been sold for arrears of revenue, out of which the government bought 13,076 acres (Innes, 1951). However, in 1904 pepper and rubber crops were exempted from assessment for three years after planting,[22] which encouraged the establishment of large plantations, albeit at the expense of the native subsistence food-growing communities.

The resettlement of Wayanad in 1926–1927 with revised land assessment rates served to further alienate land from the Kurumar. The *janmi* wetlands that were cultivated for three consecutive years and all the government *janmam* wetlands were classified as 'permanent wet' in the new assessment, and failure to cultivate such lands could not create any right to remission of assessment on them unless their registered holders had relinquished all their rights in them before a prescribed date.[23] When the Kurumar were unable to pay rent and tax, they were forced to give up all rights in their wetlands, whether *janmi* land or government *janmam*. Other wetlands that were cultivated irregularly were classified as 'fugitive wet' and were liable to assessment only when cultivated. Therefore, the Kurumar cultivated the fugitive wetlands for one season and then abandoned them before the *kolkaran* (the person in the village office responsible for measuring the plot of land) arrived to make the assessment. If they did not escape in time, they were forcefully given the tax receipt, which they had to pay.[24] The rates of land revenue on all wetlands were increased by 18.75% (Innes, 1951). As mentioned earlier, similar 'fugitive' cultivation already existed in the garden lands. For tax remissions, they had to give up all their rights in the land. If land was 'occupied' regularly, it was classified as 'developed' land and they had to pay tax and rent even for the area not cultivated, which in any case they were unable to pay. Given this situation, their only option was to become fugitives on their own land, which as pointed out earlier, had adverse consequences for future claims on land.

The concept of private property was alien to the indigenous communities, and they were not aware of the significance of titles and what it would mean for them in terms of land ownership. The fugitive nature of their existence imposed on them by the British land assessment system had grave implications for the present landlessness of the indigenous communities. However, the Chettys, Gownders and Muslims were rather well integrated into the market system and were aware of the meanings and significance of private property rights. They made use of the opportunity to acquire titles on land. In some cases the *adivasis* managed to pay tax for a few years and obtain titles, but lost the land at a later stage by pledging it as collateral to borrow money for taxes and then being unable to repay the debt. The property rights obtained as a consequence of all these processes are summarised in Table 3.1. The indigenous communities lost property rights on their own land by forces and processes that were external to them.

The idea of asymmetries of information, where the consequences for different agents having different information in a transaction or contractual arrangement, or institutional change, may be invoked in this context. The agent who has more information or better quality information has a better chance to make gains than the one who has less information or low quality information. In the case of Wayanad, the Chettys, Gownders and Muslims were better informed of the

44 *Pauperisation and proletarianisation*

Table 3.1 Property rights to agricultural land in Wayanad (1805–1930)

Communities	Ownership rights	Access rights/ Use rights/ Relation to land	Exchange rights
Kurumar	Limited number of titles to government revenue land	Individual proprietorship of titled land; Tenants on *janmi* land; fugitive cultivators on the run on government revenue land	Nil
Paniyar	Nil	Agrestic slaves/bonded labourers/plantation workers	Nil
Kattunaicker	Nil	Bonded labourers/ plantation workers	Nil
Gownders	Titles to government revenue land; titles to land expropriated from indigenous people	Individual proprietorship of titled land; tenants on *janmi* land	Individual Nil
Chettys	Titles to government revenue land; titles to land expropriated from indigenous people	Individual proprietorship of titled land; tenants on *janmi* land	Individual Nil
Nairs/Nambiars	Individual	Landlord	Individual
British planters	Individual	Individual proprietorship	Individual

consequences of private property rights in land, whereas the concept of private property rights was not present either in the ideological realm or the 'life world' of the indigenous peoples. Therefore, they were unable to take advantage of the situation. On the other hand, in systems that are defined by power asymmetries, even when an agent has an informational advantage, it may not be possible for him or her to make gains when the contracting party is in a more powerful position. In the present case, even if the indigenous peoples were aware of the concept of private property rights and its future implications for their land rights, they would not have been able to take advantage because of the oppressive system of land revenue assessment imposed by the British.

Property rights in forests (1805–1930)

When Wayanad was taken over by the British in 1805, it was claimed that most of the forests were the private property of landlords (Stebbing, 1922; Innes, 1951). William Thackeray (1807) reported, 'The forests are claimed by Nairs who pretend to the proprietary right in the soil or trees, and have actually exercised this right by selling and mortgaging the trees to the Mappilah merchants.'[25] The Report of the Joint Commission (1793) also points out the private ownership of forests by Nair chiefs who were

> ... entitled to levy the local duties in question as far as they still remain at their own disposal, for a considerable part of them appear to be now mortgaged to certain Mappilah merchants, who exercise of course the rights of the original proprietors.[26]

These interpretations were later criticised by others. For example, Innes points out that it was unfortunate that 'instead of asserting the State's right to wastelands, they adopted the presumption that every acre of land was the private property of some janmi' (Innes, 1951: 319). Logan argued that there must have been 'wide stretches of primeval forests, unreclaimed wastes and sandy tracts, and hills and waste lands used from time immemorial as common grazing grounds and places where the people at large cut grass and fuel'.[27] According to Sir Henry Winterbotham, 'the pestilential legal fiction that all waste land must have a private owner' had the effect of 'a direct standing invitation for the preferment of unfounded preposterous individual claims' (quoted in Innes, 1951: 319).

The British had made early attempts to monopolise the rights over forests. However, they could get control over only certain territories that had fallen to them through conquest, escheat (land belonging to Pazhassi Rajah and the prominent landlords who fought the British) or purchase. As mentioned earlier, most of the forests were deemed to have been the *janmam* property of the *janmis*. The British did not want to displease the landlord class by taking over the forests, as this class was useful in suppressing the peasant rebellions (Karunakaran, 1992; Panoor, 1989). The court orders were also in favour of recognising the private rights of *janmis* over forestlands. Moreover

> ... [t]he instructions of the Court of Directors of 1800 indicated that their object was to obtain a regular supply of timber for public purposes, from unappropriated lands, to which alone the proclamation was intended to apply. It was not intended to invade private property.
>
> (Stebbing, 1922: 70)

However, soon after the conquest of Wayanad, a commission was appointed to report on the composition of forests and the proprietary rights existing in them; that is, they had to report on what could be regarded public forests and to distinguish them from groves and plantations forming private estates. Based on the commission's report a proclamation was made on 25 April 1807, according to which the royalty rights in teak were vested with the East India Company and all unauthorised felling of teak by private individuals was prohibited (Stebbing, 1922). However, this proclamation did not define the term 'sovereignty', nor did it specify the forests over which sovereignty was extended. Captain Watson, the then Conservator of Forests, made use of this opportunity to set up a timber monopoly in Malabar and practically abolished almost all private rights in the forests by assuming their non-existence (Ribbentrop, 1900). Private timber trade was completely annihilated and even '[t]he privilege of cutting fuel for private use, which had been practised at will by all from time immemorial, was also invaded and prohibited, a short-sighted step of amazing folly' (Stebbing, 1922: 71). But due to widespread discontent among the *janmis* and timber traders, and the protests of the peasants indignant at the restrictions on fuel cutting, the monopoly and the conservatorship were abolished in 1823. The *janmis* once again took possession of the forests.

The large-scale timber operations in the forests disrupted the lives of the indigenous people, and they were driven more and more into the inaccessible forest areas to find land for shifting cultivation (Kurumar) and for hunting and gathering (Kattunaicker). The British attitude at the time towards forests was from a purely utilitarian point of view (Stebbing, 1922). They viewed forests as a source of timber, and all other issues were disregarded. They refused to recognise the fact that the interests of the *ryotes* were closely interwoven with the forestry question. 'Whilst energetically supporting the rights of private ownership they forgot the equal rights of the community which were gravely imperilled' (Stebbing, 1922: 73). Thus, from the very beginning, the British forest policies in Wayanad were detrimental to the interests of the indigenous communities, who were agriculturists as well as hunters and gatherers.

The government leased-in vast areas of forestland from *janmis* for cultivating teak. This meant large-scale depletion of natural forests. The multiple species and varieties of trees, as well as other vegetation, including roots and tubers in the dense rainforests, which were more valuable to the life and livelihoods of the *adivasis*, and to the ecosystem, were systematically removed and replaced with teak which was important for the colonial commercial interests. The indigenous people and other agricultural populations who were directly or indirectly dependent on natural forest resources did not in any way benefit from the profits of teak introduction and trade (Kunhikrishnan, 1987). Large areas of forestlands were either bought or leased-in by British companies to establish tea and coffee plantations. All these meant that the forests, as well as the forest produce accessible to the *adivasis*, were drastically reduced in terms of both quantity and quality.

Fencing the forests

A memorandum issued by the British in 1855 marked the beginning of the official closure of India's forests to the local population. This was later replaced by the Indian Forest Act of 1865, which was further amended in 1878. The objective was to extend state control over forest areas all over India.[28] This Act was based on the proposal of Baden-Powell, who advocated that all rights in forests should be vested with the state (Baden-Powell, 1875 cited in Guha, 1996). This legislation resulted in the enclosure of the vast majority of Indian forests and demarcating them as state forests, owned and controlled by the state. The rights of the indigenous peoples and other forest-dependent communities were severely attenuated. Though there was a provision for the constitution of village forests to be owned and controlled by the villagers, this option was exercised by the government only in a few isolated cases (Ribbentrop, 1900). Legal provisions existed for the contestation of forest takeovers by the state. However, the villagers were mostly illiterate and unfamiliar with legal procedures, and they were often unaware that a survey was in progress to enclose their forestlands (Poffenberger *et al*, 1996).

Following the Indian Forest Act, large areas of forest tracts in Wayanad were brought under the control of the British state, either by purchase or lease, in addition to the escheat forests that were already under state control. A considerable extent still remained under the control of the *janmis*. Shifting cultivation in the forests was already banned by an order issued by the government of Madras in May 1860 (Stebbing, 1922). This had a serious impact on the Kurumar who were traditionally shifting cultivators. The *adivasis* who were living in the forests from time immemorial 'were permitted to make clearings for *punam* cultivation where they pleased, but they are now confined to prescribed areas' (Innes, 1951: 241). These interventions severely curtailed the access rights of the indigenous peoples.

Meanwhile, the colonial government passed the Madras Forest Act in 1882. According to the Act, the best-quality forests were classified as 'reserve forests'. These forests contained the most commercially valuable timber and were deemed to be amenable to sustained exploitation by the colonial state. The relatively poor-quality forests were classified as 'revenue forests' or 'protected forests', and the forests belonging to the *janmis* were retained as 'private forests'. Reserve forests were under total state control with practically no access for any one, including the indigenous people. However, those indigenous people who were already living in these forest areas continued to live there, but were dispossessed of all their rights in these forestlands and resources. The process of declaring an area as reserve forest had been more intricate and prolonged in Malabar than in any other part of the Madras presidency (Indhrani, 1982, cited in Kunhikrishnan, 1987). This is mainly because the civil appellate courts accepted the proposition that no forest in Malabar was at the disposal of the government unless acquired by escheat, purchase or contract. Therefore, the onus of proof was with the government: 'All forests and unoccupied lands in the old province of Malabar have been considered to be private property' (Browne, 1929).[29] Therefore no action was taken to extend government ownership over private forests other than through due process of law.

The colonial government adopted its first Forest Policy in 1894. Severe restrictions were imposed on the rights traditionally enjoyed by the forest dwellers. This had a detrimental effect on indigenous people's access to forest resources and led to malnutrition, impoverishment and indebtedness among forest dwellers. Moreover, it led to the overexploitation of the forests that remained accessible to them after the government had closed all other forests to them (Fernandes *et al*, 1988). Forests were classified into (1) reserve forests – in which the right of the state would be almost absolute; (2) protected forest – forests which were burdened with legal rights, whether prescriptive or granted; and (3) village forests – forests settled and managed by village communities. However, this classification could not be extended to Madras, as the Madras government was of the opinion that if it was desirable to protect an area, it was essential to reserve it absolutely and bring it under the control of the Forest Department.[30]

48 *Pauperisation and proletarianisation*

Consequently, in Malabar the government forests were classified as reserve forests and protected forests. No village forests served as common property for the indigenous people and other villagers. Nevertheless, the role of the village forests in Malabar was, to a large extent, satisfied by the private forests. 'The state forests cover such a small proportion of the forest land of the district that there is little or no friction with the people, who can as a rule graze their cattle and gather fuelwood in the private forests free of cost' (Innes, 1951: 245). The revenue forestlands in Malabar later became de facto open-access forests. People were allowed to cultivate this land by paying rent and taxes. As in the case of the government *ryotwari* land (revenue land), the rule was that if a plot of land was cultivated continually for three years, the cultivator had to pay tax in cash and obtain the title from the village *adhikari*. The indigenous people were unable to pay the tax and became fugitive cultivators. Thus they lost their future claims or chances of acquiring private property rights, as had happened in the case of revenue lands. Table 3.2 summarises the changes in property rights in forests during the period. The changes depict how a dominant property rights regime dispossessed a community which operated under common property regime and for whom the concept of private property was alien. The indigenous communities lost access to forests through statisation and privatisation processes.

During this period a major shift in economic activities occurred for all categories of indigenous populations. One significant feature was the emergence of wage work for the indigenous peoples in the plantations and forests. However, the participation of the indigenous people in wage work was rather low because most of them, especially the Paniyar, were attached to the Nairs/Nambiars, Gownders and Chettys as bonded labour or other patron-client ties. They were not familiar with the kind of work they were expected to do in the plantations, and the working conditions in the plantations were dismal. Although some Kattunaicker became wageworkers in the plantations and in the forests, especially working with elephants, most of them withdrew into the forest interior. The Kurumar preferred to

Table 3.2 Property rights to forests in Wayanad (1805–1930)

Communities	Ownership rights	Access rights/ Use rights/ Relation to land	Exchange rights
Kurumar	Nil	**Private forests** Tenants; commons	Nil Nil Nil
		Revenue forests Tenants Fugitive cultivators Workers Commons	
		Reserve forests Restricted access for collection of minor forest produce	

Communities	Ownership rights	Access rights/ Use rights/ Relation to land	Exchange rights
Paniyar	Nil Nil Nil	**Private forests** Commons **Revenue forests** Workers Commons **Reserve forests** Restricted access for collection of minor forest produce	Nil Nil Nil
Kattunaicker	Nil Nil Nil	**Private forests** Commons **Revenue forests** Workers Commons **Reserve forests** Restricted access for collection of minor forest produce Workers with elephants	Nil Nil Nil
Gownders	Nil Nil Freehold	**Private forests** Open access for grazing cattle Tenants **Revenue forests** Tenants De facto open access Titled private property	Nil Nil Free exchange right
Chettys	Nil Nil Freehold	**Private forests** Open access for grazing cattle Tenants **Revenue forests** Tenants De facto open access **Titled private property**	Nil Nil Free exchange right
Nairs/ Nambiars	Freehold Nil Nil	**Private forests** Landlord **Revenue forests** **Reserve forests**	Free exchange right Nil Nil
British planters	Nil Freehold Nil Freehold	**Private forests** Lessee Owner (purchased from landlords) **Revenue forests** Lessee Owner (purchased from landlords)	Nil Free exchange right Nil Free exchange right

be their own masters and continued with their cultivation activities. *Adivasis* were also kept as captive workers in the British plantations (Ravi Raman, 2000, 2002).

Settler period (1930s–1947)

Property rights in agricultural land

This is the period during which large-scale in-migration to Wayanad occurred. In the early period Christian planters from Travancore and planters from the neighbouring regions of Tamil Nadu came to Wayanad and opened up new plantations of tea, coffee and cardamom.[31] The land for establishing plantations was mainly obtained by leasing-in government revenue land (*ryotwari* land), revenue forestland and private forestlands or agricultural lands from *janmis*. This meant that the indigenous peoples living in these areas were forced to move to other areas, relinquishing their traditional rights to these areas. The labour requirement in these plantations was mostly met by recruiting workers from the drought-affected areas of Tamil Nadu and Mysore states (George and Tharakan, 1986).

The spreading of plantations in the forest areas of Wayanad opened up facilities for the cultivation of new lands in these tracts, which attracted many enterprising cultivators from Travancore, who were in search of new cultivable lands due to the scarcity of land in Travancore (Varghese, 1970). Unlike the late in-migrants who were mainly marginal farmers and landless labourers, those who migrated to northern Kerala in the 1940s were mainly large planters from Travancore (Tharakan, 1984). They were looking for land to invest the surplus earned from the plantations in southern Kerala, as there were complications with the tenancy system that prevailed in Travancore at the time. The in-migrants were also attracted by the prospects of buying land at cheap prices. For example, whereas in Muvattupuzha (a place in Travancore), the price of land was Rs. 697.48 per acre in 1925, it was only Rs. 4.00 per acre in Malabar. In 1931 the corresponding figures were Rs. 807.20 and Rs. 10.00 (Tharakan, 1984). Although in-migration of peasants from Travancore and Cochin to Malabar started in the late 1920s, peasant in-migration to Wayanad became active only in the 1940s. The spurt in the population growth of Wayanad during the decade 1941–1951 proves this exodus. There was a 59.2% increase in the total population of Wayanad from 1941–1951 (Tharakan, 1976). The lands available to them in Wayanad at the time included government revenue land, revenue forestland, *janmi* land and reserve forestland (legally not available). The mode of acquiring property rights in these lands varied considerably.

Establishing property rights in revenue land[32]

On arrival, the in-migrants or settlers would establish claim on a certain area of land by marking the trees on the four boundaries. Then they would proceed to clear the land for cultivation. Though cutting of teak and rosewood were illegal, the settlers cut and burnt them. On the cleared land they grew chama (a cereal), rice, lemongrass, cassava, yams and vegetables. Some of the lands within the boundaries of the claimed lands or nearby areas would already have been occupied and cultivated by indigenous people, especially Kurumar. The lands would have been cultivated either 'fugitively' (without paying tax or rent to the government) or legally by paying what is due to the government and obtaining tax receipt and title. In such cases the settlers would buy the land from the *moopan* (land was collectively owned by the community and the title would be in the *moopan*'s name) by paying a nominal sum of money, which was much lower than the market price. In most cases the sales agreement was written in a white paper as '*theeradharam*'; that is, all rights in the land, along with crops, trees and other assets available on the land, were irreversibly transferred to the new owner. In some cases these agreements were registered at the government registrar's office. After this, the settler would start paying the government tax and get the receipt, thus establishing undisputed private property rights in this land. Moreover, the indigenous people did not have a concept of area or measurement of land in modern terms like acre or hectare. Their ignorance was taken advantage of by the settlers, who got control over areas much larger than that agreed upon by the Kurumar in paper. There would also be cases where the settler would ask the *moopan* for permission to cultivate a portion of the land controlled by a sub-lineage. The *moopan* would give permission, as was the traditional practice of the community for centuries. The settler would then build a house on the plot, start cultivation, pay tax to the government and establish rights in the land. As mentioned earlier, the indigenous people were often unable to pay the tax and had to relinquish the land to settlers. Only a small fraction of indigenous people were able to pay the tax and retain control over their lands. In many cases they had to borrow money from the Chettys, Gownders, Muslim traders and other money lenders or settlers to pay the tax by pledging their land, crops or cattle as collateral. Often, they were unable to repay the debt along with the high interest, and then they would be forced by threats to write the *theeradharam* over to them, thus losing the sub-lineage's claim on the land. Field discussion with the older generation of *adivasis* also revealed that they lost land in various ways.

The indigenous people admitted in the field discussions that they did not recognise the value of land in the market sense or the meaning of 'ownership' in the modern sense of private property ownership with the attendant rights and privileges, including excludability and the irreversibility of the transaction. Therefore, they did not take efforts to claim private property as the others did; neither could they afford to do so due to lack of money to pay the government tax and rent. Private property was an alien concept imposed on them, and they were unaware of the future implications underlying the concept. This is an example of how the modern concept of private property rights, which is characteristic of the market economy, when imposed on a traditional community which was not yet integrated into the market system, cheated them out of their means of production, livelihood and their dwellings. The Kattunaicker, if present in the revenue lands claimed by the settlers, would move farther into the forest interiors.

Establishing property rights on janmi *land*

As mentioned earlier, large tracts of land in Wayanad were owned by *janmis*. Land was leased from them by indigenous people like the Kurumar and Kurichiyar,

Chettys, Gownders, some Nairs and Muslims. The cultivators had to pay rent to the landlords and tax to the government. This was also a major source of land for the settlers. They leased-in land directly from the *janmis* for the specified rent and tax rates. The contract or agreement, called a *marupattam*, was signed between the *janmi* and the tenant. According to this agreement, the tenant had the right to sell the lease to another tenant who would then pay the rent to the *janmi*.

At the time the settlers arrived, the Kurumar had large tracts of *janmi* land under their control under a *marupattam* agreement. The settlers acquired this land either by paying a nominal sum or they encroached on the Kuruma lands, cultivated it and paid rent to the *janmi* and tax to the government and established rights in the land. The *janmi*'s main concern was rent, and the government's main concern was tax revenue. It was not in their interest to be concerned with who cultivated the land and paid the rent and tax. In many cases, the settlers bought land from the *janmi* by *theeradharam*, but these lands may already have been occupied by the Kurumar, and they were evicted. Moreover, when there was demand for land from the settlers, the *janmi* forcefully evicted the Kurumar and leased the land to the settlers at a higher rent. This was called '*melcharthu*'. There were also situations where the land controlled by the Kurumar would be leased out to settlers by the *janmi* without their (the Kurumars') knowledge or consent. Then the settlers, together with the *janmi* and with the support of the government officers, would force the Kurumar out of their lands. Once the land was leased-in, the settler would pay rent to the *janmi* and tax to the state and obtain possession rights on the land. In many cases, the deals the settlers made with the *janmi* were verbal (Tharakan, 1976). Then they paid tax to the government and made the land their own.

All of this was made easier by the Malabar Tenancy Act that was passed in 1930. Though there were provisions for fair rent and fixity of tenure, the potential advantages of these were nullified by the other provisions.[33] The Act was largely in favour of the landlord class. The landlord had the right to demand one year's rent in advance or equivalent security, the right to force renewals on customary *verumpattamkars* (tenants-at-will) and the right to treat rents due to them as a statutory charge on the interests of the tenants. Provisions were also there for the landlords to use the lands for their own cultivation or for cultivation by family members. The Act failed to confer security of tenure to non-cultivating *verumpattamkars* and renewal rights to *kanams* that were mere mortgages. All these provisions were detrimental to the interests of the *adivasi* communities, who fell largely under the category of tenants-at-will. It was difficult for them to raise one year's rent as advance payment; neither did they have the security to pay in lieu of it, which nullified the 'security of tenure' provision. Moreover, the landlords could easily evict them under the pretext of resuming land for their own cultivation or for that of family members and lease out the land to the newly arriving settlers at much higher rents, or even sell the land. The 'fair rent' fixed by the Act was still high compared to the incomes obtained from farming. All of this meant further loss of access to land by the indigenous peoples. Those who managed to stay on became permanently indebted to the landlords.

The British authorities held a 'sterile' legal attitude to all these complex issues; they had imported their legal machinery to India. All problems regarding land rights and tenancies were to be settled through civil courts. Litigations, however, required a large expense on the part of the tenants. The indigenous people, who were already dispossessed and impoverished and poorly integrated into the market, were not in a position to approach civil courts and engage in protracted legal processes. Moreover, the court decisions were infamously in favour of landlords (Varghese, 1970). Apart from this, the indigenous people were neither literate nor familiar with legal procedures. They were easily intimidated by the all-powerful landlords, who were also in many cases the village *adhikaris* (village revenue officers of the colonial government), and the early settlers were known for their ruthlessness.[34] Thus, the Malabar Tenancy Act of 1930 provided fertile grounds for the settlers and at the same time the indigenous people lost the grounds from under their feet. Table 3.3 gives a summary of the nature of property rights in agricultural land during this period.

The Paniyar who lived on the edges of the *janmi* land were further marginalised. Slavery was abolished, and in many cases they became unattached to the land, but bonded labour in many forms still continued. When the *janmi* land was leased-in by settlers, the Paniyar who were living on the edges of these lands were also forced to move. The Kattunaicker, if they happened to be living on *janmi* land, were also forced out when the land was bought or leased-in by the settlers. They withdrew farther into the forests. Thus the indigenous people living on the *janmi* land or revenue land faced the same fate – they were dispossessed of their means of production and living space.

Property rights in forest land

As mentioned, the forests of Wayanad were classified into reserve forests, revenue forests and private forests. The methods adopted by the settlers for claiming property rights on these three types of forests were different. The reserve forest was exclusively owned by the government. The settlers gained access to this land by illegal encroachment. They cleared the forestland and started cultivation. The Kattunaicker community was by now mostly living in the reserve forest areas, as this was the only undisturbed area where they could live and forage for their livelihood. They were driven farther into the interior of the forests due to the encroachment of settlers. Because the encroachment took place in remote areas, the government authorities could not take much action to prevent it.

The settlers established property rights on revenue forestlands by leasing the land from the government. Cutting and burning was the method adopted by settlers for clearing the land. Though it was illegal to cut teak and rosewood, they were cut and burnt to facilitate agriculture. Large quantities of valuable timber were turned into ashes during this period. The initial period of the lease was twelve years, but it could be renewed. On these lands, the settlers were not allowed to cultivate perennial crops like coffee, pepper, jack trees and so on. Therefore, they mainly grew annual and seasonal food crops like chama, finger millet, rice, cassava, banana and yams and cash crops like ginger and lemongrass.

Table 3.3 Property rights to agricultural land in Wayanad (1930–1947)

Communities	Ownership rights	Access rights/ Use rights/ Relation to land	Exchange rights
Kurumar	Limited number of freehold titles to government revenue land, but many lost it to settlers	Individual proprietorship, but in most cases title for a sub-lineage in the chief's name	De jure exchange rights, but de facto regulated by the chief
Paniyar	Nil	Bonded labourers to *janmis*, Gownders and Chettys Plantation workers Wage workers on settler farms	Nil
Kattunaicker	Nil	Bonded labourers to *janmis*, Gownders and Chettys Plantation workers Wage workers on settler farms	Nil
Gownders	Freehold titles to government revenue land Freehold titles to land taken over from indigenous people	Individual proprietorship of titled land Tenants on *janmi* land	Free exchange rights *Marupattam* exchange
Chettys	Freehold titles to government revenue land Freehold titles to land taken over from indigenous people	Individual proprietorship of titled land Tenants on *janmi*'s land	Free exchange rights *Marupattam* exchange
Nairs/Nambiars	Freehold	Landlord	Free exchange rights
British planters	Freehold	Individual proprietorship	Free exchange rights
Settlers	Titles to government revenue land Titles to government revenue land taken over from indigenous people	Private ownership of titled land Tenants on *janmi*'s land Tenants on *janmi*'s land taken over from indigenous people	Free exchange rights *Marupattam* exchange *Marupattam* exchange

Some extent of revenue forestlands was still under the control of the indigenous Kurumar agricultural community, either legally cultivated by paying tax and rent or under fugitive cultivation. The settlers took over much of these lands as a forest lease, in many cases without the knowledge of the community concerned. Here was a community who did not grasp the differences between the different land classifications – government revenue land, revenue forestland, and *janmi* forestlands – and the implications involved when living on and cultivating these lands. They were also not in a position to comprehend the significance of legally leasing-in revenue forestland vis-a-vis living and cultivating the land traditionally through generations. Thus the 'modern' mechanisms employed for assigning property rights in land by external agents, including the state, dispossessed them of their ancestral lands. Most of the indigenous people were reduced to the status of landless workers. The Malabar Tenancy Act of 1930 also adversely affected their chances of leasing-in wastelands as *kuzhikanam* tenure, as they had to pay rent and renewal fees in addition to the lease fee.

The Kattunaicker, whose livelihoods were intricately interlinked with the forests, were forced to move even farther into the interior. However, they could no longer meet their sustenance needs from the forests as the extent and quantity of accessible forests declined. There were also serious restrictions on what could be collected from the forests. Therefore, more and more of them became bonded labourers and wageworkers. The food requirements of the Paniyar were to a large extent met by gathering from forests. However, as the accessible forests decreased in area and quality, they also were forced to work more and more as bonded labourers to the *janmis*, and as wageworkers in the settler farms and plantations. Many of them were wageworkers in name only, as they were in a debt trap and therefore in effect bonded workers to the debtors.

Though de facto private property rights were established in large extents of revenue forest lands by settlers, which were now converted into agricultural lands, the remaining revenue forests were still treated as common property by the indigenous communities with regard to access and use rights. The community norms, rules and regulations according to the *Aivu* were still observed by them, while the same forests were treated as a de facto open-access resource by outsiders. Here is a case where a community that followed the rules of resource use in a common property regime lost out to outsiders who did not acknowledge and respect the rights of these communities in the resource. This resulted in resource depletion, or ruining of the commons, and in the process the dominant communities maximised profits and the weaker communities lost their resource base and livelihoods.

The British government had reserved vast areas of revenue forest for the Wayanad colonisation scheme, according to which land was allotted to the veterans of the Second World War. This also resulted in reduced access to land by the indigenous communities living in the nearby areas. Some *adivasi* households who were inhabitants of this area were also allotted land, but most of it was later lost to the settlers.

The settlers also leased-in private forestland from the *janmis* for cultivation. In some cases, land was bought from the *janmis*, as land prices were very low in Wayanad at that time. In many cases the *janmi* either sold or leased out to the settlers lands that were traditionally controlled by the Kurumar without their knowledge, and they were forced out of the lands. There were also cases where the settlers bought land from the Kurumar as per *theeradharam* after paying a nominal amount of money. The indigenous people were not well informed of the market value of land, and the settlers took advantage of this situation. A Kuruma settlement (Kurumakudy) consisting of twenty-five to thirty households may have had about 300 to 500 acres of land under their control, which they managed as common property. However, as mentioned earlier, they were not familiar with the 'modern' measures of acres or hectares. The Kuruma *moopan* would point to the area and say that those three or four hills and the surrounding valleys belong to their *kudy* (settlement). The settler might ask the *moopan* to sell five acres of land to him, and the *moopan* would sign the *marupattom* agreement for the same.[35] The settler may in fact have written a much higher area on the agreement paper (say, for example, fifteen acres) and this would not be detected, as the indigenous people were mostly illiterate at the time. The settler would then mark the boundaries for an even larger area (say, twenty-five acres). This would not be detected as well, as they were not familiar with the measurements. Another settler might come and ask for land, and the *moopan* would agree to sell some land and the same process would be repeated. Thus, many Kurumakudys lost much of their lands. There were also cases where forceful occupation of the Kuruma lands by the settlers occurred. The indigenous people were by and large peaceful people and were afraid of outsiders. Therefore, they were easily subjected to exploitation.

The private forests were utilised by all the *adivasi* communities, especially by the Kattunaicker and Paniyar, as common property for trapping small birds and small animals and gathering food materials, which contributed to a large share of the household food requirement; grazing cattle; collecting fuelwood; raw materials for artisanal work; house construction materials and so on. However, as more and more of the private forest lands were taken over by the settlers for cultivation, the indigenous people lost even more access to these resources. During this period the scale of deforestation was very high and a large extent of land was brought under cultivation by the settlers.[36] The indigenous communities were largely alienated from the land and forest resources. This was the situation at the time of Indian independence in 1947.

Though there was no major shift in the economic activities of the indigenous communities during this period, the number of wageworkers increased to a large extent. This was mainly due to the dispossession of land incurred by the Kurumar, the release of more and more Paniyar and Kattunaicker from bonded labour and the increased demand for labour created by the increased spread of agricultural activities with the arrival of the settlers.

Post-independence period

Property rights in agricultural land

The flow of in-migrants from Travancore and Cochin to Wayanad continued in the post-independence period. The migration process gathered momentum in the late 1940s with the 'grow more food' campaign of the government of India. Various push and pull factors were in operation.[37] Our concern here is the consequent changes in the property rights of the indigenous communities.

Under the Wayanad colonisation scheme, the land which was already reserved for the ex-service men from the Second World War was allotted to them in 1948. The project area included 9,802 acres of '*pattayam*' land[38] and 24,000 acres of revenue forestland spread over three villages in South Wayanad namely, Sulthan Bathery, Ambalavayal and Nenmeni (Mohandas, 1992). Large-scale in-migration to Wayanad was triggered by this project. The in-migrants (settlers) continued to acquire land by various means, as described in the earlier section. The unification of Malabar with Travancore and Cochin in 1956 to form Kerala state opened up new opportunities, and this triggered further in-migrations to Wayanad. As the scale of migration increased, land continued to grow scarcer. This in turn placed more demands on the lands under the control of the indigenous communities. During this period, alienation from their land reached its peak. The sixties and seventies were also the periods that witnessed mass in-migrations of marginal farmers and landless labourers to Wayanad.[39] The intensity of in-migration into Wayanad can be discerned by comparing the decennial population growth of Wayanad district and Kerala state (Table 3.4).

The settlers then formed a pressure group, negotiating and bargaining with the state for the provision of well-defined property rights – that is, titles to the land they leased-in and encroached on the revenue forestlands and the encroached lands in the reserve forests. They formed their own political party, called the Kerala Congress Party, that had considerable influence in the conservative coalition of Kerala led by the Congress Party of India.[40] Consequently, the government of Kerala supplied the settlers with titles to their land four times since the formation of Kerala state in 1956. These government decisions "regularised" occupations that occurred before 1 April 1957, 1 January 1960, 1 January 1968 and 1 January 1977 (Sivanandan *et al*, 1986). Granting titles to the land encroached upon and otherwise occupied by the settlers became a way of amassing popular political support, especially for the conservative coalition.[41] However, the Forest Conservation Act of 1980 passed by the government of India stipulated that any change in land use allocation in the reserve forest areas could be made only with the prior concurrence of the Central government.

The process of obtaining titles to land was cumbersome, involving protracted bureaucratic procedures that included filling in several application forms, producing

Table 3.4 Decadal variation in the populations of Wayanad and Kerala from 1951–1991

District/State	Decadadal variation in population (%)					
	1941–51	*1951–61*	*1961–71*	*1971–81*	*1981–91*	*1991–2001*
Wayanad	59.17	62.60	50.35	33.87	21.32	17.04
Kerala	22.82	24.76	26.29	19.24	14.32	9.42

Source: Census of India 2001, Series 33, Kerala, Provisional Population Totals

evidence of duration of stay and possession and innumerable other documents. It also involved high expenses in the form of fees to the government and bribes to rent-seeking officials. Therefore, a large number of indigenous people failed to file applications to obtain titles to the meagre lands that remained in their possession because of illiteracy, unfamiliarity with bureaucratic procedures and lack of money to pay the fees and bribes and to meet the travel expenses to go to the town office.[42] Therefore, the alienation of land continued further. As we have discussed earlier, the in-migrants in the late phase of migration were mostly marginal farmers and landless workers. They employed both overt and covert means to take possession of the land. They obtained small plots of land from the indigenous peoples by paying a small amount as an advance, with promises to pay more later; in some cases, a few bottles of liquor or a few bundles of chewing tobacco were offered as payments. The in-migrants then applied for titles and got them in their names, and the promised money was never paid.[43]

The apparent contradiction is that the indigenous people, particularly a large section of the Kattunaicker and some Paniyar and a small number of Kurumar, who had been traditionally living in the forest areas for generations, were not given titles because, by accident, they happened to be living in forest areas now classified as reserve forests. Earlier, many of them were living in forest areas now classified as 'vested forests',[44] revenue forests, or revenue lands. They were driven to the present 'reserve forest' areas by the outsiders as a result of the connivance of the *janmis* and aided and abetted by the state. Thus, it is evident that a dominant property rights regime (private property) sub-serving the market economy, in collusion with the state, effectively succeeded in dispossessing a community which was largely outside the market regime and which was unfamiliar with the concept of private property rights.[45]

The land reforms and after

The introduction of the Agrarian Relations Bill in the Kerala Assembly in 1959 has been pointed out as a major factor that triggered in-migration to Wayanad in the sixties (Mohandas, 1992). This bill proposed to confer ownership rights to all those holding land under various tenure systems. According to the Kerala Land Reforms Act of 1963, all kinds of tenancy systems were abolished and the tenants became the owners of the land they cultivated, subject to a ceiling of five hectares per family. However, this ceiling limit was not applicable to commercial plantations like tea, coffee, cardamom and rubber. Once the *janmis* and settlers got wind of these provisions of the Act, they proceeded to convert large extents of land to tea and coffee plantations. In the case of lands cultivated with other crops, many transferred the lands above the ceiling limits to their relatives. This considerably reduced the surplus land available for expropriation in Wayanad. Thus, according to the Land Reforms Act, titles were granted to the settlers who were holding *janmi* land and those who were cultivating the land belonging to the Kurumar according to some verbal agreement or other. In this process a small number of indigenous people, especially Kurumar and Kurichyar, who were able to hold on to some land also got titles to their land. But the area now under their control was

Pauperisation and proletarianisation 59

miniscule when compared to the settlers.[46] During this period, they also had to undergo harassment from the *janmis*, who tried to oust them from their lands, and from the settlers, who tried to take over the lands they controlled. Much land was lost by the indigenous communities, including Kurumar, Paniyar and Kattunaicker, in the frantic attempts by the *janmis* and the settlers to gain control over land on the eve of granting titles. Manipulations and corruption abound in the actual implementation of the land reforms. Collusion between the implementing officers, *janmis*, Chettys, Gownders and settlers negated much of the potential benefits that otherwise would have accrued to the indigenous communities.

The land reforms had made some provisions for squatters or hutment dwellers, who were landless labourers living on the landlord's land. Most of the Paniyar and some Kattunaicker were living as squatters. Each family was entitled to ten to twenty-five cents of land and the huts in which they lived. They were threatened and harassed in various ways to leave the land. Many were thus forced to leave, thereby relinquishing their right to the land and the hut. Those who managed to stay were granted titles to the land and the hut. A limited number of the landless indigenous people were allotted twenty-five cents to one acre of land from the surplus lands expropriated. However, many were unable to take possession of the lands allotted to them, as the land in question was under protracted litigation.[47]

The Kattunaicker were mostly living a nomadic life, moving from one place to another in the forests. Thus, a large population of this community could not be included in any category – neither tenants nor squatters. Though the government has now settled them on the edges of the forests, they cannot claim ownership to the land, as they are living on forestlands that belong to the state. At the same time, they are also not allowed to collect fuelwood and other forest products, except a few items classified as minor forest products, and that, too, with special permits for which they have to pay a fee. This is the present state of a community who once had unrestricted access to the forest space and resources. Table 3.5 summarises their present position with regard to land rights.

The foregoing analysis shows that the Kurumar, a traditional landowning group, obtained a limited number of titles to their lands. Moreover, the extent of area involved was rather small. They lost access to all other types of agricultural lands and therefore most of them ended up as wageworkers. The Paniyar became disembedded from land and were released into the labour market as free wageworkers, but without any skills except in rice cultivation. The Kattunaicker were settled on the edges of forests, disembedded from the actual forests and thrown into the labour market without any entitlements and capabilities. This was a situation of internal colonisation in which the settlers usurped the assets of the original inhabitants and left them dispossessed and pauperised.

Property rights in forest lands

New trends in the management of forests began to emerge in the post-independence period. The colonial forest policy was re-formed, and the National Forest Policy of free India was formed in 1952. However, the essence of the policies remained

Table 3.5 Property rights to agricultural land in Wayanad (post-independence period)

Communities	Ownership rights	Access rights/ Use rights/ Relation to land	Exchange rights
Kurumar	Further loss of titled land. Gained limited number of titles to tenancy land due to land reforms	Individual proprietorship of titled land. Workers on private plantations. Workers on settler farms. Workers on farms owned by Chettys, Gownders and former *janmis*	Exchange to non-indigenous communities prohibited by law in 1975[1]
Paniyar	Gained titles to *kudikidappu* plots[2]. Gained limited number of titles to surplus lands redistributed by the state	Individual proprietorship. Workers on private plantations. Workers on government plantations. Workers on farms owned by settlers, Gownders, Chettys and former *janmis*	Exchange to non-indigenous communities prohibited by law in 1975
Kattunaicker	Gained a minuscule number of titles to *kudikidappu* plots. Gained limited number of titles to surplus lands redistributed by the state	Individual proprietorship. Workers on private plantations. Workers on government plantations. Workers on farms owned by settlers, Gownders, Chettys and former *janmis*	Exchange to non-indigenous communities prohibited by law in 1975
Gownders	Titles to government revenue land. Titles to land taken over from the indigenous people. Titles to tenancy land	Individual proprietorship	Free exchange right
Chettys	Titles to government revenue land. Titles to land taken over from the indigenous people. Titles to tenancy land	Individual proprietorship	Free exchange right
Nairs/Nambiars	Freehold	Individual proprietorship	Free exchange right

1 The Tribal Land Alienation Act was passed in 1975 with a retroactive effect from 1960. However, the transfer of land from indigenous people to outsiders continued until 1986 without any hindrance. See Kjosavik (2004).

2 *Kudikidappu* plots are the squatter plots on the landlord's land where the squatters lived in a small hut. The squatters gained titles to ten to twenty-five cents (one acre is equal to 100 cents) of land, together with the hut.

the same. The powerful sections of society continued to be the beneficiaries of the forest administration. The exclusion policies with regard to the indigenous peoples also continued with renewed vigour. The 1952 policy led to further erosion of the legitimacy of the traditional claims of the indigenous communities (Gadgil and Guha, 1992). At the same time, the policy statement was a reassertion of the state monopoly over the forests (Guha, 1990). The post-independence drive for industrialisation led to a process of 'sequential overexploitation' of the forests (Gadgil and Guha, 1992). The consequence was that benefits often accrued to societies far removed from the forests, while the forest-dependent communities became more and more deprived of their resources.

In the Constitution of India, forest was listed as a provincial or state subject. The government of Kerala's priorities with regard to the forests were to extend the agricultural areas and to increase government revenues. As mentioned earlier, large tracts of forest in Wayanad were under private ownership. Necessary supplies of timber were obtained through private channels. We have seen that the land tenure regimes in Malabar, especially during the nineteenth century, were so harsh that there was very little incentive for the peasants from the midlands and lowlands to clear forests on a large scale for cultivation. This and the bonded nature of labour in Wayanad obviated for a long period the necessity to protect the forests from encroachment (Kunhikrishnan, 1987). Moreover, people's need for fuel and timber were met from the rich variety of tree species available in the home gardens of the midlands and coastal areas.

These factors contributed to the relatively high level of forest cover in Wayanad even at the end of the British period, even though in-migration from Travancore and Cochin had commenced in the late British period. Private ownership of forestlands continued for some time even after independence. Confusion and vacillations by the state government and the Central government, as well as judicial interventions, prevented the state from taking over the forests soon after independence.[48] The Madras Preservation of Private Forest (MPPF) Act of 1949 was the first post-independence attempt to establish some regulation over private forests. This Act applied to private forests with a contiguous area exceeding 100 acres (Vasudevan and Sujatha, 2001). According to this Act, the owner was not allowed to sell, mortgage, lease or otherwise alienate the whole or any portion of the forest without the prior sanction of the district collector. The MPPF Act also prevented cutting of trees, clearing the forests, cultivating the forestland, building houses on forestland, etc. Such offences were punishable with imprisonment of up to six months or a heavy fine. 'Forests' in this Act also included waste or communal land containing trees and shrubs, pasturelands and any other class of land declared by the government to be a forest by notification in the gazette.

Our discussions with elderly settlers in Wayanad revealed that a few of the early settlers were imprisoned for violating the MPPF Act. Though the *janmis* could not sell their forestlands, the *janmi* forestlands that were under the possession of Kurumar were bought by the settlers under a *marupattam* agreement, or without any documents. Thus the MPPF Act was circumvented by the settlers and the *adivasi* communities were further dispossessed of the forestlands they controlled. As has been mentioned, the private forests in Wayanad served as the village forests (village commons) for the indigenous people for grazing their cattle, collecting fuelwood, fodder, food gathering and collection of minor forest produce and other raw materials in the absence of de jure village commons. With the settlers gradually taking over these lands, the indigenous people were further squeezed out of their traditional commons.

After the formation of the Kerala state, Wayanad, which was in Malabar, became a part of Kerala. This provided an added impetus to the ongoing peasant migration to Wayanad from Travancore-Cochin (Tharakan, 1976). When the Communist Party was elected to power in Kerala in 1957, the state made an attempt to take over private forests by passing the Kerala Private Forests Act of 1957. The intention was to protect the forests and to redistribute degraded forestland to landless people. However, it could not be implemented due to the dismissal of the Communist government by the then-Central government led by the Congress Party.[49] When the 'highly enterprising' peasants of Travancore got wind of the imminent statisation of private forests, the exodus gained an added momentum. There was a 'land rush' and the frontiers practically became a 'free-for-all'. The result was large-scale encroachment of private forests and revenue forests and even reserve forests. These encroachments had been regularised at various points due to the highly organised political clout of the settlers. However, the 1980 law of the government of India stipulating the state governments to get central concurrence for such regularisations prevented further regularisations.

The Kerala Forest Act of 1961 was passed with the objective of having a unified law for the forests of the whole of Kerala – that is, Travancore, Cochin and Malabar – as the forests in these regions were under different rules. In 1962, the Congress government of Kerala passed another bill for the purchase of private forests at market price, but it was not approved by the government of India (Vasudevan and Sujatha, 2001). Following this, the Kerala Private Forests (Vesting and Assignment) Act was passed in 1971, and it received the president of India's assent on 23 August 1971. The purpose of this Act was to provide for vesting in the government the private forests of Kerala and for the assignment of these forestlands to small peasants and agricultural labourers for cultivation. Accordingly, the government of Kerala took over the private forests of Wayanad and designated them as vested forests. By this time, large areas were already occupied by the settlers. The total area of private forests in Malabar in the early 1950s was estimated to be 0.35 million hectares, but by the time it was taken over by the state in 1971, it was reduced to 0.18 million hectares.

Forest projects for indigenous peoples

Recognising the fact that the indigenous communities had been historically alienated from their lands and had become mostly free wageworkers, the government decided that each tribal family should have access to two hectares of land for their rehabilitation. The forest projects implemented in Wayanad with this objective include the Chingeri Extension Scheme, the Sugandhagiri Cardamom Project,

Pookot Lake Dairy Project, and Priyadarshini Tea Estate.[50] For the Chingeri Project, 540 acres of revenue forestland was allotted in 1958 to rehabilitate 100 tribal families. They were to plant coffee in these lands. However, the plantation was managed by the Harijan Welfare Department and the *adivasis* were working as wageworkers. As there was no regular and assured work in the project and the families were not paid regular wages, many left in search of work in private plantations and small farms. The scheme failed to achieve its objectives and later it was handed over to the Agricultural Research Station, Ambalavayal.

The South Wayanad Girijan Joint Farming Co-Operative Society, known as the Sugandhagiri Cardamom Project, was started in 1976. Each tribal family selected to settle in this project area was assigned two hectares of land under the provision of the Kerala Private Forests (Vesting and Assignment) Act of 1974. The conditions were that both the husband and wife should work as labourers in the project and that they must become members of the Joint Farming Co-Operative Society for cultivation of cardamom in the project. The land assignees had to mortgage their land to the co-operative society, which then undertook cultivation of cardamom. They were not allowed to mortgage the land elsewhere or sell it. The Pookot Lake Dairy Project was designed to rehabilitate 110 tribal families who were former bonded labourers. The project area included 420 hectares of vested forestlands, of which 245 hectares were grasslands. A portion of the land was used for growing various crops like cardamom, coffee and cacao. The target was to acquire 300 milch cows by the end of the third year of the project. However, the project turned out to be economically nonviable and was running at a loss. Later, this land was handed over to the Kerala Agricultural University to establish the College of Dairy Sciences. In addition to this, there are a few tea, coffee and pepper plantations on vested forestlands established for the purpose of providing employment to the indigenous people. These plantations were run by the Forest Department and in 2001 they were transferred to the Forest Development Corporation. Many of these projects are running at a loss and fail to provide regular employment to the *adivasis*. Though the indigenous people are the rightful owners of these project lands, they have no role in the management decisions and are mere wageworkers.

Encroachment and leasing-in of revenue forests by settlers continued even more aggressively after independence. This led to further marginalisation of the agricultural community of Kurumar. For the Paniyar, these forests were the commons for food gathering, and for the Kattunaicker it was their commons as well as their dwelling place. Both these communities' access to resources, as well as dwelling possibilities for the Kattunaicker, were adversely affected by the influx of settlers. The private property rights of settlers in these lands were later recognised by the state and titles were granted to them. Thus, whether it is agricultural land or forestland, the usurpers gained private property rights with the collusion of the state at the expense of the traditional indigenous rights-holders.

The freeing of wage labour was completed during this period. Even the former landowning community of Kurumar was largely dispossessed and the members released into the labour market. The former landlords and tenants became owner cultivators. Even when land was assigned to the indigenous communities according to the Kerala Private Forests (Vesting and Assignment) Act, these lands were held in co-operatives and the indigenous peoples were mere wageworkers on their own land.

Conclusion

The empirical material and analysis presented in this chapter have shown how the lives and livelihoods of the indigenous communities of Wayanad were impacted by the land policies and governance structures and practices of the colonial raj and the post-colonial governments of Kerala. The prime motive behind the colonial policy was to take greater control over land resources and their utilisation in order to raise revenue, promote commercial plantations and, of course, impose a more effective administrative system. The colonial rulers created a local ally in the form of a class of upper-caste landowners whose interests were closely linked to theirs. Indigenous people were turned into insecure tenants who had to pay their rent to the newly created landlords and taxes in cash to the colonial state. Inability to pay taxes and rents led to loss of access to land and consequent pauperisation. The land policy encouraged in-migration of foreign and local investors in plantation agriculture, and a rural agricultural proletariat class emerged as a result. Rising indebtedness and pauperisation also contributed to the more widespread incidence of bonded labour. The progressive appropriation of forests and their classification into different categories, along with the fencing of a large extent of land by the state and the transfer of forests to private investors for the creation of monoculture plantations, forced large sections of the *adivasi* population out of their habitat and sources of livelihood. The dispossession and deprivation caused by the colonial land policy led to an uprising of the indigenous people in 1812, which was one of the earliest agrarian revolutions in the region. Wayanad continued to attract migrants in the early years after independence, as well as after the formation of the Kerala state in 1956. The land reforms benefitted only a small minority of the indigenous people in Wayanad. This chapter lends empirical evidence to our thesis of pauperisation and proletarianisation and that the class-indigeneity intersection involves a variety of transitional social locations, with pauperisation being the dominant tendency. The analysis raises questions regarding the inclusivity of the Kerala model of development. We shall be addressing the issue of integration and exclusion in the next chapter.

Notes

1 Cf. Farmer, *Report to the Governor of Bombay Presidency in 1793* (quoted in Innes, 1951); Major Walker, *Report on the Land Tenures of Malabar, 1801*; William Thackeray, *A Report on Revenue Affairs of Malabar and Canara, 1807*; Thomas Warden, *Report on the Revenue System of Malabar, 1813*. See also Varghese (1970).
2 Mr. Farmer's report (Voucher No. 39) to the Bombay Presidency, dated 25 February 1793 (quoted in Innes, 1951: 306).
3 Major Walker's *Report on the Land Tenures of Malabar*, 1801 (quoted in Innes, 1951: 307).

Pauperisation and proletarianisation 65

4 Mr. Thackeray's *Report to the Board of Revenue*, dated 4 August 1807 (quoted in Innes, 1951: 307).
5 Mr. Warden's *Report to the Board of Revenue*, dated 12 September 1815 (quoted in Innes, 1951: 308).
6 Sullivan, *Report on the Provinces of Malabar and Canara to the Chief Secretary to the Madras Government*, Fort St. George, 1841, para 27 (quoted in Varghese, 1970: 26).
7 See Innes (1908: 301–302), Baden-Powell (1972: 170) and Logan (1951).
8 *Report on Malabar Land Tenures*, p. 122 (G. O. No. 500, Political, dated 29 July 1884 (quoted in Innes, 1951: 313).
9 See Innes (1951: 313–317) for a detailed account.
10 Discussion with former Poothady *adhikari*.
11 See also Panoor (1989) and Johnny (2001).
12 See also Ravi Raman (2000).
13 See George and Tharakan (1986) and Ravi Raman (2002) for detailed accounts of the oppressive conditions of production that prevailed in the British colonial plantations in Kerala.
14 Logan, *Malabar Special Commissioner's Report on Malabar Land Tenures, 1881–82, Vol. 2,* Appendix 1, Chapter 4, para. 100 (quoted in Varghese, 1970).
15 Discussions with former Poothady *adhikari*.
16 Moberly (1900), *Report of the Settlement of Malabar District*: Madras (cited in Varghese, 1970)
17 This section is based on discussions with Poothady *adhikari* and elders of indigenous communities.
18 Discussions with elders of the Kuruma community.
19 This was a modified version of *vallikettu*, the agrestic slavery practice in Wayanad for centuries, by which the indigenous communities of Paniyar and Adiyar had been bonded for life. (See Panoor (1963) and Johnny (2001) for details of the practice.)
20 Discussions with elders of Kuruma community.
21 Discussions with former Poothady *adhikari*.
22 G. O. No. 797, Revenue, dated 25 July 1904 (in Innes, 1951).
23 See Innes (1951) and Varghese (1970) for details of the settlement.
24 Discussions with former Poothady *adhikari*.
25 William Thackeray (1807: 3), *A Report on the Revenue Affairs of Malabar and Canara* (quoted in Kunhikrishnan, 1987).
26 Report of the Joint Commission of Bengal and Bombay, 1792–93, para 445 (quoted in Kunhikrishnan, 1987).
27 Logan's *Collection of Treaties, etc., Part II*, No. XXXIX (quoted in Innes, 1951: 319).
28 This Act with minor modifications is still in vogue in India. See also Fernandes *et al* (1988) and Guha (1996).
29 Browne, R. S. 1929, *Revised Working Plan for Malabar*, Madras (quoted in Kunhikrishnan, 1987).
30 *A Manual of Administration for Forest Range Officers in Madras Presidency*, Madras, 1929, p. 2 (cited in Kunhikrishnan, 1970).
31 *Plantation Enquiry Committee Report*, Government of India, 1956 (cited in Varghese, 1970).
32 The sections on establishing property rights by settlers are mostly based on interviews with the village *adhikari*; elders of Kurumar, Paniyar and Kattunaicker communities; and elderly settlers.
33 See Varghese (1970) for a discussion on the various provisions of the Act.
34 See Panoor (1963, 1989).
35 Only the *moopan* had the right to sell land belonging to the *kudy*.
36 See Varghese (1970), Tharakan (1976) and Joseph (1988) for details.
37 See Tharakan (1976) and Joseph (1988, 1997) for a detailed study of the causes of migration from Travancore-Cochin to Malabar.

38 Land with legal title already owned by private owners.
39 See also Mohandas (1992).
40 The Conservative coalition, led by the Congress Party of India, and the Left coalition led by the Communist Party of India (Marxist), have been alternating power in Kerala state since the first elections in 1957 after the formation of the state in 1956.
41 See Moench (1990) for the politics of 'regularisation' of leased-in and encroached forestlands and revenue lands in highland Kerala. See also Hoeschele (1998).
42 Discussion with elders of the indigenous communities.
43 According to a sample survey conducted in Wayanad, following the large-scale in-migration of settlers, two-thirds of the indigenous households lost approximately half of the land area held by them prior to the in-migration. More than nine-tenths of these land transfers were to the settlers (Mohandas, 1992).
44 The private forests owned by the *janmis* were taken over by the state in 1971 as per the Vested Forest Act of 1971. These forests are classified as vested forests.
45 See also Kjosavik (2010).
46 See Kjosavik and Shanmugaratnam (2004) for an analysis of the impact of land reforms on the indigenous communities of Kerala.
47 Discussions with the village officer, *Irulam* and the indigenous people.
48 See also Karunakaran (1992) and Kunhikrishnan (1987).
49 See Nossiter (1982, 1988) for expositions of the factors leading to the dismissal of the Kerala government in 1959. See also Kjosavik and Shanmugaratnam (2004).
50 See Mohandas (1986).

References

Baden-Powell, B. H., 1875, 'On the Defects of the Existing Forest Law (Act XIII of 1865) and Proposals for a New Forest Act', in Baden-Powell, B. H. and Gamble, J. S. (eds.), *Report of the Proceedings of the Forest Conference, 1873–74*. Calcutta: Government Press.

Baden-Powell, B. H., 1972, *The Indian Village Community*. Delhi: Cosmo Publications.

Brown, H., 1953, 'Parrys of Madras – A Story of British Enterprises in India', in Speer, S. G. (ed.), UPASI 1893–1953. New York: MacMillan.

Gadgil, M. and Guha, R., 1992, *This Fissured Land: An Ecological History of India*. New Delhi: Oxford University Press.

George, T. K. and Tharakan, P. K. M., 1986, 'Penetration of Capital into a Traditional Economy: The Case of Tea Plantations in Kerala, 1880–1950', *Studies in History*, 2(2): 200–229.

Guha, R., 1990, *The Unquiet Woods: Ecological Change and Peasant Resistance in the Himalaya*. Berkeley: University of California Press.

Guha, R., 1996, 'Dietrich Brandis and Indian Forestry: A Vision Revisited and Reaffirmed', in Poffenberger, M. and McGean, B. (eds.), *Village Voices, Forest Choices: Joint Forest Management in India*. Delhi: Oxford University Press: 86–100.

Hoeschele, W. R. W., 1998, *Land Degradation, State Power, and Peasant Livelihood in Attappadi (Kerala State, India)*. Doctoral dissertation, Pennsylvania: Pennsylvania State University.

Indhrani, K., 1982, *The Forest Policy and Administration of the Madras Presidency Under the Crown, 1858–1935*. Doctoral thesis, Madras: University of Madras.

Innes, C. A., 1908 (1997 rpt), *Malabar Gazetteer Vol. I and II*. Trivandrum: Kerala Gazetteers.

Innes, C. A., 1951, *Madras District Gazetteers: Malabar*. Madras: Government Press.

Johnny, O. K., 2001, *Wayanad Records – A Regional History*. Calicut: Pappiyon.
Joseph, K. V., 1988, *Migration and Economic Development of Kerala*. Delhi: Mittal Publications.
Joseph, K.V., 1997, 'Peasant Migration from Travancore to Malabar', in Zachariah, K. C. and Irudaya Rajan, S. (eds.), 1997, *Kerala's Demographic Transition: Determinants and Consequences*. New Delhi: Sage: 249–268.
Karunakaran, C. K., 1992, *Kerala Forests Through Centuries*. Trivandrum: Kerala State Language Institute.
Kjosavik, D. J., 2010, 'Politicising Development: Re-Imagining Indigenous People's Land Rights and Identities in Highland Kerala, South India', *Forum for Development Studies*, 32(2): 243–268.
Kjosavik, D. J. and Shanmugaratnam, N., 2004, 'Integration or Exclusion? Locating Indigenous Peoples in the Development Process of Kerala, South India', *Forum for Development Studies*, 31(2): 231–273.
Kunhikrishnan, K. V., 1987, *The British Indian Forestry: Malabar Experience*. M. Phil. dissertation, Calicut: University of Calicut.
Kurup, K. K. N., 1986, *Vijnanakairali*, quoted in Johnny, O.K., 2001, *Wayanad Records – A Regional History*. Calicut: Pappiyon.
Logan, W., 1951, *Malabar, Vol. 1*. Madras: Government Press.
Moench, M. H., 1990, *From Forest to Agroforest: Land Use Dynamics and Crop Succession in the Western Ghats of Kerala, South India*. Doctoral dissertation. Berkeley: University of California.
Mohandas, M., 1986, *Impact of Development Projects in the Western Ghat Region on the Forest Dependent Population: Case Study of Wayanad District in Kerala*. Trichur: College of Co-operation and Banking, Kerala Agricultural University.
Mohandas, M., 1992, *Impact of New Settlers in the Western Ghat Region on the Socio-Economic Conditions of the Tribal Population: The Case of Wayanad District in Kerala*. Trichur: College of Co-operation and Banking, Kerala Agricultural University.
Nossiter, T. J., 1982, *Communism in Kerala: A Study in Political Adaptation*. Berkley: University of California Press.
Nossiter, T. J., 1988, *Marxist State Governments in India: Politics, Economics and Society*. New York: Continuum International Publishing Group.
Panoor, K., 1963, *Kerala's Africa*. Kottayam: National Book Stall.
Panoor, K., 1989, *Kerala's America*. Kottayam: National Book Stall.
Poffenberger, M., McGean, B. and Khare, A., 1996, 'Communities Sustaining India's Forests in the Twenty-first Century', in Poffenberger, M. and McGean, B., (eds.), *Village Voices, Forest Choices: Joint Forest Management in India*. Delhi: Oxford University Press: 17–55.
Ravi Raman, K., 2000, 'Intervention in the Western Ghats: An Inquiry into the Historical Processes of Loss of Biodiversity and Community Sources of Livelihood', in Pushpangadan, P., Ravi, K. and Santhosh, V. (eds.), *Conservation and Economic Valuation of Biodiversity, Vol. 2*. New Delhi: Oxford and IBH: 525–544.
Ravi Raman, K., 2002, *Bondage in Freedom: Colonial Plantations in Southern India c. 1797–1947*, Working Paper No. 327. Trivandrum: Centre for Development Studies.
Ribbentrop, B., 1900, *Forestry in British India*. Calcutta: Government Press.
Sivanandan, P., Narayana, D. and Nair, K. N., 1986, 'Land Hunger and Deforestation: A Case Study of Cardamom Hills in Kerala', *Economic and Political Weekly*, XXI(13): 546–550.

Stebbing, E. P., 1922, *The Forests of India*. London: The Bodley Head Limited.
Tharakan, P. K. M., 1976, *Migration of Farmers from Travancore to Malabar from 1930 to 1960: An Analysis of Its Economic Causes*. M. Phil. dissertation, Trivandrum: Centre for Development Studies.
Tharakan, P. K. M., 1984, *Intra-Regional Differences in Agrarian Systems and Internal Migration: A Case Study of the Migration of Farmers from Travancore to Malabar 1930–50*, Working Paper No. 194. Trivandrum: Centre for Development Studies.
Varghese, T. C., 1970, *Agrarian Change and Economic Consequences: Land Tenures in Kerala 1850–1960*. Bangalore: Allied Publishers Private Limited.
Vasudevan, C. V. and Sujatha, V., 2001, *Forest Laws of Kerala*. Cochin: Ganesh Publications.

4 Not a frozen class

Indigenous people (*adivasis*) in the Kerala model of development

Introduction

In this chapter we revisit the Kerala model of development and its performance with special reference to indigenous communities. The *adivasis*, who were thrown into the rural labour market either after their release from slavery and bonded labour or through dispossession, were largely unskilled and unfamiliar with the new agricultural crops and technology introduced by the settler farmers. Earlier, the British planters – and later, the local planters – brought workers from the neighbouring states of Tamil Nadu and Karnataka, who were either familiar with the cultivation of these crops or were willing to work under oppressive conditions at very low wages. In fact, a different form of bonded labour – 'contract' labour, without any right to negotiate fair wages or decent living conditions for the workers – prevailed in the plantation sector.[1] The *adivasis* were often unwilling to work in the plantations, and many were still attached to landlords through debts and other forms of patron-client ties. Later, in the second half of the twentieth century, the in-migration of large numbers of landless workers from the lowlands and midlands created an excess supply in the labour market. Consequently, in the ensuing competition, *adivasi* workers were forced by circumstance to work for substantially lower wages or be unemployed.

Conceptualisation of indigenous people in the Kerala model

It would seem that, at a certain level, the Kerala model regarded the indigenous communities together with the lower castes as 'frozen classes'. This conceptualisation has had its problems, although a certain correspondence is discernible between class and caste/ethnicity at an empirical level, particularly when it comes to oppressed castes and a large majority among the indigenous communities.

However, the inequality question in India cannot be reduced merely to the economic realm. The caste system and ethnicity questions relating to indigenous communities are at the root of economic and social inequalities. Hindu society has been divided and subdivided into various groups, called *castes*, which are arranged hierarchically in complex ways; each caste's position is primarily defined by its location in the ritual hierarchy, which usually coincides with that of the social – and, consequently, the economic – hierarchies. Therefore, the genesis of economic inequalities could arguably be located in the ritual hierarchies.[2] The indigenous communities historically were outside the rubric of the caste structure.[3]

Class, in a Marxian sense, is defined by the fundamental criterion of relationship to the means of production. In a class society, one group of people can appropriate the labour of another because of the different places they occupy in the socio-economic system; the location of the groups is determined by their relation to the means of production, by their role in the social organisation of labour and, consequently, by the dimension and mode of acquiring a share of social wealth.[4] In the class-caste debate in India, following independence, the term *class* has been used loosely to denote particular communities or caste groups or indigenous groups, in contrast to the concept of class in social theory. All the Articles in the Constitution of India – except one in Part XVI titled 'Special Provisions Relating to Certain Classes' – deal with Scheduled Castes, Scheduled Tribes and the Anglo-Indian community. Whenever reference is made to backward classes, as in Article 338(3) or in Article 340, it appears to mean the aforementioned categories (Béteille, 1994). Thus class is treated as a logical category obtained by means of one or another logically consistent classification system, and the classes mentioned in the Indian Constitution reflect this. Analysts of the Indian Constitution often argue that the only logical way of classifying the Indian peoples is on the basis of castes and communities. For example, the Karnataka Backward Classes Commission Report states:

> Class is synonymous with caste or tribe, so far as Hindus are concerned. Class is synonymous with tribe, or racial group, so far as tribal communities are concerned. Class is synonymous with section or group, so far as Muslim, Christian and other religious communities and denominations are concerned.
> (Havanur, 1975: 98–99, quoted in Béteille, 1994: 31)

The use of the term *class* in this sense is clearly inconsistent with the conception of class in social theory. 'The grouping of castes, or tribes, or races in terms of even purely economic criteria does not give us classes, but ranked divisions of some other kind' (Béteille, 1994: 91–92).

The caste–class debate in India thus failed to make any conceptual distinction between class, caste and other subordinate groups. In fact, all of them were collapsed into a common category. When one views this from the inside, it would seem that this semantic usage of the term *class* to connote caste categories or indigenous communities was sufficient for the purpose of affirmative action policies. Nevertheless, in the Kerala context, this takes on larger dimensions. The founders of the Kerala model introduced policies for the oppressed castes and the *adivasis*, bringing them under the rubric of a 'frozen working class' that had been denied mobility for generations. One could say that the Marxists had a point when they conceived of caste as frozen class, especially in the case of the Scheduled Castes with regard to their relation to the means of production. The characteristic of this 'class' was that the members were propertyless (in the sense that they did not own any means of production), but were bounded within a structure that denied them the mobility enjoyed by workers in a modern capitalist society.[5] Nevertheless, being part of a larger social system, the Scheduled Castes were eventually able to derive gains from the various reform policies, social-sector investments and welfare programmes targeted at them, and were included in the legal framework that legitimised trade-union activism as well as certain other rights. These programmes included the public distribution system, free health care and education, welfare programmes for the various categories of wage workers, the Agricultural Workers' Act, the Industrial Workers' Act, the Plantation Labour Act and other initiatives to protect trade unions in various sectors.

However, the case was not the same when it came to the indigenous communities. In the late 1950s, when the Kerala model began to emerge, the vast majority of indigenous peoples could be included in the category of proletarians based on their relation to the means of production. They had been dispossessed of their ancestral lands by statisation and privatisation processes, and they became casual and seasonal workers in plantations, small farms and state forests. As mentioned earlier, the proletarianisation process of the *adivasis* was very different; they had not yet been integrated into the mainstream of Kerala society and were on the margins of the market. Their dispossession made them potential participants in the labour market, but lack of employment opportunities and, more importantly, lack of employable skills pushed them into pauperism. Geographical isolation, cultural specificities, socio-economic organisation, protracted patron-client ties, and other institutional constraints prevented them from emerging as a regular proletariat and taking advantage of programmes targeted at the labour class. Various welfare programmes bypassed the *adivasis*, as they did not fall neatly into the specific categories of workers. In hindsight, it would seem that the problem was inadequately grasped by the proponents of the model when they treated the *adivasis* as a 'frozen working class' like the Scheduled Castes. The class reductionism that informed the conceptualisation of indigenous communities as a 'frozen class' was largely ineffective in fine-tuning development programmes and welfare measures to meet their specific needs. It lost sight of the dynamic intersection between indigeneity and class. While we are aware of the ongoing theoretical debates on issues of indigeneity in India, our concern here is to show how *adivasi* communities were conceptualised within the Kerala model and the implications of this for the socio-economic integration of these communities.[6]

The government of India's approach to the development of indigenous peoples

Post-colonial India adopted a strategy of integration with regard to indigenous peoples. Several provisions were made in the constitution for this purpose. For example, Article 46 makes states responsible for taking special care to promote the educational and economic interests of Scheduled Tribes and Scheduled Castes, and for protecting them from social injustice and all forms of exploitation. The Fifth Schedule of the Constitution includes special provisions for the administration and control of the Scheduled Areas (regions where indigenous communities are concentrated, and which are often remote and not easily accessible) and Scheduled Tribes in eight states.[7] Article 244 lays out special provisions for the administration of Scheduled Areas, Scheduled Tribes and Tribal Areas. In Article 342, indigenous communities are listed under the category of Scheduled Tribes, thereby targeted for affirmative action and various special development programmes. Article 275 allows central grants-in-aid to states for promoting the welfare of Scheduled Tribes. Articles 330 and 332 provide for reservation of seats in the parliament and the state assemblies, while Article 335 provides for job reservation in central and state services. According to the provisions of Article 339, the government of India can direct a state to implement certain specific schemes deemed necessary for the welfare of Scheduled Tribes in that state (Patel, 1998).

Starting with the First Five-Year Plan, efforts have been made to further the development of indigenous communities through programmes providing them with direct economic, educational and social benefits. Special Multipurpose Tribal Blocks were set up for this purpose. In the Third Plan, these were modified as Tribal Development Blocks, with each block covering 25,000 persons in areas where two-thirds of the population was indigenous. In the Fifth Plan (1973–1978), there was a discernible change in the development strategy. It was felt that rather than a blanket approach to the indigenous development problem, attention had to be focused on each identifiable community or area. Therefore, it was decided that programmes had to be directed towards (1) areas of tribal concentration, (2) dispersed tribals, and (3) 'primitive' tribal communities. The result was the adoption of the Tribal Sub-Plan (TSP) strategy, according to which contiguous Tribal Areas were brought under a separate sub-plan of the general state plan. Guidelines for the formulation of the TSP were issued to the states by the Planning Commission of India. Accordingly, TSP areas were delineated at the macro-, meso- and micro-levels, taking into consideration the natural resources of a region, geographic peculiarities, the level of development of the indigenous communities inhabiting the region and other socio-economic conditions (Patel, 1998). The TSP approach is still being followed by the government of India.

Kerala's approach to indigenous peoples' development

Kerala was not able to harness significant benefits from the earlier programmes of the government of India because its indigenous population was a minuscule percentage of the overall population and because the state had no areas designated as Scheduled Areas. The *adivasis* of Kerala, however, eventually benefited considerably from the sub-plan approach to development due to its special focus on individual families, in the case of dispersed indigenous groups, and its identification of 'primitive tribal communities' – that is, the most disadvantaged indigenous groups – for which special programmes could be tailor-made, in addition to the focus on spatial units where the communities were concentrated. It became possible to cover the entire *adivasi* population of Kerala under the TSP. However, due to the late take-off of the programme, precious time was lost – nearly two decades – before the whole *adivasi* population was able to benefit.

With regard to the indigenous people, Kerala followed the broad approach of the national government. Most of the programmes implemented were also within the framework provided by the Central government, and it was mandatory for the state to abide by it. In the process, it was inevitable that many development issues specific to the *adivasis* of Kerala were overlooked. The development of these communities has, therefore, been incremental and disjointed. However, it would seem that the *adivasis* have been able to achieve some gains from the policies of the state within the general framework of the Kerala model, though not at the same pace or to the same extent as that of Scheduled Castes, due to reasons we have already outlined. Investments in the education sector, as mentioned earlier, were a primary focus in the Kerala model. The following tables show that the indigenous communities benefited from the provision for universal education. Substantial improvements in literacy were achieved by them and the Scheduled Castes (Table 4.1). Holders of secondary school leaving certificate (SSLC) and higher qualifications also increased. By 1981, the indigenous communities were able to catch up with the Scheduled Castes in this respect.

The leftist government elected in 1987 launched a series of programmes called 'New Democratic Initiatives' at the grassroots level. The objectives of these were to undertake massive campaigns for total literacy, to install energy-efficient stoves in a bid to solve the fuelwood crisis, and to undertake a campaign for resource mapping at the local level that would form the basis of future local planning for sustainable development.[8] Large-scale mobilisation of *adivasis* occurred during these campaigns. The substantial leap in their literacy level during this period bears testimony to this.

The disaggregated data on school enrolment reveals that the state's investment in educational infrastructure has also paid substantial dividends to the indigenous communities. Table 4.2 shows that there is proportional representation of *adivasi* students (Scheduled Tribes) in the total school enrolment (1.14% against a population share of 1.10%). However, the dropout rate is much higher among students from indigenous communities, as evidenced by the fact that their share in the total

Table 4.1 Literacy and education levels in Kerala by population categories

Year	Percentage of literates			Holders of SSLC* and higher qualifications		
	General Population	Scheduled Castes	Scheduled Tribes	General Population	Scheduled Castes	Scheduled Tribes
1961	46.15	24.44	17.26	6.45	2.51	1.56
1971	60.42	40.21	25.72	10.01	4.39	3.36
1981	70.42	55.96	31.79	NA	5.00	5.00
1991**	89.22	79.66	57.22	NA	NA	NA

Source: Sivanandan (1989)
**State Resource Centre (2002).
*Secondary school leaving certificate.

74 *Not a frozen class*

Table 4.2 Disaggregated data on school enrolment in Kerala (2000)

School level	Percentage of total enrolment		
	General Population	*Scheduled Castes*	*Scheduled Tribes*
Lower primary school	87.78	10.75	1.47
Upper primary school	88.25	10.72	1.03
Secondary school	88.76	10.38	0.86
Total	88.23	10.63	1.14
Kerala's population* (%)	88.99	9.91	1.10

Source: State Resource Centre (2002).
* Population % pertains to the year 1991.

enrolment is only 0.86% at the secondary school level. The Kerala model appears to have a beneficial impact on the education of indigenous communities, as shown by the fact that the dropout rate of Scheduled Tribe students in Kerala is 31.4%, while the average for India is 77.7% (State Resource Centre, 2002).

The general investments in rural infrastructure and the provision of basic services have also been beneficial to the indigenous population, both directly and indirectly. For instance, 100% of Kerala villages have primary schools and 99% have secondary schools and ration shops (outlets for the supply of basic food and fuel at subsidised prices) within two kilometres. There is easy access to health services, as indicated by the presence of health dispensaries in 91% of villages, health centres within two kilometres of 47% of the villages and hospitals within a distance of five kilometres of 78% of the villages.[9]

Agrarian reforms and indigenous communities

The land reforms implemented in 1970 were the major policy component in the Kerala model that effected fundamental structural changes. The reforms have had a positive impact on indigenous communities, although the gains they made, especially in the case of traditional land-holding groups, were not significant in relation to the historical land alienation they had suffered. However, certain communities such as the *Kurumar* and the *Kurichiyar*, who were tenants, were able to secure ownership rights to the land they cultivated, subject to a ceiling of two hectares. A large number of former bonded labourers among the *Paniyar* and the *Adiyar*, and a limited number of *Kattunaicker*, who were squatters on the landlord's land, obtained ownership rights to ten to twenty-five cents of land,[10] together with the huts they lived in. A limited number of landless households obtained ownership rights on between twenty-five cents and one acre of land through the redistribution of surplus land – that is, land exceeding the limit of two hectares, which was expropriated by the state from large land-owners. The beneficial impact of land reforms on the *adivasis* is evident from the decrease in landlessness among them in the post–land reform period (Table 4.3). In 1964–1965, 57.69% of the *adivasi*

Table 4.3 Landlessness among the *adivasi* households in rural Kerala

Rural households	Percentage of households without land		
	1964–1965	1974–1975	1983–1984
Adivasi households	57.69	28.70	20
All households	33.20	17.10	6.70

Source: Adapted from Sivanandan (1989) and Oommen (1994).

households were landless, whereas five years after the implementation of land reforms – that is, in 1974–1975 – this decreased to 28.70%. As the implementation of the reforms proceeded, the proportion of landless households further decreased to 20% in 1983–1984.

The landlessness among indigenous communities is more than three times that of Kerala state as a whole. Now the question could be raised as to why the gap in landlessness between indigenous households and the rest of the Kerala households remained high in the post–land reform phase. It is in this context that the class-indigeneity intersection becomes relevant. The historical, geographical, ecological and socio-economic specificities of the *adivasis* were subsumed in the class reductionism that informed the land reforms. They were treated on a par with the Scheduled Castes and the general population with regard to the means of production and the relations of production. It would seem that the architects of the Kerala model failed not only to take into consideration the customary land tenure systems of the *adivasis*, but also to include any provision in the land reforms for the establishment of forest commons. Such a provision would have helped reduce the problem of landlessness, at least to a limited extent, since forest commons had historically been a part of the livelihood system of the *adivasis*. Evidently, the reformists approached the land question merely in terms of private and state property regimes.

The land question of the *adivasis* was thus articulated within the framework based on the notion of a 'frozen class', which as we see now, did not bring them as much benefit as it should have, had their land question been treated with due regard to its particular eco-historical features. Some provisions, however, were included to safeguard their interests, as well as those of the Scheduled Castes. Accordingly, 75% of the expropriated surplus lands were to be distributed to *adivasi* and Scheduled Caste households. The Kerala Land Assignment Rules (1964) provide for distribution of at least 25% of the *puramboke*[11] land to these groups. However, the major beneficiaries of these provisions have been Scheduled Castes, as opposed to indigenous communities. Much of the *puramboke* land had already been occupied by the Scheduled Castes, and allocation was mostly limited to giving titles to the existing occupiers. The extent of *puramboke* land in the highlands was limited and scattered in various regions. Given the traditional clustered settlement pattern of the indigenous communities and the socio-ecological embeddedness of their lives and livelihoods, it was not in their interest to receive tiny scattered plots of land outside their familiar environment.

In this context we must also elucidate some of the constraints faced by the protagonists of the reforms. Although 'land to the tiller' was the slogan of the times, a large section of the real 'tillers' constituting the rural proletariat could not get any substantial amount of land for cultivation. To explain this, one has to look at Kerala as part of the Indian Union. Land reforms were a major plank of rural development in independent India. According to the Congress Agrarian Reforms Committee, a 'tiller' is a farmer engaged in 'personal cultivation', that is, one who contributes 'physical labour and participates in actual agricultural operations' (AICC, 1949, quoted in Oommen, 1994). The Planning Commission's guidelines to the states, however, also include 'supervision' in the definition of 'personal cultivation'. Consequently, this was included in the Kerala Land Reforms (Amendment) Act of 1969, passed by the conservative coalition government. This took the teeth out of the Agrarian Relations Bill of 1959 passed by the left-wing government, which was radical and oriented towards the 'land to the tiller' initiative, both in words and spirit. The model for land reforms laid out in the Five-Year Plans had clearly left out the agricultural proletariat (Oommen, 1994). However, within this restrictive framework, Kerala managed to include some provisions by incorporating squatters' rights to at least ten cents of land and to the huts they occupied, and by placing ceilings on holding size and expropriating surplus land for redistribution to the landless workers.[12] The Kerala Agricultural Workers' Act of 1974, which was aimed at protecting the rights of agricultural workers with regard to working hours and work conditions, and to guarantee wage employment on the farms;[13] the Kerala Plantation Labour Act of 1964; and so on can be considered offshoots of the larger Agrarian Relations Bill of 1959.[14]

Many of the benefits of land reforms for the *adivasis* were in the form of rights to squatter plots and, to a limited extent, ownership rights to tenants. The ceiling on holdings and expropriation provisions, intended for the redistribution of surplus land, did not have a significant beneficial impact on these communities for various reasons. Agrarian reforms, including a ceiling on holdings, were envisaged as soon as the Communist Party came to power in 1957. However, implementation could not be effected until January 1970. This long time lag provided sufficient time for large landowners to transfer land on paper to various family members and relatives or to make other voluntary transfers, including market sales. Land transfers in various forms were treated as valid by the state until 16 August 1988.[15] These mostly consisted of transfers of the surplus land in the highlands that should have been redistributed to the indigenous communities. Another important factor was the exemption on ceilings given to holdings growing plantation crops such as rubber, tea, coffee and cardamom, according to the stipulations of the Planning Commission of India. Tea, coffee and cardamom are the major crops grown in the highlands, and rubber is largely grown in the midlands. This meant that it was hard to find significant surplus land in these areas. Moreover, given the time lag between the conception and implementation of the reforms, many large landowners converted their land to plantations of these crops, thus circumventing the ceiling laws. Therefore, the amount of surplus land expropriated in highland Kerala was negligible, with negative consequences for the indigenous communities. In northern Kerala, historically, *adivasis* had access and use rights in large areas of forestland, although the latter was owned by landlords. The conversion of these forests to plantations that happened during this period was also condoned and was exempted from ceilings by the government.

The land ceiling provision of the larger land reforms was thus a double-edged sword for the indigenous communities. On the one hand, the state's failure to extract surplus lands in the highlands resulted in them not gaining much land. On the other hand, the legitimisation of conversion of private forests in northern Kerala to plantations resulted in their losing access to the forestland and resources. This situation is reflected in the higher incidence of landlessness among *adivasis* of northern Kerala as compared to those of southern Kerala even after the implementation of land reforms (Table 4.4).[16]

This assumes significance given the fact that more than two-thirds of the indigenous population live in the highlands of northern Kerala, particularly Wayanad district, which is home to 35.82% of Kerala's indigenous people. In spite of all the exemptions, evasions and other loopholes, the state did manage to expropriate a small amount of surplus land in this district. Some of this land had been assigned on paper to *adivasi* families by the state as early as 1980; however, the families have been unable to take possession, as the land is still tied up in protracted litigations. Our discussions with the land assignees in Wayanad revealed that they did not have the economic resources necessary to seek legal assistance and that the state, represented by the bureaucracy, shows a general apathy with regard to this issue.

Currently, the *adivasi* land question in Kerala is articulated outside the framework of the land reforms. In the late 1960s and early 1970s, the radical Left movement led by the Marxist-Leninist Communist Party of India (CPI-ML) made inroads into the indigenous landscape and kindled a revolutionary spirit among the communities. Since then, the politics of the *adivasis* have centred on the land question. The Marxist Leninist movement, which adopted the Maoist ideology of peasant insurgency,[17] was soon crushed by the state machinery, but left a lasting impression on the hearts and minds of the indigenous people.[18]

Table 4.4 Extent of landlessness among *adivasis* in northern and southern Kerala

Regions	Percentage of landless adivasi households	
	1976*	1982**
Northern Kerala	30.47	8.56
Southern Kerala	4.83	0.91

Source: Computed from Sivanandan (1989).
* Figures are based on a survey of all *adivasi* households in the state.
** Figures are based on a survey of 48% of the total *adivasi* households in the state. A comparison between the years 1976 and 1982 may not give the right inference, as one is based on the entire population and the other on a sample. It is important to note that most of the non-landless households had only homesteads of 5 to 10 cents.

78 *Not a frozen class*

Table 4.5 Restitution effected by March 1991

Region	Area to be restituted (hectares)	Number of applications filed	Area involved (hectares)	Number of applications processed	Area restituted (hectares)	Number of applications pending
Northern Kerala	7,146.63	5,472	7,608	203	461.87	5,249
Southern Kerala	2,217.84	3,282	2,301	240	82.69	3,042
Total	9,364.47	8,754	9,909	443	544.56	8,291

Source: Statement filed by government of Kerala dated 4 April 1991. From the records of the Foundation for Educational Innovation in Asia (FEDINA), Sulthan Bathery, Wayanad.

In response to the mounting pressure from the *adivasi* groups, and as directed by the government of India, the Kerala state passed the Kerala Scheduled Tribes (Restriction on Transfer of Lands and Restoration of Alienated Lands) Act in 1975. The two key provisions in this Act are aimed at prevention of further land alienation and restitution of already alienated land. Accordingly, the transfer of land from indigenous peoples to others is prohibited,[19] and the land that had been alienated from them since 1 January 1960 should be retrieved and handed back to them. Following this, there was a decade of absolute impasse until 1986, when the state framed the necessary rules for the implementation of the act. Tribal land tribunals were set up in the districts, with the district revenue officer as the chief arbitrator. The *adivasis* were to file applications, supported by the necessary proof, to the tribunal for restitution of their land. Thus, the process of restitution was initiated. A statement filed by the government of Kerala in 1991 shows that the extent of legal restitution effected has been negligible (Table 4.5). Even the legally restituted land has not been physically restored to the *adivasis* due to organised resistance from the non-*adivasis* who currently occupy this land.

However, the whole process is at a standstill currently due to the enactment of new bills and acts by the state and protracted litigation involving the present landowners, settlers' organisations, the state, pro-*adivasi* activists and *adivasi* organisations. The *adivasis* have been engaged in various forms of land struggles, including 'direct action', for nearly two decades now.[20] We address these issues in detail in Chapters 6 and 7.

Alternative state initiatives to address the indigenous land question

Based on the guidelines provided by the government of India, Kerala initiated programmes for the rehabilitation of former bonded labourers and landless workers belonging to indigenous communities since the late 1950s. Rehabilitation projects were set up for this purpose as early as 1958 under the Integrated Tribal Development Programme.[21] By 1964, the problem of alienation of *adivasi* land to non-*adivasis*, especially the in-migrant settlers, traders and moneylenders, was recognised as a major impediment to the further socio-economic development of these communities (Government of Kerala, 1964).[22] The forests that were under private ownership were taken over by the state under the Kerala Private Forests (Vesting and Assignment) Act of 1971,[23] and the rules were framed in 1974. Rule 8 stipulates that 50% of the lands available for assignment should be allotted to members of the *adivasi* communities who were willing to engage in agriculture as a means of livelihood; preference would be given to those residing in the private forests vested in the government (Vasudevan and Sujatha, 2001).

The Madhava Menon Commission,[24] a commission formed by the state to make recommendations for allotment of vested forestland, recommended an allotment of 8,470 hectares distributed over fourteen *panchayats* in Wayanad district to the *adivasis* (Solidarity, 1995). However, given the widespread occurrence of transfer of land from indigenous people to others, the state decided to form Joint Farming Co-operative Societies, with indigenous people as members, instead of granting ownership rights to individual households (personal discussion with Madhava Menon).[25] Each member household was to have two hectares of land as its share. The intention was to make sure that the land would not be alienated from them. Several such co-operatives were formed in the vested forestland acquired by the state in Wayanad. These societies were initially to be run by the state bureaucracy, with the *adivasis* as workers, and a share of the profits was to be distributed to the members. Under this programme, tea, coffee and cardamom plantations and a dairy farm were established in Wayanad. The idea was that the state would run the projects until they 'took off' and then they would be handed over to the members of the society. However, this has not happened so far, even after nearly three decades. Moreover, these projects have been steeped in controversy, have been prone to severe disputes between workers and the management (bureaucracy) and have been running at a heavy loss.[26] Thus, they have not proved effective in solving the landlessness and associated development issues of the *adivasis*, though some employment was generated. The state was not in a position to redistribute this land to the *adivasis*, as, according to the Forest Conservation Act of 1980, the state required the concurrence of the government of India to make any decision on forestland. The bureaucracy was also trying to thwart any attempt by the government to distribute this land.

The State Forest Department established a few coffee and pepper plantations in the vested forestland earmarked for distribution to the indigenous communities. The proposed purpose of these plantations was to provide employment to *adivasis*. However, our discussions with the *adivasis* in Irulam Village, Wayanad district, revealed that non-*adivasi* workers are also employed in these plantations. The *adivasi* casual labourers have to compete with them for the scarce labour days.[27] In one of the plantations we visited, *adivasis* constituted a mere 8% of the permanent workers. This shows that the *adivasis* are clearly being marginalised, even in the special projects initiated for them. The plantation management's version is that at the establishment stage of the plantation in the late 1970s, they needed a large labour force to get the plantation started. At the time, there was a scarcity of *adivasi* labour, as the *adivasis* were not interested in working regularly on the plantation. Therefore, to keep the plantation going, other workers had to be recruited. Later, these workers organised themselves into trade unions and claimed the status of permanent workers under the provisions of the Plantation Labour Act of 1964 and they were granted that right. The management pleaded helplessness on the issue. However, our discussions with the *adivasi* workers provided another story. According to their version, when the plantation was started in 1978, many of them went to work there, but the wages were low compared to the agricultural wages in the open labour market. Further, wages were not paid regularly, but whenever the Forest Department got funds from the government. This created a difficult situation for the *adivasis*, as they did not have any other source of income to fall back on. They needed the wages to be paid daily so that they could buy their daily food requirements. This forced many *adivasis* to leave the plantation and work for settler farmers so that they could get daily wages. The non-*adivasi* workers were recruited to meet the shortage thus created. The plantations had been running at a loss, and in the year 2000 they were transferred from the Forest Department to the Forest Development Corporation of Kerala for more 'efficient' management. Predictably, the *adivasi* workers had also been recruited to the various trade unions along with the other workers. However, their influence is not as effective as that of the other categories of workers who dominate the unions, and the special problems pertaining to them often get subsumed in the general question of the rights of workers as a class. This is an instance of how class reductionism has been detrimental to the interests of the *adivasi* workers.

Currently, the state has more than forty development and welfare programmes specifically targeting the indigenous communities, and each family benefits from one or more such programmes (discussion with tribal development officer, Sultanbathery, Wayanad district). Most of these have been formulated and implemented under the guidelines of the Tribal Sub-Plan. However, not all communities are able to respond to the various programmes.[28] Most of the development programmes are related to agriculture, animal husbandry and allied activities that require assured access to land and fodder. Under these programmes, financial assistance in the form of loans for self-employment or other activities requires land as collateral. Therefore, only a small landed section is able to take advantage of these programmes and make a real change in their socio-economic situation. For example, in Wayanad district, Kurumar and Kurichiyar are the two *adivasi* communities that own some land. However, they constitute only about 25% of the total *adivasi* population of the district. The other 75% includes the landless or near-landless communities such as the Paniyar, Adiyar, Uralis and Kattunaicker, and a large number of development programmes bypass them. They are only able to take advantage of the welfare programmes, which help them to take one day at a time, with no real chance of any socio-economic mobility. Within the framework of the Kerala model, the state has twenty-seven major social security and welfare schemes currently targeting various categories.[29] Many of these programmes, designed for the various categories of the labour class, do not consider the indigenous communities, as they fall outside those categories; exceptions include a few schemes such as the

Agricultural Workers' Welfare Scheme, the Kerala Widow Pension Scheme, the Kerala Destitute/Old Age Pension Scheme and the Leprosy and Cancer Patients' Pension Scheme.

Although these programmes have contributed substantially to the reduction of absolute poverty, as well as to improvements in access to basic health care and education, they have not been able to provide momentum for socio-economic mobility of these communities. The absence of non-agricultural economic opportunities reinforces the contention that gaining access to land for cultivation is the single major factor that can contribute to their mobility, be it on the economic or the social front.

Civil society interventions in the development of indigenous peoples

Parallel to the state, civil society organisations have also been intervening in the development of indigenous communities. Foremost among them have been the Christian Church–based organisations and, at a later stage, other non-governmental organisations (NGOs). With the in-migration of a large Christian population from southern Kerala since the late 1920s, the Church began to play a major socio-economic and political role in the region in addition to its spiritual mandate. The initial approach of the Church was paternalistic and welfare based.[30] However, with the formation of Church-based social service societies in the highlands, especially in Wayanad, Palakkad and Idukki districts[31] in the 1970s, there was a radical shift in their approach to the *adivasi* development question. Inspired by the ideals of liberation theology and a new commitment to genuine social change, these organisations embarked on conscientisation and educational programmes to enable the indigenous people to struggle for their rights. A decade of their work made significant changes in the lives of the indigenous people, and they began to be more assertive. This radicalism, however, was not in the interests of certain groups, particularly the political leaders of certain factions, the state bureaucrats responsible for the *adivasi* development and welfare programmes and the mainstream Church. Therefore, the Church-based organisations were forced to 'contain' their radicalism, perhaps fearing 'the danger of *conscientizacão*' (Freire, 1996: 17) and the consequent anarchist tendencies.

In the 1980s, the more radical elements from the Church-based organisations distanced themselves from the Church and went on to found separate NGOs to further the cause of the indigenous people. They used the classic method of Paulo Freire[32] to educate them, and this resulted in the creation of a 'critical mass' who became attuned to taking up minor local issues and in the process getting mobilised (Cheria *et al*, 1997). Our interactions with some Church-based organisations and NGOs in Wayanad and discussions with the *adivasis* revealed that no real divide exists between them currently.[33] What we observed is a constructive division of labour, where the more radical political activity of organising is mostly undertaken by the NGOs. The Church-based organisations focus more on the socio-economic developmental activities, which also serve as a means of empowerment.

Facilitated by the NGOs and various political parties, the *adivasis* began to organise themselves into various associations, some with allegiance to left-wing political parties, some to the Congress Party, and others with no preferred political allegiances. In addition, they have organisations based on specific *adivasi* groups. For example, the *Mekhala Paniya Samajam* (Regional *Paniya* Association) and the *Kuruma Samudaya Samrakshana Samithy* (*Kuruma* Community Welfare Association) are organisations in northern Kerala primarily focused on the *Paniya* and *Kuruma* communities, respectively. Similarly, the *adivasis* of southern Kerala, like the *Kanikkar*, the *Uralis* and other groups, have their own community-based organisations. The formation of community-based organisations indicates that each community feels the need for separate agency and advocacy, as each community perceives that its interests and issues are different from those of the other groups. This is due to the specific historical processes that are reflected in the current socio-economic differentiation between them. The indigenous communities of northern Kerala are a highly heterogeneous group. Socio-economic hierarchies and practices akin to that of the caste Hindu society have been widely prevalent among these communities and still exist to a certain extent. The landed *adivasi* groups such as the *Kurichiyar* and *Kurumar* consider themselves superior, ritually and socially, to other communities such as the *Paniyar* and *Adiyar*, who were historically agrestic slaves and/or bonded labourers, and the *Kattunaicker*, who were traditionally hunters and gatherers. Of late, the Hindu fundamentalist Bharatiya Janata Party (BJP) has made some inroads, though minuscule, into the *Kurichiya* and *Kuruma* communities by playing on their 'upper caste' sentiments.

However, despite their prevailing differences, the communities have found a common terra firma to stand on: their identity as indigenous peoples, the *adivasi*. This new awakening paved the way for the founding of the *Adivasi Aikya Samithy* (United *Adivasi* Forum), the different units of which coalesce at a higher level to form the *Adivasi Vikasana Pravarthaka Samithy* (*Adivasi* Development Activists' Forum). These processes occurred mainly in the late 1970s through the 1980s. A critical mass of radical activists and leaders emerged through these developments.

Several international events in the late 1980s and early 1990s provided an impetus to the *adivasi* mobilisation process in Kerala. Convention No. 169 of the International Labour Organisation in 1989 provided an international legal framework with regard to the rights of indigenous peoples. Part II of the convention, including Articles 13 to 19, covers issues related to land and territories of indigenous peoples.[34] This was a great leap forward for the *adivasis* in their struggle for land. The World Bank's Operational Directive No. 4.20 (1991) and the United Nations Working Group on Indigenous Populations (UNWGIP) of the UN Commission on Human Rights, especially the Draft Declaration on the Rights of Indigenous Peoples, agreed to by the UNWGIP in 1993, marked another step forward in the struggle for *adivasi* rights. The year 1993 was declared the International Year of Indigenous Peoples by the United Nations (UN), and the period 1995–2004 has been declared the UN Decade of Indigenous Peoples. In April 2000, the UN Human Rights Commission decided to set up a permanent forum on indigenous issues.

These developments have provided international legitimacy to the struggles of the *adivasis* of Kerala. Networking of *adivasi* organisations with those of neighbouring states and other regions of India, largely facilitated by the NGOs, was a major development that furthered the mobilisation process. The *Sangamom,* a coming together of the indigenous peoples of South India, organised in Wayanad district a week-long sharing of experiences and chartering of future agendas. It lasted from 12–19 October 1992, and was a major event in the history of *adivasi* struggles. Following the *Sangamom,* the South Zone *Adivasi* Forum (SZAF) was formed, the mandate of which was to be a forum for struggles.[35] A woman from the *Adiyar* community, C. K. Janu, was chosen as the president. Almost all the subsequent struggles for land have been led by Janu. Gender struggles within the *adivasi* organisations, although mostly covert, are also a frequent phenomenon. Our discussions with activists revealed that, given the currently dominant patriarchal ideology among *adivasi* communities, a woman's leadership is frequently questioned and criticised.

Some radical left groups – for example, the Communist Party of India (Marxist Leninist-Red Flag) (CPI-ML Red Flag) and the Kerala Communist Party (KCP), which are fallouts from the former Communist Party of India (Marxist Leninist) – have been supporting the *adivasi* land struggles, although they address the land question from a different ideological platform: the Maoist ideology of peasant insurgency, as mentioned previously. They are critical of the pacifist approach of the indigenous people's movement. The movement of the Scheduled Castes of Kerala, known as the *Dalit* movement,[36] actively co-operates with the *adivasi* struggles for land. The intense agitation for land organised in July to August 2001 was spearheaded by the *Adivasi-Dalit* Action Council. The women's movement of Kerala is in solidarity with the *adivasi* movement. On many occasions, the women's movement, represented by *Kerala Sthree Vedi* (the Kerala Women's Forum, which is a network of feminist groups and fellow-travellers), has joined hands with the *adivasis* in their struggles. Of late, the Communist Party of India (Marxist), which is at present the leading opposition party in the Kerala Legislative Assembly, is increasingly taking part in the *adivasi* land struggles. For example, in May 2002 they supported a struggle by the indigenous people in Irulam Village, Wayanad district, where the agitators entered the vested forestland and built traditional *adivasi* huts among the teak trees using wild grasses and rice straw. It was a symbolic agitation to remind the state of the 'promised land' in the earlier agitation of 2001. The state, currently governed by the Congress coalition, reiterated its promise, and the *adivasis* ended the agitation and peacefully dismantled their huts. In February 2003 they intensified the agitation and forcefully occupied the forestland in Muthanga Wildlife Sanctuary in Wayanad district. The state brutally suppressed this agitation, and in the ensuing violence unleashed by the state police force, one *adivasi* man and a policeman were killed and several agitators wounded. Several leaders of the struggle, including C. K. Janu, were imprisoned. The Communist Party came out in support of the *adivasis*. The saga of the *adivasi* movement, especially the struggle for land in the past decades, has been highly turbulent and eventful, spread out over time and space (see Kjosavik, 2004).[37]

Crisis of the Kerala model and the indigenous people

The 'crisis' of the Kerala model of development has been a subject of debate in the last decade[38] initiated by scholars and political activists of a leftist persuasion.[39] It would seem that the most important feature of the crisis faced by the Kerala model is of a fiscal nature,[40] with consequent implications for investments in the social as well as economic sectors. The centre-state fiscal relations characterising Indian polity have not been favourable to the interests of Kerala. In centre-state fiscal transfers, Kerala is a net loser on two counts. First, the economic sectors in which the state has an advantage – for example, cash crop agriculture and fisheries – are under the purview of the centre with regard to tax revenues from both interstate trade and exports to other countries. When Kerala was drafted into the Indian Union after independence, the state lost its control over customs revenues, which had been the mainstay of its open economy. The service sector in Kerala has been growing much faster than the secondary sector, but tax revenues from this go to the centre. About 31% of Kerala's net State Domestic Product is constituted by remittances from abroad by out-migrants from Kerala (Jeromi, 2003). Taxes on the remittances accrue to the Central government. Second, transfer of funds from the centre to the state is not proportional to the state's contribution to the centre, and has in fact been declining over time.[41]

The stagnation of the agricultural and industrial sectors has been pointed to as a factor contributing to the crisis. Various theses exist as to the reasons for stagnation in these sectors, but there is no apparent consensus.[42] A Central government unwilling to change its position on fiscal issues and vacillations in Kerala's electoral politics have also gone a long way in contributing to the crisis of the model. The Congress coalition has been in power almost continually at the centre since independence, except for a few short breaks. At the same time, the Congress coalition has been alternating with the leftist coalition to form governments in Kerala. The impact of this on the state's development has been characterised by some local commentators as 'two steps forward, one step back'. The radical reforms conceived and implemented by the governments of the left would either be made ineffective or blunted by the Congress coalition when in power. The state's Congress coalition has had the blessing of the Congress governments at the centre in this endeavour. However, due to the powerful agency of the mass movements in Kerala, it has never been possible to completely reverse a process once underway. The conservative coalition led by the Congress Party, together with various smaller parties, plays a significant role in Kerala's dynamic democratic process. The concern we raise, however, relates to some tendencies in the conservative coalition that have not been helpful in moving forward the positive policies initiated by the Left in the larger interest of the state and its people. We have already discussed how the Congress Party, then in opposition, sabotaged the radical clauses in the land reforms in collusion with the Central government. Sathyamurthy (1985) points to at least three occasions when the Congress government at the centre manipulated food supplies to the state to demoralise the leftist government.

The state has been constantly discriminated against in terms of fund allocations, especially with regard to non-plan and other special funds that form a major part of the state's expenses in the social sector. The conservative coalition in the state, when in power, seems to be more concerned with serving the interests of the powers that be at the centre than with trying to secure the rightful share for the state. At the state level, its efforts are directed more towards undoing the progressive policies of the Left than towards formulating innovative policies and programmes or implementing existing programmes efficiently. Examples include the adult literacy campaign, the peoples' resource mapping programme for land and resource literacy, the group farming programme and the district councils of the late 1980s, and more recently, the decentralised planning process. Thus Kerala's development process unfolded in a political and institutional environment constrained by limited autonomy, interventions from the Central government,[43] and an opposition political coalition that is at ideological loggerheads with the protagonists of the model. India's democratic federal framework, which provided the space for the Kerala Communists to implement radical reforms in the first place, also serves as a constraint to the success of some of those policies. Therefore, any critique of the Kerala model has to address this dynamic framework.

The general crisis of the Kerala model has had adverse consequences for the indigenous communities. The stagnation in the agricultural sector, in particular, affected their opportunities for wage labour. The trends in cropping pattern, with the change from labour-intensive food crops such as rice, cassava and banana to less labour-demanding plantation monocultures, were especially harmful with regard to their employment opportunities. Nevertheless, as a large part of the funds for the TSP was still transferred from the Central government,[44] the state was able to implement development and employment-generating programmes that benefited *adivasi* communities. A small percentage was able to obtain gainful employment through affirmative action policies. Moreover, the overall social security and welfare programmes of the Kerala model that were still continuing, including the public distribution system, provided a safety net for these marginal communities.

Nevertheless, the situation took a downturn with the implementation of neo-liberal programmes in the early 1990s by the government of India. The crisis of the Kerala model has since then been exacerbated by liberalisation and structural adjustment policies. Stringent fiscal 'discipline' imposed on the state government, with strict directives to cut down on social-sector expenditure, and the decreased transfer of funds from the centre to the state have substantially diminished the prospects for social security of the marginal communities, particularly the *adivasis*. The crash in agricultural prices engendered by indiscriminate trade liberalisation in the agricultural sector has further reduced wage labour opportunities for them. At the same time, the state is not in a position to implement the affirmative action policies effectively, as few jobs are being created in the state sector where the policy is applicable, due to the increased drive for privatisation. The neoliberal policies have thus initiated a process of 'new social exclusion' with regard to indigenous communities.

86 *Not a frozen class*

The leftist government that came to power in Kerala in 1996 initiated the decentralised planning process through the people's plan campaign as a strategy to combat the adverse effects of the neoliberal policies. Substantial fiscal and administrative powers were devolved to elected bodies at the local level – *panchayats* and municipalities. These local bodies were given the power and responsibility to plan and implement development programmes.[45] Funds were earmarked at the local level for the implementation of development programmes for the indigenous communities. There was a leap forward in their advocacy and agency that was facilitated by, among other things, the reservation of 10% of seats in local bodies for indigenous peoples. Thus, the decentralised planning process has been a continuation, with further reinforcement, of the 'inclusive' development policies followed by the leftist governments in Kerala. However, the various changes in the decentralised planning process brought about by the conservative coalition that came to power in 2001 have in many ways undone this 'inclusiveness'. As a result of the currently diminished decentralised planning and the relentless implementation of neoliberal policies, the 'new social exclusion' of the indigenous communities continues.

Conclusions

This chapter took a critical look at the Kerala model of development and analysed how the workings of the model, in conjunction with forces external to it, have impacted the development of the indigenous communities. The radical policies initiated by the leftist government in 1957, which became the defining characteristics of Kerala's development, led to high levels of social development at relatively low levels of economic growth. Our question was how this development process addressed the condition of the *adivasis*. With regard to the general development strategy of the state, Kerala took advantage of the federal polity and attempted a departure from the mainstream growth-led development path to a predominantly distribution-based development. However, with regard to the *adivasis*, Kerala followed the guidelines of the federal government at the centre, which was not very conducive to their development for various reasons.

The conceptualisation of the indigenous communities as a 'frozen class' in the Kerala model seems, in hindsight, to have been a shortcoming of the development approach. A development strategy that gave due regard to eco-historical processes would have brought them more socio-economic benefits than did the class reductionist approach. Our analysis shows that the *adivasis* have made both economic and social gains, albeit to a limited extent, through the workings of the Kerala model, particularly in literacy, education and access to land. Our contention is that although they are still an 'outlier' category, they have not been excluded from the development approach followed by the Kerala model. On the other hand, the various policies have, in general, tried to integrate the *adivasis* into the process. However, the forces that precipitated the setback of the Kerala model and the present crisis, including hostile Central governments, electoral vacillations and opposition politics, have also had negative implications for the development of the *adivasis*. We have highlighted the case of land reforms and how the attempts to expropriate surplus land to be distributed to the *adivasis* were thwarted, despite the best efforts of the protagonists. Alternative attempts by the state to address the land question, outside the framework of land reforms, have also not come to fruition. The 1975 Act that provides for restitution of alienated land to the *adivasis* has not been implemented for various reasons. We identify landlessness as the major development issue of the *adivasis* of Kerala at present. Access to land for cultivation is a precondition for generating surpluses and thereby fuelling the building of cultural capital through education in agrarian communities in general and in embedded communities such as the indigenous people in particular.

Recent trends in Kerala's development, following the adoption of neoliberal policies, have engendered a process of 'new social exclusion'. In the chapter that follows, we address the question whether the *adivasis* of Kerala are now trapped in a development triangle – the Kerala model of development, neoliberal policies and decentralised planning. While the development that unfolded through the Kerala model helped the integration process to a great extent, the workings of the liberalisation and structural adjustment programmes have shown exclusionary tendencies. The initial phase of the decentralised planning process contributed to the further integration of the indigenous people into the socio-economic and political mainstream. The later phase, however, showed reverse tendencies, which also coincided with the aggravated impact of the neoliberal imperatives. It would seem that the forces of exclusion are currently gaining the upper hand with regard to the indigenous people of Kerala. We explore these in the next chapter.

Notes

1 The plantation workers did not have any legal protection, while the planters enjoyed full protection. For example, according to the Workmen's Breach of Contract Act of 1859, the workers had to sign a contract for a specific period of time and, if violated, he or she was subject to prosecution. Therefore workers from Kerala were not willing to work in the plantations, and workers had to be brought in from the drought-affected areas of Tamil Nadu and Karnataka. In 1896, 80% of the workers in plantations of northern Kerala (Wayanad) and southern Kerala (Travancore) and 96% of the workers in central Kerala (Cochin) were brought in from outside (George and Tharakan, 1986).
2 Though the existence of caste as a structure and practice is widely admitted, its conceptualisation and the historical trajectories of caste formation are contested. There are also regional variations in caste structures and practices and in the extent of interaction between different castes, and between castes and *adivasis*. See Hutton (1969), Béteille (1969), Berreman (1970, 1971, 1993), Dumont (1972), Gupta (1980), Thapar (1984), Khare (1984), Chakravorty (1985), Chakrabarty (1989), Mukherjee (1991, 1999), Quigley (1993) and Bahl (1995, 2004) for conceptualisations and discussions of the caste system in India.
3 There are more than 700 *adivasi* groups in India scattered over a wide range of geographic regions and ecological niches, and with varying intensities of socio-economic and political interaction with the other populations. Singh (1982) claims that the 'tribes' that are included in the Scheduled Tribes category according to the Constitution of India share many of the characteristics of tribes included in the anthropological literature, such as relative isolation, homogeneity and settlement in a well-defined habitat. In the Indian context, however, 'tribe' as a conceptual category is problematic. See Ambasta

(1998) for an account of the debate on tribe as a conceptual category vis-à-vis analytical category. See also Pathy et al. (1976), Pathy (1982, 1988, 1992), Roy Burman (1983), Cinemart Foundation (1984), Béteille (1986), Sengupta (1988a, 1988b, 1988c, 1988d, 1988e), Corbridge (1989), Shah (1992) and Devalle (1992).
4 See Lenin (1952), Dahrendorf (1959), Bendix and Lipset (1966), Giddens (1981), Stavenhagen (1970), Ossowski (1963) and Tharamangalam (1981) for discussions on the concept of class.
5 In Kerala there are no village commons, which can contribute to the livelihoods of landless people. The forests – reserve forests and protected forests – are owned and managed by the state. In northern Kerala some of the forests were owned by landlords but were taken over by the state in 1971. Although *adivasis* have restricted access to the forests for the collection of certain minor forest produce, others – including oppressed castes – are denied access to forest resources.
6 See Barnes (1995), Kingsbury (1995, 1998), Gray (1995a, 1995b) and Jentoft (2003) for general discussions on the concept of indigenous peoples; Bates (1995), Betteille (1998), Xaxa (1999), Karlsson and Subba (2006) and Rycroft and Dasgupta (2011) for discussions of the concept in the Indian context.
7 To date, Kerala still has no designated Scheduled Areas. Recently, however, the state government has conceded to the demand from the indigenous peoples' movement and agreed to request the Central government to designate areas of tribal concentration in the state as Scheduled Areas.
8 See Franke and Chasin (1994a), Thomas Isaac and Franke (2002).
9 See Franke and Chasin (1994a).
10 One acre is equal to 100 cents.
11 Plots of land by roadsides and river banks and other such land not owned by private individuals have been classified as *puramboke* land.
12 About 0.3 million proletarian households benefited from the squatters' rights provision and about 67,000 hectares of surplus lands were expropriated by the end of 1988 in accordance with the ceiling provision to be distributed to the proletariat, out of which 25,000 hectares have been distributed to 126,000 landless households. Nearly 87% of the surplus lands have been reserved for the settlement machinery to settle disputes between landowners and labourers. About 3 million tenants became owners of the land they cultivated (Oommen, 1994).
13 Subject to certain constraints, such as cash-crop farms, continual employment for a certain number of days per year, giving due advance notice, and so on.
14 Paulini (1979), Oommen (1971, 1979, 1985), Mencher (1980), Herring (1980, 1983), Nossiter (1988), Radhakrishnan (1989) and Jannuzi (1994), among others, provide detailed expositions of Kerala's land reform experience.
15 See also Oommen (1994).
16 Feudal relations of production had been abolished to a great extent in southern Kerala (Travancore) by the Royal Proclamation of 1865 and the Landlord-Tenant (*Janmikudiyan*) Proclamation of 1867. As a consequence of this progressive legislation, the indigenous communities of southern Kerala also gained land-ownership rights, which would in part explain the lower incidence of landlessness among those in southern Kerala.
17 Some extreme factions attempted 'elimination of the class enemies'. Ajitha (1990) gives an account of their activities in Wayanad.
18 This is captured in the following statement made by an elderly *Paniyar* woman in Wayanad, with whom we had discussions: 'Those were the days with high expectations. Comrade Ajitha, Comrade Varghese and others brought us a renewed dignity and spirit that had been crushed time and again, for centuries, by outsiders who dominated Wayanad hills. For the first time we felt that we were not alone, that there was a group of people fighting for our cause. But the state, together with the upper classes, crushed our movement, but we will never allow them to crush our spirits once again.'

Not a frozen class 89

19 With certain exceptions and with special permission from the district revenue officer (collector).
20 'Direct action' includes forceful occupation of land to be restituted, land that is tied up in litigations and state forestland.
21 See Mohandas (1986) for a review of a rehabilitation project in Wayanad district, northern Kerala.
22 See also Mohandas (1992).
23 Large extents of forests in northern Kerala were under the ownership of landlords.
24 The commission was named after Chairperson Madhava Menon.
25 See also Panoor (1989).
26 See Mohandas (1986) for a review of two such projects. See also Sasikumar (1993).
27 We had discussions with the plantation management and the workers in May 2001.
28 Antony (1995) found that the landowning indigenous group Kurichiyar was more responsive to the programmes of the state than the largely landless Paniyar community.
29 See State Resource Centre (2002) for a list of the programmes.
30 See Cheria *et al* (1997).
31 These are districts with a high concentration of indigenous people.
32 Freire (1996) uses the term *conscientizacão* to refer to learning to perceive social, political and economic contradictions, and to take action against the oppressive elements of the society. In his *Pedagogy of the Oppressed*, Freire argues that the condition of ignorance and lethargy among the poorer classes of the society is directly linked to their economic, social and political domination by the powerful groups. The right kind of education rooted in the everyday life experiences, continued shared investigations and the action-reflection-action process would serve to develop a critical awareness in any oppressed class, however poor or illiterate it might be.
33 We had interactions with two Church-based organisations – Shreyas (the Bathery Social Service Society) and the Wayanad Social Service Society (WSSS) – and three NGOs – Solidarity, High Land Development Association (HILDA) and Federation for Educational Development in Asia (FEDINA) which were offshoots of former Church-based organisations.
34 See Patel (1998), Xaxa (1999) and AICFAIP (2001).
35 See Cheria *et al* (1997) for an account of the *Sangamom*.
36 The term '*dalit*' is used to refer to the former oppressed castes.
37 Kjosavik (2004) gives a detailed analysis of the indigenous peoples' struggles for land.
38 For recent debates on the Kerala model of development by authors of different political persuasions, see Tharamangalam (1998), Franke and Chasin (1998), Omvedt (1998), Heller (1998), Parel (1998), George (1998), Parameswaran (1998), Törnquist (1998), Alexander (1998), Parayil (1998, 2000), Kannan (1999) and Parayil and Sreekumar (2003).
39 See, for example, Thomas Isaac and Mohanakumar (1991), Franke and Chasin (1994b, 1994c) and Thomas Isaac and Tharakan (1995a, 1995b).
40 See George (1990, 1994, 1999).
41 According to the decision of the Eleventh Finance Commission, Kerala's share in central taxes would be reduced from an average of 3.85% during 1995–2000 to 3.06% during 2000–2005. The state would incur a net loss of about US$734 million as a result of this (Government of Kerala, 2001).
42 See, for example, Kannan and Pushpangadan (1990), Narayana (1990) and Sivanandan (1994) on Kerala's agricultural sector; Subrahmanian (1990, 1994), Albin (1990), Nanda Mohan (1994), Pillai (1994), Padmanabhan (1990), Thampy (1994) and Sankaranarayanan and Meera Bhai (1994) on Kerala's industrial sector. See also Heller (1995, 1996, 1999) and Kannan (1998).
43 See Sathyamurthy (1985) for an account of the government of India's interventions in Kerala politics.

44 There was a strict directive from the centre not to divert TSP funds for any other programmes or purposes.
45 See Thomas Isaac and Harilal (1997) and Thomas Isaac and Franke (2002) on the decentralised planning process in Kerala. See also Véron (2001).

References

AICFAIP, 2001, *Voices of the Adivasis/Indigenous Peoples of India*. New Delhi: All India Coordinating Forum of the Adivasis/Indigenous Peoples.

Ajitha, K., 1990, 'Reminiscences from Wayanad', in Sen, Ilina (ed.), *A Space Within the Struggle*. New Delhi: Kali for Women: 19–24.

Albin, A., 1990, 'Manufacturing Sector in Kerala: Comparative Study of Its Growth and Structure', *Economic and Political Weekly*, September 15: 2059–2070.

Alexander, W. M., 1998, 'Economics as If People Mattered: The Kerala Case', *Bulletin of Concerned Asian Scholars*, 30(4): 44–46.

Ambasta, A., 1998, *Capitalist Restructuring and Formation of Adivasi Proletarians: Agrarian Transition in Thane District (Western India) c. 1817–1990*, Ph D thesis. The Hague: Institute of Social Studies.

Antony, P., 1995, *The Food Economy of Tribals in Kerala: A Comparative Study of Kurichiyar and Paniyar*, M. Phil. dissertation. Trivandrum: Centre for Development Studies.

Bahl, V., 2004, 'Terminology, History and Debate: "Caste" Formation or "Class" Formation', *Journal of Historical Sociology*, 17 (2/3): 265–318.

Barnes, R. H., 1995, 'Introduction', in Barnes, R. H., Gray, A., and Kingsbury, B. (eds.), *Indigenous Peoples of Asia*. Michigan: The Association for Asian Studies, University of Michigan: 1–12.

Bates, C., 1995, '"Lost Innocents and the Loss of Innocence": Interpreting *Adivasi* Movements in South Asia', in Barnes, R. H., Gray, A. and Kingsbury, B. (eds.), *Indigenous Peoples of Asia*. Michigan: The Association for Asian Studies, University of Michigan: 103–119.

Bendix, R. and Lipset, S. M., 1966, 'Karl Marx's Theory of Social Classes', in Bendix, R. and Lipset, S. M. (eds.), *Class, Status, and Power: Social Stratification in Comparative Perspective*. New York: The Free Press: 6–11.

Berreman, G. D., 1970, 'Pahari Culture: Diversity and Change in the Lower Himalayas', in Ishwaran, K. (ed.), 1970, *Change and Continuity in India's Villages*. New York: Columbia University Press: 73–103.

Berreman, G. D., 1971, 'The Brahmanical View of Caste', *Contributions to Indian Sociology*, December 5: 16–23.

Berreman, G. D., 1993, *Hindus of the Himalayas: Ethnography and Change*. Delhi: Oxford University Press.

Béteille, A., 1969, *Caste: Old and New. Essays in Social Structure and Social Stratification*. Bombay: Asia Publishing House.

Béteille, A., 1986, 'The Concept of Tribe with Special Reference to India', *European Journal of Sociology*, XXVII(2): 297–318.

Béteille, A., 1994, *The Backward Classes in Contemporary India*. Delhi: Oxford University Press.

Béteille, A., 1998, 'The Idea of Indigenous People', *Current Anthropology*, 39(2): 187–191.

Chakrabarty, D., 1989, *Rethinking Working Class History*. New Jersey: Princeton University Press.

Chakravorty, U., 1985, 'Toward a Historical Sociology of Stratification in Ancient India: Evidence from Buddhist Sources, *Economic and Political Weekly*, 20(9): 356–360.

Cheria, A., Narayanan, K., Bijoy, C. R. and Edwin, 1997, *A Search for Justice: A Citizen Report on the Adivasi Experience in South India.* Bangalore: St. Paul Publications.

Cinemart Foundation, 1984, *Scenario of the 7 Per Cent, Vol. 1.* New Delhi: Cinemart Foundation.

Corbridge, S., 1989, 'Tribal Politics, Finance, and the State: The Jharkhand India, 1900–1980', *Ethnic and Racial Studies*, 12(2): 175–207.

Dahrendorf, R., 1959, *Class and Class Conflict in Industrial Society.* Stanford: Stanford University Press.

Devalle, S. B. C., 1992, *Discourses of Ethnicity – Culture and Protest in Jharkhand.* New Delhi: Sage.

Dumont, L., 1972, *Homo Hierarchicus: The Caste System and Its Implications.* London: Paladin.

Franke, R. W. and Chasin, B. H., 1994a, *Kerala: Development Through Radical Reform.* San Francisco: The Institute for Food and Development Policy.

Franke, R. W. and Chasin, B. H., 1994b, 'The Relevance of the Kerala Model in the Emerging World Order', Paper presented at the First International Congress on Kerala Studies, August 27–29, Trivandrum: A. K. G. Centre for Study and Research.

Franke, R. W. and Chasin, B. H., 1994c, 'Report on the First International Congress on Kerala Studies, 27–29 August, 1994', *Bulletin of Concerned Asian Scholars*, 26(3): 72–73.

Franke, R. W. and Chasin, B. H., 1998, 'Kerala: A Valid Alternative to the New World Order', *Bulletin of Concerned Asian Scholars*, 30(3): 25–36.

Freire, P., 1996, *Pedagogy of the Oppressed.* London: Penguin.

George, K. K., 1990, 'Kerala's Fiscal Crisis: A Diagnosis', *Economic and Political Weekly*, September 15: 2097–2105.

George, K. K., 1994, 'Whither Kerala Model?', *Proceedings of the International Congress on Kerala Studies,* vol. 1: 65–77.

George, K. K., 1998, 'Historical Roots of the Kerala Model and Its Present Crisis', *Bulletin of Concerned Asian Scholars*, 30(4): 35–40.

George, K. K., 1999, *Limits to Kerala Model of Development.* Trivandrum: Centre for Development Studies.

George, T. K. and Tharakan, P. K. M., 1986, 'Penetration of Capital into a Traditional Economy: The Case of Tea Plantations in Kerala, 1880–1950', *Studies in History*, 2(2): 200–229.

Giddens, A., 1981, *The Class Structure of the Advanced Societies.* London: Hutchinson University Library.

Government of Kerala, 1964, *Report of the Evaluation Committee on the Welfare of Scheduled Castes, Scheduled Tribes and Other Backward Communities in Kerala State with the Orders of Government on Its Recommendations,* Trivandrum: Government Press.

Government of Kerala, 2001, *White Paper on State Finances,* Trivandrum: Finance Department, Government of Kerala.

Gray, A., 1995a, 'Who Are Indigenous People?' in Büchi, S, Erni, C., Jurt, L. and Rüegg, C. (eds.), *Indigenous Peoples, Environment and Development.* Copenhagen: IWGIA: 15–18.

Gray, A., 1995b, 'The Indigenous Movement in Asia', in Barnes, R. H., Gray, A. and Kingsbury, B. (eds.), *Indigenous Peoples of Asia.* Michigan: The Association for Asian Studies, University of Michigan: 35–58.

Gupta, D., 1980, 'From Varna to Jati: Indian Caste System from Asiatic to Feudal Mode of Production', *Journal of Contemporary Asia*, 10(3): 249–271.

Havanur, L. G., 1975, *Karnataka Backward Classes Commission Report*, vol. 1, part1. Bangalore: Government of Karnataka: 98–99.

Heller, P., 1995, 'From Class Struggle to Class Compromise: Redistribution and Growth in a South Indian State', *The Journal of Development Studies*, 31(5): 645–672.

Heller, P., 1996, 'Social Capital as a Product of Class Mobilization and State Intervention: Industrial Workers in Kerala, India, *World Development*, 24(6): 1055–1071.

Heller, P., 1998, 'Problematizing the Kerala Model', *Bulletin of Concerned Asian Scholars*, 30(3): 33–35.

Heller, P., 1999, *The Labour of Development: Workers and the Transformation of Capitalism in Kerala, India*. Ithaca: Cornell University Press.

Herring, R. J., 1980, 'Abolition of Landlordism in Kerala: A Redistribution of Privilege', *Economic and Political Weekly*, 5(26): A59–A69.

Herring, R. J., 1983, *Land to the Tiller: The Political Economy of Agrarian Reform in South Asia*. New Haven: Yale University Press.

Hutton, J. H., 1969, *Caste in India: Its Nature, Function and Origin*. Delhi: Oxford University Press.

Jannuzi, Tomasson F., 1994, *India's Persistent Dilemma: The Political Economy of Agrarian Reform*. Boulder: Westview.

Jentoft, S., 2003, 'Introduction', in Jentoft, S., Minde, H. and Nilsen, R. (eds.), *Indigenous Peoples: Resource Management and Global Rights*. Delft: Eburon: 1–18.

Jeromi, P. D., 2003, 'What Ails Kerala's Economy: A Sectoral Exploration', *Economic and Political Weekly*, April 19: 1584–1600.

Kannan, K. P., 1998, *Political Economy of Labour and Development in Kerala*, Working Paper No. 284, Trivandrum: Centre for Development Studies.

Kannan, K. P., 1999, 'Rural Labour Relations and Development Dilemmas in Kerala: Reflections on the Dilemmas of a Socially Transforming Labour Force in a Slowly Growing Economy', *Journal of Peasant Studies*, 26(2 &3): 140–181.

Kannan, K. P. and Pushpangadan, K., 1990, 'Dissecting Agricultural Stagnation in Kerala: An Analysis Across Crops, Seasons and Regions', *Economic and Political Weekly*, September 1–8: 1991–2004.

Karlsson, B. G. and Subba, T. B. (eds.), 2006, *Indigeneity in India*. London: Kegan Paul.

Khare, R. S., 1984, *The Untouchable Himself: Ideology, Identity and Pragmatism Among the Lucknow Chamars*. London: Cambridge University Press.

Kingsbury, B., 1995, '"Indigenous Peoples" as an International Legal Concept', in Barnes, R. H., Gray, A. and Kingsbury, B. (eds.), *Indigenous Peoples of Asia*. Michigan: The Association for Asian Studies, University of Michigan: 13–58.

Kingsbury, B., 1998, '"Indigenous Peoples" in International Law: A Constructivist Approach to the Asian Controversy', *American Journal of International Law*, 92(4): 414–457.

Kjosavik, D. J., 2004, 'Contested Frontiers: Re-imagining *Adivasi* Land Rights and Identities in Highland Kerala, South India', Paper presented at the XI World Congress of Rural Sociology – Globalisation, Risks and Resistance, 25–30 July, Trondheim, Norway.

Lenin, V. I., 1952, *Selected Works*, vol. 2. Moscow: Foreign Language Publishing House.

Mencher, J., 1980, 'The Lessons and Non-Lessons of Kerala', *Economic and Political Weekly*, 15(41–43): 1781–1802.

Mohandas, M., 1986, *Impact of Development Projects in the Western Ghat Region on the Forest Dependent Population: Case Study of Wayanad District in Kerala*, Trichur: College of Co-operation and Banking, Kerala Agricultural University.

Mohandas, M., 1992, *Impact of New Settlers in the Western Ghat Region on the Socio-Economic Conditions of the Tribal Population: The Case of Wayanad District in Kerala*, Trichur: College of Co-operation and Banking, Kerala Agricultural University.

Mukherjee, R., 1991, *Society, Culture, Development.* New Delhi: Sage.
Mukherjee, R., 1999, 'Caste in Itself, Caste and Class or Caste in Class', *Economic and Political Weekly*, 34(27): 1754–1761.
Nanda Mohan, V., 1994, 'Recent Trends in the Industrial Growth of Kerala', in Prakash, B.A. (ed.), *Kerala's Economy: Performance, Problems, Prospects.* New Delhi: Sage: 217–236.
Narayana, D., 1990, *Agricultural Economy of Kerala in the Post-Seventies: Stagnation or Cycles?*, Working Paper No. 268, Trivandrum: Centre for Development Studies.
Nossiter, T.J., 1988, *Marxist State Governments in India.* London: Pinter Publishers.
Omvedt, G., 1998, 'Disturbing Aspects of Kerala Society', *Bulletin of Concerned Asian Scholars*, 30(3): 31–33.
Oommen, M.A., 1971, *Land Reforms and Socio-economic Change in Kerala.* Madras: CLS.
Oommen, M.A., 1979, *Kerala Economy Since Independence.* New Delhi: Oxford and IBH.
Oommen, M.A., 1994, 'Land Reforms and Economic Change: Experience and Lessons from Kerala', in Prakash, B.A. (ed.), *Kerala's Economy: Performance, Problems, Prospects.* New Delhi: Sage: 117–140.
Oommen, T.K., 1985, *From Mobilization to Institutionalization: The Dynamics of Agrarian Movement in Twentieth Century Kerala.* Bombay: Popular Prakashan.
Ossowski, S., 1963, *Class Structure in the Social Consciousness.* London: Routledge and Kegan Paul.
Padmanabhan, N., 1990, 'Poor Performance of Private Corporate Sector in Kerala', *Economic and Political Weekly,* September 15: 2071–2075.
Panoor, K., 1989, *Keralathile America*, Kottayam: National Book Stall.
Parameswaran, M.P., 1998, 'Kerala "Model" – What Does It Signify?', *Bulletin of Concerned Asian Scholars*, 30(4): 40–42.
Parayil, G., 1998, 'The Perils of Trying to Be Objective Without Being Reflexive: The Kerala Model Revisited', *Bulletin of Concerned Asian Scholars*, 30(3): 28–31.
Parayil, G., 2000, *Kerala – The Development Experience: Reflections on Sustainability and Replicability*, London: Zed Books.
Parayil, G. and Sreekumar, T.T., 2003, 'Kerala's Experience of Development and Change', *Journal of Contemporary Asia*, 33(4): 465–492.
Parel, A., 1998, 'Is the Unexamined Life Worth Living, Even in Kerala?', *Bulletin of Concerned Asian Scholars*, 30(3): 35–36.
Patel, M.L., 1998, *Agrarian Transformation in Tribal India.* New Delhi: M.D. Publications.
Pathy, J., 1982, *Agrarian Structure in Tribal Gujarat and its Implications for Tribal Policies*, New Delhi: ICSSR.
Pathy, J., 1988, *Ethnic Minorities in the Process of Development.* Jaipur: Rawat Publications.
Pathy, J., 1992, 'The Idea of Tribe and the Indian Scene', in Chaudhuri, B. (ed.), 1992, *Tribal Transformation in India, Volume III, Ethnopolitics and Identity Crisis.* New Delhi: Inter-India Publications: 43–54.
Pathy, J., Suguna, P., Bhaskar, M., and Panda, J., 1976, 'Tribal Studies in India: An Appraisal', *The Eastern Anthropologist*, 29(4): 399–417.
Paulini, T., 1979, *Agrarian Movements and Reforms in India: The Case of Kerala.* Saarbrücken: Verlag Breitenbach.
Pillai, M.P., 1994, 'Performance of State Sector Enterprises in Kerala', in Prakash, B.A. (ed.), *Kerala's Economy: Performance, Problems, Prospects.* New Delhi: Sage: 259–278.
Quigley, D., 1993, *The Interpretation of Caste.* Oxford: Clarendon Press.
Radhakrishnan, P., 1989, *Peasant Struggles, Land Reforms and Social Change: Malabar, 1836–1982.* New Delhi: Sage.

Roy Burman, B. K., 1983, 'Transformation of Tribes and Analogous Social Formations', *Economic and Political Weekly*, XVIII(27): 1172–1174.
Rycroft, D. and Dasgupta, S. (eds.), 2011, *The Politics of Belonging in India: Becoming Adivasi*. London: Routledge.
Sankaranarayanan, K. C. and Meera Bhai, M., 1994, 'Industrial Development of Kerala – Problems and Prospects', in Prakash, B. A. (ed.), *Kerala's Economy: Performance, Problems, Prospects*. New Delhi: Sage: 298–315.
Sasikumar, M., 1993, 'Tribal Resettlement in Wayanad, Kerala – An Emic View', *Man and Life*, 19(3–4): 249–258.
Sathyamurthy, T. V., 1985, *India Since Independence: Studies in the Development of the Power of the State. Vol. 1, Centre-State Relations: The Case of Kerala*. Delhi: Ajanta.
Sengupta, N., 1988a, 'Reappraising Tribal Movements – I', *Economic and Political Weekly*, 23(19): 943–945.
Sengupta, N., 1988b, 'Reappraising Tribal Movements – II', *Economic and Political Weekly*, 23(20): 1003–1005.
Sengupta, N., 1988c, 'Reappraising Tribal Movements – III', *Economic and Political Weekly*, 23(21): 1054–1055.
Sengupta, N., 1988d, 'Reappraising Tribal Movements – IV', *Economic and Political Weekly*, 23(22): 1111–1112.
Sengupta, N., 1988e, 'Reappraising Tribal Movements – I', *Economic and Political Weekly*, 23(23): 1153–1154.
Shah, G., 1992, 'Tribal Issues: Problems and Perspectives', in Chaudhuri, B. (ed.), *Tribal Transformation in India, Volume II, Socio-Economic and Ecological Development*. New Delhi: Inter-India Publications: 113–141.
Singh, K. S., 1982, *Economies of the Tribes and Their Transformation*. New Delhi: Concept Publishing.
Sivanandan, P., 1989, *Caste and Economic Opportunity – A Study of the Effect of Educational Development and Land Reforms on the Employment and Income Earning Opportunities of the Scheduled Castes and Scheduled Tribes in Kerala*. Ph D thesis. Trivandrum: Centre for Development Studies.
Sivanandan, P., 1994, 'Performance of Agriculture in Kerala', in Prakash, B. A. (ed.), *Kerala's Economy: Performance, Problems, Prospects*. New Delhi: Sage: 141–159.
Solidarity, 1995, *Report of a Survey of Adivasis in Wayanad*, Mimeo, Mananthavady: Solidarity.
State Resource Centre, 2002, *Kerala: Facts and Figures*, Trivandrum: State Resource Centre.
Stavenhagen, R., 1970, *Agrarian Problems and Peasant Movements in Latin America*. New York: Doubleday.
Subrahmanian, K. K., 1990, 'Development Paradox in Kerala: Analysis of Industrial Stagnation', *Economic and Political Weekly*, September 15: 2053–2058.
Subrahmanian, K. K., 1994, 'Some Facets of the Manufacturing Industry in Kerala', in Prakash, B. A. (ed.), *Kerala's Economy: Performance, Problems, Prospects*. New Delhi: Sage: 237–258.
Thampy, M. M., 1994, 'Development of Organised Small-scale Industries: Some Issues', in Prakash, B. A. (ed.), *Kerala's Economy: Performance, Problems, Prospects*. New Delhi: Sage: 279–297.
Thapar, R., 1984, *From Lineage to State*. Bombay: Oxford University Press.
Tharamangalam, J., 1981, *Agrarian Class Conflict: The Political Mobilization of Agricultural Labourers in Kuttanad, South India*. Vancouver: University of British Columbia Press.

Tharamangalam, J., 1998, 'The Perils of Social Development Without Economic Growth: The Development Debacle of Kerala, India', *Bulletin of Concerned Asian Scholars*, 30(1): 23–34.

Thomas Isaac, T. M. and Mohanakumar, S., 1991, 'Kerala Elections, 1991: Lessons and Non-Lessons', *Economic and Political Weekly*, 26(9): 2691–2704.

Thomas Isaac, T. M. and Tharakan, P. K. M., 1995a, 'Kerala: Towards a New Agenda', *Economic and Political Weekly*, 30(31–32): 1993–2004.

Thomas Isaac, T. M. and Tharakan, P. K. M., 1995b, 'Kerala – The Emerging Perspectives: Overview of the International Congress on Kerala Studies', *Social Scientist*, 23(1–3): 3–36.

Thomas Isaac, T. M. and Harilal, K. N., 1997, 'Planning for Empowerment: People's Campaign for Decentralised Planning in Kerala', *Economic and Political Weekly*, 32(1): 53–58.

Thomas Isaac, T. M. and Franke, R. W., 2002, *Local Democracy and Development: The Kerala People's Campaign for Decentralized Planning*. New York: Rowman and Littlefield.

Törnquist, O., 1998, 'Beyond Romanticism: Remarkable Popular Organizing', *Bulletin of Concerned Asian Scholars*, 30(4): 43–44.

Vasudevan, C. V. and Sujatha, V., 2001, *Forest Laws of Kerala*. Cochin: Ganesh Publications.

Véron, R., 2001, 'The 'New' Kerala Model: Lessons for Sustainable Development', *World Development*, 29(4): 601–617.

Xaxa, V., 1999, 'Tribes as Indigenous People of India', *Economic and Political Weekly*, 34(51): 3589–3595.

5 *Adivasis* in a development triangle
Decentralisation, neoliberalism and the Kerala model

Introduction

This chapter examines the experiences of decentralisation under successive political regimes in Kerala in the context of neoliberal policies and an eroding Kerala model, with reference to the impact on the lives of *adivasi* (indigenous) communities. The term *decentralisation* is often used to refer to the disaggregation and delegation of political, economic and administrative powers and responsibilities to a wide range of institutions and actors – local and regional governments, para-statal agencies, non-governmental organisations (NGOs), local resource use groups, co-operatives, community-based organisations and private enterprises. In the current development policy discourse, decentralisation has become more explicitly articulated and prescribed as a market-led process and a part of the larger reform of rolling back the state and privatising and liberalising the economy. This decentralisation is closely associated with destatisation, which involves reallocation of tasks performed by the state to non-governmental and private agencies, a redefinition of the public–private divide and a shift from government to governance (Jessop 2002). Destatisation, while clearing the way for privatisation to move ahead, is supposed to enhance the freedom of civil society and enable it to play an active role in development, especially in providing certain social services that markets fail to deliver and promoting the expansion of a market economy. Thus civil society is regarded as the source of necessary non-market alternatives to the state in order to develop and sustain a market economy.

Kerala is an interesting case to examine the experiences of decentralisation under two successive governments with opposing ideological leanings. The neoliberal prescription was adopted in 2001 by the newly elected Congress Party–led government in Kerala, where the outgoing government led by the Communist Party of India–Marxist (CPI(M)) had been implementing a home-grown, state-led programme of decentralisation since 1996. The result was conflict and tension between the two divergent approaches in this highly politicised state in which two coalitions, one led by the CPI(M) and the other by the Congress Party, have been wielding power alternately through democratic elections. The Left coalition introduced its new policy of decentralised planning when it regained power in 1996 and was actively implementing it through a 'People's Planning Campaign' (PPC). In line with the policy of the central government, the newly elected Congress-led government adopted a neoliberal approach to development and decentralisation, with little role for the state bureaucratic and political actors in mobilising people for planning and implementing projects at the local level, which inevitably meant making amendments in the programme institutionalised by the previous government. Not surprisingly, this situation led to controversies over the different approaches to decentralisation in Kerala, and one of the areas of concern was how these would affect the poor and marginalised groups. Kerala has been known for its positive achievements in social development through radical reforms. It is also well known that these reforms and their implementation were state led. Indeed, Kerala went through a process of social democratisation under Communist Party–led governments since 1957 within the parliamentary democratic framework of India until the central government decided to adopt structural adjustment as a national policy in 1991.

This policy shift had more serious implications for Kerala than for any other state in India, because this state had gone furthest with state-led development. Thus the withdrawal of the state from social and economic sectors was more complicated and bound to lead to more problems here than in the other Indian states. Among the affected groups were those that did not have the resources to participate in the emerging competitive market economy. Signs of new social exclusion were becoming visible among the indigenous communities and other resource-poor groups. As discussed in the previous chapter, the radical reformist Kerala model was, to a considerable extent, inclusive of the indigenous people (*adivasis*), despite many shortcomings (see also Kjosavik and Shanmugaratnam, 2004).

In this chapter, we look at how the previous government's decentralised planning and the policy shift of 2001 have affected the state's indigenous people as a group that has historically suffered exclusion. The Indian Constitution has special provisions to protect groups such as Scheduled Tribes from social injustice and exclusion. From a careful reading of the various Articles of the Constitution that deal with these provisions, it would seem reasonable to believe that the authors of the Constitution did envisage a direct role for the state to enforce these provisions. The question now is whether the provisions can be met by the current policy, which is premised on destatisation and liberalisation.

In the next section, we discuss the decentralised planning in Kerala and its implications for indigenous communities. This is followed by an analysis of the emerging trends in Kerala's development in the context of the neoliberal policies and their consequences for indigenous people. We then analyse recent trends in decentralised planning in the changing political context with reference to *adivasi* communities. We conclude by highlighting that the policy change in 2001 was not favourable to the indigenous communities with regard to their development and empowerment.

Decentralised planning in Kerala

The Constitution of India was amended in 1992 to provide a legal basis and a mandate for the states to devolve power to the *panchayats* (democratically elected bodies at sub-regional levels). In accordance with these amendments, the government of Kerala, led by the Congress coalition, passed the Kerala *Panchayat Raj* Act in 1994. Kerala accepted the three-tier *panchayat* system proposed by the central government, and elections were held in 1995 to establish elected bodies at the village level (*grama panchayat*), block level (block *panchayat*) and district level (*jilla panchayat*). In 1996, when the Left coalition returned to power in the state, it undertook fiscal and administrative decentralisation,[1] which represented a major step toward democratic decentralisation.

The authors of Kerala's decentralised planning rejected the neoliberal position that regarded the state and civil society as binary oppositional categories. They also rejected the theoretical framework of the new social movements, in which an autonomous civil society is positioned against the state and the market, as well as the romantic visions of civil society as non-hierarchical and non-exploitative.[2] Instead, it would seem that the massive PPC for decentralised development initiated by the Left coalition was more in line with the 'state-in-society' approach of Migdal *et al* (1994) where state and society mutually shape each other (see also Véron, 2001). Rather than treating state and society as two conflictual/antagonistic spheres, the emphasis is on state–society relations (Tornquist, 1999; Fox, 1997) and on strategic engagement and disengagement between different factions of the two (Stokke and Mohan, 2001). This perspective acknowledges the existence of a multiplicity of links between actors within the state bureaucratic and political systems and actors in civil society. Such a conceptualisation of state–society relations is helpful in grasping the proactive potential of both the state and civil society to engage each other.

Evans (1995) developed the concept of 'embedded autonomy' to understand state–society relations in a developmental state. The bureaucratic apparatus in a developmental state is expected to have a certain kind of autonomy arising from a sense of corporate coherence. At the same time, it differs from the Weberian ideal type that is insulated from society. In a developmental state, the bureaucracy is 'embedded in a concrete set of social ties that binds the state to society and provides institutionalised channels for the continual negotiation and renegotiation of goals and policies' (Evans, 1995: 12). This combination of autonomy and connectedness, Evans calls embedded autonomy. While the connectedness in general may be with the entrepreneurial class within a society, Evans highlights Kerala as a variant in that the connectedness is with the working class rather than with the entrepreneurial class. We stretch the concept of embedded autonomy to gain a more nuanced understanding of state–society relations in Kerala in the context of the decentralised planning introduced by the Left coalition and the later decentralisation programme of the conservative coalition. In our view, the case of Kerala shows that embedded autonomy is mediated by changes in political power within a parliamentary democratic framework. This has to do with the fact that Kerala has a functioning parliamentary democratic system in which political power shifts between the Left and the Conservatives through the electoral process. While it is true that the reformist agenda instituted by the Communist Party–led government in 1957 set the stage for the policies of future governments, left or conservative, the dynamics of embeddedness tend to vary with the government in power. It could be said that the connectedness to the peasants, working class, indigenous communities, women and other marginalised groups is stronger when a Left coalition government is in power, and it shifts in favour of the entrepreneurial and landed classes when a conservative coalition takes over. The dynamic nature of embeddedness could help understand the differential experience of indigenous people's development through decentralised planning under different regimes.

The democratic decentralisation through the PPC in 1996 was clearly an instance of the state's engagement with civil society, initiated by the left forces within the state. This instance has to be distinguished from the historical mass mobilisation by civil society to engage the state in Kerala in the late nineteenth and early twentieth centuries.[3] From the late 1930s, however, the mobilisation of Kerala's civil society to engage the state has largely been led by the leftist political parties and left-leaning individuals. Since the Communist Party formed the first government in Kerala in 1957,[4] the state–society relations had thickened due to the institutionalisation of various rights and reforms demanded in the mass struggles. Therefore, it was no coincidence that when the Left coalition formed the government in 1996, they initiated a form of re-engagement with civil society through the PPC to address development issues posed by the new policy regime. This moment of re-engagement required the Communist Party to make a shift from its traditional stance of democratic centralism to democratic decentralisation.

The Left coalition government started addressing questions of growth and equity by renewing its earlier programmes aimed at expanding the material production base with the support of mass movements, and at the same time defending the redistributive gains from the past. Substantial fiscal and executive powers were devolved to the elected local bodies. It devolved about 35% to 40% of the plan funds to the *panchayats* for the implementation of development programmes formulated with the people's participation. A massive campaign, involving state agencies and bureaucrats, NGOs, trade unions, other civil society organisations and activists, was organised to provide training for elected representatives, resource persons and local people in project formulation and implementation.[5] Significant institutional reforms and procedural innovations were adopted so as to enable people's participation at the grassroots level. This extensive mass mobilisation actively mediated by the state has had a positive impact on the *adivasis*' participation in the political, economic and social realms. Transparency was built into the process to pre-empt possible corruption and nepotism. It was also widely seen as a mass resistance movement against the ongoing liberalisation and structural adjustment policies. The prescription for rolling back the state was disregarded by the Left government in 1996, on the grounds that it did not leave space for building the state–society synergy that was necessary to achieve growth with equity.

The successes and failures of Kerala's decentralised planning have been greatly debated (see Das, 2000; Chathukulam and John, 2002; Mohanakumar, 2002, among others). The vision for Kerala's decentralised planning was an economic policy that emphasised self-reliance and a broadening of the domestic market (Patnaik, 2001). This was not consistent with the neoliberal economic agenda of the central government. Such a situation was bound to place serious constraints on the project of decentralisation as envisaged by the Left, with the state being an integral part of the Indian economy and polity. Moreover, Kerala's decentralisation had been beset with conflicts between the then-ruling Left front and the opposition Congress coalition. There were also conflicts within the government – between the bureaucracy that largely resisted decentralisation and the proponents of decentralisation represented by politicians of a leftist persuasion and some committed bureaucrats. Gurukkal (2001) alleges that the conflicts of interest within state and within civil society delimited the radical objectives of decentralised planning in spite of the leftist agenda of effecting changes in the existing structural distribution of power. Kerala has a highly politicised civil society, which had been the prime mover of the state's achievements in social development. Civil society in Kerala has been understood as a heterogeneous and contested terrain where mass organisations have also been engaged in organised political action in order to achieve collective goals such as radical land reforms, workers' rights, enhancing of public entitlements, women's rights and environmental protection.

The decentralised planning initiated by the left-wing government had been actualised through the PPC where the state acted in partnership with civil society at various levels. With the introduction of Robert Putnam's conception of social capital as located in networks of associations and organisations residing in depoliticised local spaces and places – that is, in civil society (Putnam, 1993) – and its co-optation by the World Bank, 'over-politicisation' of civil society has been highlighted as the major cause of all the developmental ills of Kerala (Tharamangalam, 1998). With regard to decentralised planning, Tharakan (2004) holds that over-politicisation leads to major failures. On the other hand, it has been argued that the reformists within the CPI(M) focused more on 'de-politicising' the local space than on 're-politicising' it and this had led to major failures (Tornquist, 2004). Our contention is that the highly politicised civil society has been both enabling and constraining at the same time with regard to the PPC. It is the politicisation of Kerala's civil society that made the PPC possible in the first place. Contestational politics and conflicts of values and ideologies are essential elements of democracy. We would argue that it was through politicisation, including the inevitable party politicisation in a multi-party democracy, that Kerala's marginalised and excluded groups gained whatever bargaining power they have vis-à-vis the dominant groups. While it may be true that the PPC could have achieved more if the differences between political parties had been minimised, which in any case is a counterfactual condition, the so-called 'over-politicisation' cannot be considered a criticism of the PPC per se.

Indigenous communities in decentralised planning

While controversies over the decentralised planning approach abound, our task here is to analyse the ways in which decentralised planning contributed to the socio-economic and political empowerment of the *adivasis*. Participatory approaches, although advocated in development programmes for indigenous peoples, have seldom been practised in Kerala. For example, the *adivasis*' participation in poverty reduction programmes implemented under the Integrated Tribal Development Programme had been very low. This is a major reason for the ineffectiveness of various tribal development programmes implemented by the state (Vijayanand, 1997). The embedded participation of *adivasis* in the socio-economic and political processes is important to enable them to take control of their development. The decentralised planning introduced through the PPC provided a meaningful participatory space for them. This was ensured by the reservation of 10% of the seats in the local bodies for indigenous communities. Funds were earmarked for them by creating a Tribal Sub-Plan (TSP) at the local level. While the overall transfer of state funds to the local bodies was only 36%, 75% to 80% of the total TSP funds were devolved (Isaac, 2001). Depending upon the size of the *adivasi* population and the extent of their deprivation, the local bodies had the flexibility to decide on the share of funds to be allocated for programmes for these communities. Accordingly, in six *grama panchayats* and four block *panchayats*, the share of the TSP and special component plan for scheduled castes exceeded 50% of the total allocation – the real flow of funds to the weaker sections reached a record high in 1997–1998 (Isaac and Franke, 2002). Several safeguards were included to reduce corruption and misuse of funds, such as ensuring greater participation of *adivasis* in the campaign and setting up special subject groups in the *grama sabhas*[6] and development seminars to discuss special issues related to the development of *adivasis*. A task force chaired by an elected representative of indigenous people was responsible for overseeing the drafting of projects under the TSP. Individual beneficiary projects were encouraged rather than infrastructual projects; if infrastructural projects such as irrigation were to be implemented, the condition was that at least 51% of the beneficiaries had to be *adivasis*. These stipulations were intended to ensure that the funds allocated for the *adivasis* would actually be used to address their specific development concerns. Projects for drinking water, housing and sanitation were emphasised. In the production sphere, the emphasis was on vegetable cultivation, as it could be practised in small parcels of land, and animal husbandry, as fodder could be obtained from the neighbouring forests and plantations and the summer rice fallows could be used for grazing. Schemes for employment training for *adivasi* men and women were also prioritised in many regions.

Apart from these tangible benefits, perhaps the most important achievement as far as the *adivasis* were concerned was their empowerment. The various platforms that were created, mandated and institutionalised by the PPC provided space for advocacy and agency of the indigenous peoples. Their participation in the *grama sabhas*, development seminars and other project planning and decision-making bodies was fairly high. Mobilisation by NGOs and political activists played a major role in this. The institutions were designed in such a way as to enable the participation of all sections of the population, particularly the marginalised communities such as *adivasis* and oppressed castes. In the first year of decentralised planning (1996), the participation rate of the Scheduled Castes and Scheduled Tribes in the *grama sabha* was lower than that of the general population (Chaudhuri and Heller, 2003). However, in the second year (1997), there was a dramatic increase. The increased participation in the second year was due to certain procedural changes that were intended to facilitate participation and increase the transparency of fund targeting. Large-scale training programmes targeting these groups were also undertaken in addition to increased mobilisation by the CPI(M) and the People's Science Movement (KSSP) (Chaudhuri and Heller, 2003).

The participation of elected members of *adivasi* communities in the local bodies, and as presidents in 10% of the local bodies, ensured that the community's voices were heard in matters of decision making, not only at the local level, but at the higher levels as well. In Poothady *Panchayat* of the Wayanad district, where our field study was conducted, we encountered an *adivasi* population articulating and addressing their development issues with enthusiasm. The Left coalition had a majority in the *Panchayat* body during 1996–2001, while in the period 2001–2005, the conservative coalition dominated. About 18.5% of the population of this *panchayat* belonged to *adivasi* communities. Of the fourteen elected representatives, two were from indigenous communities – a woman and a man.[7] A study of the pattern of allocation of funds in this *panchayat* revealed that the development issues of the *adivasis* received priority. The fund allocation for the TSP in 1998–1999 was 35.5% of the total funds. It increased to 42.5% in 1999–2000, and in 2000–2001 the allocation was 36%.[8] This had significant positive implications for the development of *adivasis*, given that their community constituted only 18.5% of the overall population. It was an indication that the *panchayat* had given priority to issues of equity.

Housing, sanitation, drinking water, agriculture and animal husbandry were the projects that received priority with regard to the *adivasis*. Discussions with the elected representatives of the *adivasis* revealed that the total number of houses built during the four-year period from 1997–1998 and 2000–2001 was much higher than that of the total number of houses built for the *adivasis* of the *panchayat* during all the previous years since the formation of Kerala state in 1956. House construction and other project works were undertaken by the 'beneficiary committees', which provided them with employment opportunities. The quality of the works was also claimed to be much higher. Projects for self-employment targeting men and women were helpful to a certain extent in mitigating the unemployment problem. The mandatory allocation of at least 10% of the *panchayat* funds for women's development projects helped promote women's participation in the *grama sabhas*, as well as in project planning and implementation. Discussions with the *panchayat* president and other representatives revealed that there was a high level of participation of the indigenous communities in *grama sabhas* and development seminars. The educated youth among the *adivasis*, supported by activists from various political parties, NGOs and community-based organisations, played a major role in facilitating informed participation of the *adivasis* in the planning and implementation process. The PPC had seen a revival of the indigenous communities' spirits. As an *adivasi* elected representative (who was a woman) put it, 'The process has been empowering and enlightening, and all the more, it provides us with a possibility of tackling the problems of our communities based on our priorities'.

Neoliberal policies and Kerala's development: Emerging trends

With the implementation of the neoliberal policies, the central government adopted serious cuts in public spending. This has impacted government spending in the states as well due to reduced fund transfers from the centre. State governments have been advised to reduce social-sector expenditure, mainly in education, health and the public distribution system (PDS).[9] The transfer of funds to the states is currently being linked to the extent to which the state has reduced its social-sector expenses. This has clearly created a dilemma for Kerala. Moreover, the non-plan funds transferred to the state – which were already lower than those of other states (George, 1999) – have been further reduced, leaving Kerala to fend for itself in the social sector. The PDS of the state had been in part supported by the central government. Its withdrawal has negative implications for a state like Kerala, which imports more than 70% of its food grains from other regions of India. The fact that 97% of the population had until now been covered by the PDS exacerbates the problem.

The state's agricultural sector has been directly affected by the new policies. The opening up of the sector has resulted in a severe crash of the agricultural product market. In fiscal year 1999–2000, Kerala incurred a loss of about US$800 million, and in 2000–2001 it was around US$1300 million (Government of Kerala, 2001). The removal of quantitative restrictions on imports under the liberalised regime has been pointed out as the major reason for the fall in prices of agricultural commodities (Government of Kerala, 2001). For example, imports of rubber more than tripled during the period from 1998–1999 and 2001–2002. Because about 18% of the cultivated area is dedicated to rubber crop, this trend is detrimental to Kerala's agricultural economy. Moreover, the increased withdrawal of input subsidies and low investments in irrigation and other infrastructures have grave consequences for the farm sector. The agricultural economy of Kerala is dominated by perennial cash crops that have a relatively long productive life.[10] They require heavy initial investments and take several years of gestation before yielding returns. This constrains the farmers' ability to respond to market price signals by switching instantly from one crop to another. Moreover, because information about prices is incomplete, unpredictable and often delayed, the farmers are not in a position to adjust their annual outputs either.

Subrahmanian and Azeez (2000) argue that liberalisation has not resulted in any structural change in Kerala's industrial sector. The new markets, actors and rules involved in the new phase of globalisation have strong negative consequences for Kerala, as it is historically integrated into the world market as an exporter of primary goods (Parayil and Sreekumar, 2003). Terms of trade that favour manufactured goods at the expense of primary commodities or that are unfavourable to certain export crops and in favour of certain food grains are bound to affect incomes and food availability (Patnaik, 2001). This is particularly the case for a primary commodity-exporting region such as Kerala. Moreover, the institutionalisation of workers' rights and their trade union activism have now come to be regarded as disincentives for attracting international and domestic private investments to Kerala. Ironically, the basic rights that were won through historic struggles and the current democratic struggles for their defence are being portrayed as obstacles to growth and development in the new policy context.

Consequences and prospects for the indigenous communities

The *adivasis* constitute the most disadvantaged group of people in Kerala, with neither the resources nor the capabilities to participate in the market as equal players. In the earlier chapters we provided accounts of the historical processes of their alienation from land and forest resources, as well as processes by which *adivasis* were marginalised in the wage labour market and the consequent pauperisation and proletarianisation that characterise the indigeneity–class intersection. Our field study revealed that such a situation, in conjunction with the structural adjustment policies, is giving rise to certain trends that have serious negative impacts on the *adivasis*.

The shift in the policy regime has engendered a process of 'new' social exclusion; the *adivasis* are increasingly being pushed out of the market fringes they have been inhabiting and simultaneously denied the nominal welfare measures and other benefits they were entitled to earlier. A substantial proportion of the funds for *adivasi* development programmes had been from the central government. With the decrease in such transfers, development and welfare programmes for the *adivasis* have been attenuated. The general welfare programmes of the state have also been diminished by the strict regulations in social spending. One hundred per cent of the *adivasi* families depended on the PDS for a major share of their basic food and fuel consumption requirements. The dismantling of the PDS – though a nominal version still exists – means that all these households now have to incur four to five times greater expenses for food and fuel, which in turn affects their capacity to spend on other basic needs; or alternatively, that they must decrease their already low consumption levels of food and fuel. Our field discussions revealed that the pensions and unemployment benefits they are entitled to are often not paid regularly, which means that they have to buy basic food and other requirements on credit from petty traders at high interest. During field visits we observed that the landless *adivasi* families, who constituted the majority, managed, at best, one meal a day. In the lean seasons, particularly during the monsoons when they have practically no employment, they are perhaps able to have one square meal every other day. The gender-specific impact of the dismantling of the PDS was evident, too. Our discussions with *adivasi* women revealed that they had often foregone meals, particularly in the lean season, for the sake of children, husbands, fathers or brothers. They drank *kanji* water, that is, water drained after boiling rice, and let the others eat the rice.

The central pillars of the Kerala model are the education and health sectors. These sectors are now being progressively privatised. What does this foretell for the *adivasis*? The facilities in the state schools are deteriorating due to decreased funding, and the *adivasis* cannot afford to send their children to expensive private schools. Because of the state's reduced spending policy, not enough teachers are employed, even in the special schools for *adivasi* children. Allowances for books, school uniforms, umbrellas and food are not disbursed in time. Such delays in payments lead to increased school dropouts. During field visits, we met such dropouts. The parents told us that they could not send the children to school without books and uniforms, so they would allow them to drop out for a year and then send them back to school the following year if they got the money to buy books and other things needed. This is a widespread phenomenon, particularly among the landless *adivasis* of Wayanad – the *Paniyar, Kattunaicker, Adiyar* and *Urali* communities.

The expenditure cuts in the health sector are even more harmful to the *adivasis*. Their dependence on state health services is near total. Decreased government spending in this sector has affected the quality of services, and the government hospitals do not have the necessary equipment and medicines. The prices of medicines, including the most essential ones, have increased substantially following the regulations of the Trade Related Intellectual Property Rights (TRIPS) enforced by the World Trade Organization. For instance, 67% of the formulations of the top-selling seventy-three brands in the year 2000, which constitute 20% of the pharmaceutical market in India, showed a substantial price increase (Rane, 2003). This has serious implications for the health status of the *adivasis*, including the health of their children. The high-priced health services operating in the private sector are beyond their reach.

The crash in agricultural prices has seriously affected employment opportunities for the *adivasis*. The limited employment opportunities they did have were in the cash-crop sector, which consists of a large number of smallholdings and a few medium-sized and large plantations. Pepper and coffee are the major cash crops grown in the study area. According to the farmers (non-*adivasis*) with whom we had discussions, 'the agricultural sector is being destroyed by the new policies of the government'. For instance, three years ago they received about Rs. 200 per kg of pepper. The price has since then decreased to about one-third (Rs. 67 per kg in December 2003). A minimum price of Rs. 100 per kg is required to break even. A few years ago, coffee fetched more than Rs. 50 per kg, but it fell to about half of that (Rs. 27 per kg in December 2003). The break-even price for coffee is about Rs. 40 per kg. The farmers perceive this situation to be a consequence of the liberalised trade regime. Various farmers' organisations, both independent and affiliated with political parties, are active in the study area.

The fall in prices has adversely affected the capacity of the plantations and smallholders to absorb wage labour. At the same time, productivity is adversely affected due to the high price of fertilisers and other inputs. The farmers and planters are forced to save on wage labour in an attempt to break even. Discussions with planters revealed that to produce one kilogram of coffee, the labour cost incurred is at least Rs. 25, so the coffee plantations now employ workers only for pruning and harvesting. Agronomic operations such as weeding, fertiliser and pesticide application and so on have been suspended. This has reduced the number of labour days to about one-third. 'Both workers and us are suffering', said the owner of a small coffee estate. The coping strategies adopted by the farmers have serious consequences for the *adivasis*, as their employment opportunities are closely linked to the perennial cash-crop sector in the highlands. The state-owned plantations, which are supposed to provide employment for the *adivasis*, are also following the same strategy (discussions with plantation management and workers).[11] Either way, it is a no-win situation for the *adivasis*. The coffee prices were so low that it did not even pay to employ workers to harvest the produce. In many places, farmers entered into an arrangement with the workers – the workers who harvested the coffee could have half of it instead of wages, and the other half would go to the farmer.

Changing politics and *adivasi* development

The new government has introduced certain changes to the guidelines for the decentralised planning, which have considerably reduced the space for people's participation. The Area Development Scheme of the pre-decentralisation period was reintroduced by the new government. According to this scheme, each member of the legislative assembly (MLA) is allotted a sum of Rs. 2.5 million (about 25% of the current annual budget of a *panchayat*) for the development of his or her constituency. This has been a long-standing demand of the MLAs – particularly those belonging to the conservative coalition – since the beginning of decentralisation. However, this scheme, which has not been integrated with the development plan for the *panchayats*, may reintroduce the space for patronage, corruption and nepotism. Given the experience with the scheme before decentralisation, it is highly unlikely that projects that would benefit *adivasis* would be undertaken.

Another major setback for the indigenous people has been the delinking of the TSP from *panchayats* and its transfer to the line department. The new government's argument for making this decision was that the projects had not been implemented effectively under the PPC. However, many *adivasi* activists we had discussions with told us that the government's argument was contrary to the experience in many *panchayats*. They believe that the transfer of the TSP funds back to the line departments was due to pressure from the bureaucrats' lobby. Another reason given by the government was that one of the leaders of the *adivasi* groups had asked for such a delinking. When we raised this issue, the activists pointed out that the *adivasis* were a heterogeneous group with several leaders for several organisations with leanings towards different political parties. Therefore, according to these activists, the hurried delinking without wider consultations, and purportedly based on the demand from one *adivasi* leader, cannot be justified. The following statement by a *panchayat*-level official corroborates these arguments:

> The bureaucrats in the line department felt emasculated without much funds for tribal development at their disposal. The Left government antagonised the bureaucracy by taking away funds from their control. The Congress government is now giving more recognition and importance to the bureaucracy. The return of the TSP funds to bureaucratic hands was part of this new bureaucrat–politician collusion.

One avowed rationale for decentralisation raised by proponents of all political persuasions is to reduce bureaucratic control over resources. However, what is happening in Kerala at present seems to be a progressive 'recentralisation' of the devolved powers and resources. The delinking of the TSP from the *panchayat* would undoubtedly result in a substantial reduction in the funds available for the programmes for *adivasis* because there would be no room for flexibility, as there was in the case of the *panchayat* funds. We have seen earlier that six p*anchayats* had allocated more than 50% of their total funds for the TSP. In Poothady *Panchayat*, on average, up to 42.5% of the total funds had been used for projects for *adivasis*, although they constitute only about 18.5% of the population. The delinking would also increase the space for corruption and take away much of the space for the *adivasis* to participate in the development processes at the local level, as well as decision making at higher levels. It would also undermine the role of the elected representatives of the indigenous communities.

Our field visit in December 2003 revealed that many of these fears were being realised. Discussions with *panchayat* members and *panchayat*-level bureaucrats revealed that within six months of the TSP funds being transferred to the line department, it became clear that the department was in no position to implement all the projects. Consequently, the *Panchayat* Presidents' Association – with the support of other *panchayat* functionaries, elected members, indigenous people and activists, and the opposition political parties – demanded that the TSP funds be transferred back to the *panchayats* so that projects could be efficiently implemented. The government partially relented to the popular pressure and transferred 50% of the TSP funds back to the *panchayats*, while 50% was retained with the line department. The *panchayats* are fighting for full TSP funds. Caught between these struggles are the *adivasis*. Kerala's decentralised planning was intentionally named *Janakeeyasoothranam* (Peoples' Planning) by its pioneers to underline the importance of peoples' participation at the grassroots level. The new government has renamed it *Kerala Vikasana Padhathi*, meaning Kerala Development Programme. According to an *adivasi panchayat* member, the change in name itself symbolised an undermining of the peoples' role in decentralised planning.

Before it lost the election, the leftist government had established *oorukkoottams*, that is, special and separate assemblies of *adivasis* in each settlement, facilitated by trained *adivasi* activists.[12] It was a strategy to further enhance the participation and effectiveness of the planning and implementation of development projects. It was mandatory that the *oorukkoottam* meet every six months for project discussions, beneficiary selection based on preferential points, formation of beneficiary committees to implement projects and so on. The institution of the *oorukkoottam* now remains only in form; the meaning and content have changed, as an *adivasi* activist relates:

> The *Oorukkoottam* meeting has now become a ritual. Earlier, the potential beneficiaries of projects were given marks [points] at the meeting openly by the participants. But now, the marks are already given to the beneficiaries prior to the meeting and these are just read out in the meeting. This promotes corruption and partisan politics.

This shows that the transparency that was built into the procedures of project formulation, implementation and beneficiary selection is clearly being undermined. Some of the *adivasis* pointed out that the concept of 'beneficiary committee' has lost its meaning. Now, most of the projects are implemented by government agencies, NGOs, contractors and so on. This means more space for corruption, waste and undue time lags in project implementation. Earlier, a substantial share of the funds required for various projects was contributed by the beneficiary committee in the form of labour or land and, in some cases, cash. This was conducive to the implementation of more projects with less contribution from the government. Cost sharing has now taken a different form with much heavier demand on the beneficiaries. Moreover, employment opportunities for the beneficiaries and locals have been reduced, as they have to compete with 'outsiders': 'The ownership of the projects is lost from our hands', an *adivasi* activist said.

The beneficiary committee's role has become nominal even in the case of general (non-*adivasi*) projects. According to the revised rules, projects with an estimated cost of less than Rs. 50,000 can only be implemented by beneficiary committees. The more expensive projects are to be implemented by contractors or other government agencies. However, the beneficiaries have to make contributions in cash. For example, for drinking water projects, 10% of the total project cost, and for agricultural projects 20%, has to be contributed in cash in advance. The project will be implemented only after this payment is made. A *panchayat* member explained:

> It is the poor people who are in need of these projects. How can they find such large sums? Providing labour is the only way for them to contribute. That is how the projects were implemented in the earlier set-up. But now, if the payment is not made in cash in advance the project will not be implemented. Many projects thus lapsed . . . and the government can save money.

The *adivasis*' cost-sharing burden has thus increased, while their income-earning opportunities have diminished substantially – a sort of 'double squeeze' for them. According to another *panchayat* member, in the new setup, the beneficiary committees are reluctant to take up projects, as they would be harassed by the government officials who are supposed to give them technical support. The *panchayat* member said:

> They may even give wrong measurements after project completion. This will put the beneficiary committee in trouble. It has actually happened. This is their ploy to deter beneficiary committees from taking up projects. Sometimes, the beneficiary committees entrust projects with *ben ami* contractors, and they deal with the officials in the appropriate way [paying bribes and so on] and get things done. It is sad to see how things have deteriorated.

An *adivasi panchayat* member pointed out that Rs. 3 million had been allotted to Poothady *Panchayat* under the TSP in the past three years, but that this was merely a paper allotment, and no money had been handed over to the *panchayat*. The *panchayat* therefore was not in a position to implement any new projects for the benefit of the indigenous people in the past three years, but only some spill-over projects from the time of the previous government. There is also confusion about which projects are to be implemented by the *panchayats* and which ones by the line department, as one *adivasi panchayat* member explains:

> There is no clarity of roles and division of responsibilities in the matter of *adivasi* funds and development projects even nearly three years after the amendments were made. The achievements made by the *adivasis* in the first five years of peoples' planning is now being reversed.

The *adivasis* have organised under the auspices of the *Adivasi Kshema Samithi* (AKS), a left-oriented *adivasi* organisation, and are now engaged in struggles demanding the transfer of all TSP funds back to the *panchayats* and changing some of the project implementation practices that are unfavourable to the *adivasi* interests.

Inconsistency with constitutional provisions?

The changing politics and their consequences for the indigenous people take us to the question of how compatible the neoliberal policy of increasing state withdrawal from social and economic sectors is with India's constitutional provisions. As part of the affirmative action, the Constitution has provided for reserving employment for the *adivasis* both in the central and state services. However, in the new policy context, the government has adopted a strategy of non-recruitment, or minimum recruitment to state services, with negative consequences for *adivasis*. It is unlikely that the increasing privatisation of services and other economic activities will have a significant positive impact on the *adivasi* communities with regard to employment because the affirmative action policy of job reservation is not applicable in the private sector. Moreover, the *adivasis*' chances of competing in the open job market are seriously constrained because of their low education levels and lack of skills demanded by the market, such as technical and social skills, and lack of the right social and political connections.

The Constitution sees the state as a major player in both the social and the economic arena, but under the new policy regime, this particular role for the state has been drastically reduced. The socio-economic entitlements the *adivasis* had gained through state involvement in implementing the constitutional provisions are now being gradually eroded. Market-led development is unlikely to help them retain or expand their entitlements; rather, it will disentitle them, if the current trend is anything to go by. The withdrawal of the state from these sectors would thus be inconsistent with the constitutional safeguards extended to indigenous communities (Scheduled Tribes) and other marginal groups such as the Scheduled Castes.

110 Adivasis *in a development triangle*

For example, Article 275 of the Constitution provides for grants-in-aid to states for promoting the *adivasis*' welfare:

> Provided that there shall be paid out of the Consolidated Fund of India . . . to enable that State to meet the costs of such schemes of development as may be undertaken by the State . . . for the purpose of promoting the welfare of the Scheduled Tribes in that State . . .
>
> (p. 160)[13]

Article 46 states:

> The State shall promote with special care the educational and economic interests . . . of the Scheduled Castes and the Scheduled Tribes, and shall protect them from social injustice and all forms of exploitation.
>
> (p. 28)

Article 335 provides for job reservation in central and state services:

> The claims . . . of the Scheduled Castes and the Scheduled Tribes shall be taken into consideration . . . in the making of appointments to services and posts in connection with the affairs of the Union or of a State.
>
> (p. 199)

Our contention is that these constitutional provisions can be effectively implemented only with the active intervention of the state, both in the economic and social sectors. As discussed in the previous chapter, the radical policies of the Kerala model in the post-independence period facilitated an inclusive development, which enabled the *adivasis* to make gains, albeit limited, in education, healthcare, employment and social security. Their institutionalised participation in development and political processes became possible only with the implementation of decentralised planning in 1996. However, they did not have sufficient time to improve their asset base in material terms or to catch up on human development for the new generation to face the impact of the neoliberal policies. With the Congress-led government's policy on decentralised planning in place since 2001, the *adivasis* have increasingly lost control over the limited development resources they had at the local level. The vulnerability of these communities has been increasing, which is particularly disadvantageous to the younger generation, due to the lack of opportunities for quality education and healthcare. The long-term human development of the younger generation will be adversely affected, leading to the intergenerational reproduction of poverty and deprivation.

Conclusion

In this chapter we have critically examined the emerging trends in decentralisation and neoliberal policies and their implications for indigenous communities in Kerala. The decentralised planning implemented by the leftist government in 1996 through the PPC was an attempt to make the development process more inclusive of the marginal groups such as indigenous communities and to contain the 'new social exclusion' that had started setting in. We have dealt with the means by which the PPC had envisaged and institutionalised the inclusion of the indigenous communities. In the vision of decentralisation followed by the leftists, the state had a direct role in empowering people at the grassroots level. The negative effects of liberalisation, particularly in the agricultural sector, have diminished the employment opportunities for the *adivasis*, and the increased withdrawal of the state, particularly from the social and economic sectors, has contributed to further marginalisation of this community. The amended decentralisation introduced by the Congress government in 2001 resulted in a decreased role and space for the state bureaucracy in mobilising people for planning and implementing projects at the local level. At the same time, the bureaucracy intervened in ways that undermined the powers of the local bodies. We have argued that shifts in political power impact the embedded autonomy of the state and that the change of government in 2001 led to a shift that was more favourable to the entrepreneurial class and less favourable to the marginalised communities in general and *adivasis* in particular.

The new environment created by the government, being supposedly free-market friendly, is quite unfavourable to the participatory decentralised planning envisaged by the former leftist government. We have discussed how, by making certain amendments to the radical provisions of the original decentralised planning, the present government has to a large extent reversed the control over resources and decision-making powers that were extended to the local bodies by the former government, thus undermining the transparency, accountability and improved governance fostered by the PPC. These changes have also reduced the space for indigenous people's participation and increased the power of the bureaucracy. Such measures have adversely affected the indigenous people's agency and their chances of defining their own development priorities. The changes have not opened up new spaces for community initiatives either; rather, the opposite seems to be happening, due to the increased socio-economic and political exclusion. The *adivasis* are now caught in the dynamics of Kerala's politics and the larger neoliberal politics. These communities, vulnerable even when the state played an active role in the social and economic sectors, will be even more vulnerable if the current situation persists.

Notes

1 The administrative decentralisation, particularly the redeployment of administrative staff, has been incomplete due to the organised resistance – overt and covert – from the employees' trade unions (see Das, 2000 and Isaac, 2001).
2 See Mohan and Stokke (2000) and Harris *et al* (2004).
3 See Tharakan (1998) for an account of early social movements in Kerala.
4 The state of Kerala was established in 1956, and the Communist Party formed the first state government following the elections in 1957.
5 Isaac (2001) and Isaac and Franke (2002) are firsthand accounts of the people's campaign for decentralised planning in Kerala.

112 Adivasis *in a development triangle*

6 *Grama sabha* is the assembly of people from each ward in the *panchayat*. The *grama sabha* meets every six months to discuss various issues related to the planning and implementation of projects.
7 In Poothady *Panchayat*, out of the fourteen elected representatives, five are women.
8 The figures are calculated from the project reports of Poothady *Panchayat* for the relevant years.
9 A network of outlets for supplying food grains, fuel and other basic necessities at subsidised prices to low-income categories of people, including the *adivasis*.
10 See also Jose and Shanmugaratnam (1993).
11 In Irulam Village, two such plantations are currently under the forceful occupation of the indigenous people as part of the larger struggle for land.
12 See Isaac (2001).
13 The Constitution of India, as modified up to 15 April 1967, Delhi: The Manager of Publications, 1967.

References

Chaudhuri, S. and Heller, P., 2003, 'The Plasticity of Participation: Evidence From a Participatory Governance Experiment', Paper presented at the Norwegian Association for Development Research (NFU) Annual Conference – Politics and Poverty, Oslo, Norway, October 23–24.

Chathukulam, J. and John, M. S., 2002, 'Five Years of Participatory Planning in Kerala: Rhetoric and Reality', *Economic and Political Weekly*, December 7: 4917–4926.

Das, M. K., 2000, 'Kerala's Decentralised Planning: Floundering Experiment', *Economic and Political Weekly*, December 2: 4300–4303.

Evans, P., 1995, *Embedded Autonomy: States & Industrial Transformation*. Princeton: Princeton University Press.

Fox, J., 1997, 'How Does Civil Society Thicken? The Political Construction of Social Capital in Rural Mexico', in Evans, P. (ed.), *State-Society Synergy: Government and Social Capital in Development*. IAS Research Series No. 94, Berkeley: University of California.

George, K. K., 1999, *Limits to Kerala Model of Development*. Trivandrum: Centre for Development Studies.

Government of Kerala, 2001, *White Paper on State Finances*. Trivandrum: Finance Department, Government of Kerala.

Gurukkal, R., 2001, 'When a Coalition of Conflicting Interests Decentralises: A Theoretical Critique of Decentralisation Politics in Kerala', *Social Scientist*, 29(9–10): 60–76.

Harris, J., Stokke, K. and Törnquist, O., 2004, 'Introduction: The New Local Politics of Democratisation', in Harris, J., Stokke, K. and Törnquist, O. (eds.), *Politicising Democracy: The New Local Politics of Democratisation*. Houndmills: Palgrave Macmillan: 1–28.

Jessop, B., 2002, *The Future of the Capitalist State*. Cambridge: Polity Press.

Jose, D. and Shanmugaratnam, N., 1993, 'Traditional Homegardens of Kerala: A Sustainable Human Ecosystem', *Agroforestry Systems*, 24(2): 203–213.

Kjosavik, D. J. and Shanmugaratnam, N., 2004, 'Integration or Exclusion? Locating Indigenous Peoples in the Development Process of Kerala, South India', *Forum for Development Studies*, 31(2): 231–273.

Migdal, J. S., Kholi, A. and Shue, V. (eds.), 1994, *State Power and Social Forces: Domination and Transformation in the Third World*. Cambridge: Cambridge University Press.

Mohan, G. and Stokke, K., 2000, 'Participatory Development and Empowerment: The Dangers of Localism', *Third World Quarterly*, 21(2): 247–268.

Mohanakumar, S., 2002, 'From People's Plan to Plan Sans People', *Economic and Political Weekly*, 37(16): 1492–1497.

Parayil, G. and Sreekumar, T.T., 2003, 'Kerala's Experience of Development and Change', *Journal of Contemporary Asia*, 33(4): 465–492.

Patnaik, P., 2001, 'Alternative Paradigms of Economic Decentralisation', *Social Scientist*, 29(9–10): 48–59.

Putnam, R., 1993, *Making Democracy Work: Civic Traditions in Modern Italy*. Princeton: Princeton University Press.

Rane, W., 2003, 'Have Drug Prices Fallen?', *Economic and Political Weekly*, November 1: 4640–4642.

Stokke, K., and Mohan, G., 2001, 'The Convergence Around Local Civil Society and the Dangers of Localism', *Social Scientist*, 29(11–12): 3–24.

Subrahmanian, K.K. and Azeez, A., 2000, *Industrial Growth in Kerala: Trends and Explanations*, Working Paper No. 310. Trivandrum: Centre for Development Studies.

Tharakan, P.K.M., 1998, 'Socio-Religious Reform Movements: The Process of Democratization and Human Development: The Case of Kerala, South-West India', in Rudebeck, L. and Törnquist, O. (eds.), *Democratization in the Third World: Concrete Cases in Comparative and Theoretical Perspective*. London: Macmillan.

Tharakan, P.K.M., 2004, 'Historical Hurdles in the Course of the People's Planning Campaign in Kerala, India', in Harris, J., Stokke, K. and Törnquist, O. (eds.), *Politicising Democracy: The New Local Politics of Democratisation*. Houndmills: Palgrave Macmillan: 107–126.

Tharamangalam, J., 1998, 'The Perils of Social Development without Economic Growth: The Development Debacle of Kerala, India', *Bulletin of Concerned Asian Scholars*, 30(1): 3–34.

Thomas Isaac, T.M., 2001, 'Campaign for Democratic Decentralisation in Kerala', *Social Scientist*, 29(9–10): 8–47.

Thomas Isaac, T.M. and Franke, R.W., 2002, *Local Democracy and Development: The Kerala People's Campaign for Decentralized Planning*. New York: Rowman & Littlefield.

Törnquist, O., 1999, *Politics and Development: A Critical Introduction*. London: Sage.

Törnquist, O., 2004, 'The Political Deficit of Substantial Democratisation', in Harris, J., Stokke, K. and Törnquist, O. (eds.), *Politicising Democracy: The New Local Politics of Democratisation*. Houndmills: Palgrave Macmillan: 201–245.

Véron, R., 2001, 'The "New" Kerala Model: Lessons for Sustainable Development', *World Development*, 29(4): 601–617.

Vijayanand, S.M., 1997, *People's Participation in Poverty Reduction Programmes: A Case Study of the Integrated Tribal Development Project (ITDP)*, Attappady. M Phil thesis, Trivandrum: Centre for Development Studies.

6 Contested frontiers
Adivasi land restitution law and settler narratives

Introduction

This chapter examines the land restitution claims of the indigenous people of Kerala through a critical analysis of the legislative measures in place to restore land rights to the *adivasis*. The strategies of the settlers to thwart the restitution of land have led to a protracted, contested and unfinished implementation.[1] It has also created a dilemma for the state, resulting in a series of changes in legislation. The response of the state highlights the fact that the state itself is a contested arena and challenges the idea of the state as a monolithic entity with unified interests. Although the conservative coalition governments led by the Congress Party have consistently adopted a settler-friendly approach, the Left coalition governments led by the Communist Party of India (Marxist) – CPI(M) – held an ambivalent stand for a long period. However, in 1999 the Left government passed an Act which may be better contextualised with reference to the intersecting nature of class and indigeneity. The Act also coincided with the emerging rearticulation of *adivasi* sub-identities by particular communities such as the Kurumar, Paniyar and Kattunaicker, which, we would argue, enabled a more nuanced understanding of a range of locations at the intersection. We analyse the problems associated with the legislative measures for the restitution of land to the *adivasis*, the contested implementation, resistance strategies of the settlers and shifting policies in the context of changing governments.

Reclaiming land and livelihoods

Legislative measures

The Kerala Scheduled Tribes (Restriction on Transfer of Lands and Restoration of Alienated Lands) Bill was passed in 1975, with retroactive effect from 1960 (Government of Kerala, 1975). However, the rules and regulations for implementation were not framed and approved by the government until 18 October 1986, whereby all transactions of *adivasi* lands to others from 1960 to 1986 were nullified and provisions were made for the restitution of alienated lands to the original owners (Government of Kerala, 1987). The rules stipulate that the *adivasi* claimant should pay a compensation to the present owner – a sum equivalent to the amount that was paid to him or her (the *adivasi*) as entered in the deed of transfer, as well as a sum for the improvements made on the plot as decided by the district collector if the transaction occurred before 1982. The required amount would be made available through loans financed by the state, which were to be repaid within twenty years (Government of Kerala, 1987). If the transaction occurred after 1982, the present owner would not be eligible for any compensation.

Meanwhile, land transactions from *adivasis* to others continued uninterrupted until 31 December 1986, according to standard procedures of registration in the sub-registrar's offices. The government banned such land transactions only with effect from 1 January 1987. Discussions with a sub-registrar's office in Wayanad highlighted that, as the government did not issue any directions to stop registering new land transactions, these registrations continued for some years after the bill was passed in 1975. The sub-registrar's office held the position that they did not have the mandate to refuse the registration of transactions until the government issued relevant orders. Some of the settlers who had bought land from *adivasis* after 1975 told us in interviews that they were not aware that such an Act existed. As one settler put it, 'We were not told that our transaction was illegal by the officers in the sub-registrar's office. How were we to know?' A similar response was obtained from the indigenous people as well, where it was apparent that they were not aware that it was illegal to sell land to non-*adivasis*.

A delay of more than a decade before the 1975 Act was passed into law in 1986 and the continuation of land transactions through official procedures even after the 1975 Act indicate the general apathy of the various coalition governments to the land problems of the *adivasis*. In Kerala, this period was characterised by governments of bizarre coalitions; political parties with no common ideological position, leanings or even pretensions of like-mindedness shared power within the government and were coalitions of convenience rather than substantive politics.[2] The major faction of the Communist Party – the CPI(M) – was kept out of power during this decade. The period was marked by massive class struggles organised by the CPI(M). Since their focus was on workers as a class, the specificities of the *adivasi* issues did not receive adequate attention in these struggles. When the CPI(M)-led coalition formed the government in January 1980, however, the coalition partners included not only left political parties such as the Communist Party of India (CPI) and the Revolutionary Socialist Party (RSP), but also conservative parties such as factions of the Kerala Congress and the rebel All-India Muslim League. These conservative partners largely represented the interests of the landed classes. This might have played a role in preventing the CPI(M) from following up on the 1975 Act. As a minority proportion of Kerala's population, the *adivasis* did not constitute a substantial vote bank. It could be said that the ambivalence of the left regarding the *adivasi* land question was prompted by the imperatives of Kerala's electoral politics on the one hand and by class reductionism which tended to overlook the intersections inhabited by the indigenous people on the other hand.

In the 1982 elections the Congress-led coalition came to power. In 1986, under growing pressure from various activist groups, the government passed rules and regulations under the title 'Kerala Scheduled Tribes (Restriction on Transfer of Lands and Restoration of Alienated Lands) Rules and Regulations 1986' (GoK, 1987). However, implementation was stalled. The Left coalition led by the CPI(M) came to power in 1987. During this period the government started implementing the law by setting up tribal land tribunals, and some cases were adjudicated. However, it soon became apparent that the implementation would adversely affect not only a small number of large landowners and planters, but also a large number of marginal farmers who were also part of the proletariat. Therefore, when it came to physical restitution of land to the *adivasis*, the government, it would seem, was caught in a dilemma. Moreover, the Congress faction within the left-wing coalition government represented the interests of the large landowners and planters. Once again, the class loyalties of the left and the compulsions of the *realpolitik* of Kerala prevented the CPI(M)-led government from implementing the law fully. In the 1991 elections, the Congress-led coalition was returned to power. We now present a critical analysis of the 1975 Act before returning to the complexities of implementation in order to highlight its limitations and to show that, even when implemented, the law would benefit only a very small fraction of the *adivasis* of Kerala.

The 1975 Act: Some problems

Our analysis of the 1975 Act and the rules framed in 1986 show that these regulations treated the *adivasis* as a homogeneous category with one past, namely, those who owned land, and one present, that is, those who lost land. The indigenous communities, however, are a highly heterogeneous people who have had historically different relationships with land and forests, whose livelihoods and labour processes were different and who were embedded in social hierarchies that are carried into the present. These historical facts were not taken into consideration in the 1975 Act. The Act would mostly benefit only a small section of the *adivasi* communities who were traditionally agriculturists and those who could produce proof of ownership of the land alienated from them. In Wayanad there are about six major indigenous groups, out of which only two were traditionally agriculturists (the Kurumar and the Kurichiyar). These constitute only about 36% of the total *adivasi* population in Wayanad. The other communities, who constitute 64%, were traditionally agrestic slaves/bonded labourers (the Paniyar and the Adiyar), hunters and gatherers (the Kattunaicker) and artisans (the Uralis).[3] They had never 'owned' land in the formal sense of the term, except in some cases the small house plots obtained by *kudikidappu* (squatter) rights during the land reforms in 1970. By virtue of their history, they have no lands to point to as 'alienated' as defined by the Act. The Act is thus narrow in scope and excludes these communities.

The case of Irulam Village, Wayanad, where we explored these issues, demonstrates this point. The village has 672 *adivasi* families,[4] comprising the Kattunaicker (39.58%), the Kurumar (31.25%), the Paniyar (26.48%) and the Uralis (2.69%). Of the thirty-eight cases filed for restitution of alienated land in the village, the highest share (58%) was that of the Kurumar, followed by the Paniyar (26%), the Kattunaicker (6%) and none by the Uralis.[5] Several claims were rejected by the adjudicating authority, the tribal land tribunal, as the claimants failed to produce legally admissible documents. Whereas only 5.3% of the claims made by the Kurumar were rejected, 22.2% and 16.7% of claims made by the Paniyar and the Kattunaicker, respectively, were rejected. The higher rate of rejection in the case of the Paniyar and the Kattunaicker indicates that their past relations to land are negatively implicated in their present land claims under the 1975 Act. The Uralis were not even in a position to stake claims, as is shown by the absence of claims put forward by them. Judgements were made on the admissible cases, which constituted a total area of 17.1375 hectares for restitution to the claimants. Of this total, the area admissible to the Kurumar was the largest, comprising 85.4%, while the Paniyar's award was a mere 5.3%; for the Kattunaicker, it was 9.2% (Case Files of Village Office, Irulam).[6]

This lacuna of the 1975 Act did not receive adequate attention from the activists who engaged with the *adivasi* land issue in the late 1980s and facilitated their (*adivasis*') mobilisation. The entire land question of the *adivasis* has, until recently, been articulated surrounding the 1975 Act.[7] The legal battles that had been fought on their behalf also revolve around this Act.[8] This could be one of the reasons for the failure to mobilise the *adivasis* en masse for a very long time, as the majority of them had nothing to gain. A young Paniyan spoke with emotion: 'What is the use of this law for our community? We will not gain any land by fighting for the implementation of this law'. Such sentiments were expressed by the Kattunaicker as well. The historical specificities of the land question were lost sight of, and the land claims of those overlooked by the Act were not raised until much later and in a different context. We return to this issue in a later section.

The land market in Wayanad had been growing rapidly with the stream of in-migration. The earlier settlers made profits by selling portions of their lands to the later settlers, who often sold it to the next to arrive in the sequence.[9] The original settler may have obtained the land from the *adivasis*, but subsequent purchasers bought the land from the settler by paying the market price and following the legal formalities. This was not taken into consideration while formulating the Act. Our fieldwork in Wayanad shows that in many cases the alienated lands were subject to market transactions up to four times before reaching the present owner (Case Files, Irulam Village). Such a case history presents a complicating dimension when it comes to the implementation of the Act. Some of the *adivasis* we had discussions with foresee this as a major hurdle to restitution.

The 1975 Act is applicable only to lands that have been alienated from 1960 onwards. However, the greatest extent of alienation occurred before 1960, to the benefit of large planters and rich peasants.[10] The late settlers were largely small and marginal farmers or previously landless workers who acquired small or micro-holdings. The 1975 Act is, therefore, biased against the latter category whereas the early appropriators of *adivasi* lands are spared. These issues, which have significant practical implications, were not explicitly brought into the debate.

Contested implementation

Our field study in Wayanad shows that the history of implementation of the 1975 Act, according to the rules framed in 1986, is a history of the power struggle between settlers and *adivasis* mediated by the state and the judiciary. The government set up tribal land tribunals in the highland districts. The Revenue Divisional Officer (RDO) was appointed as the appellate authority to adjudicate the cases of land claims.[11] Accordingly, a tribal land tribunal was set up at the office of the RDO at Mananthavady in Wayanad district. The *adivasis* were required to file their claims with the RDO together with supporting documents to prove their previous ownership rights. The RDO would then set a date to hear the case and summon the plaintiff and the defendant. After examining the documents and listening to both parties, the RDO would adjudicate the claims. An appeal process was available to either party through the district collector, and the decision of the collector would be final.[12] Although the Left coalition government began implementing the Act in the late 1980s, the bureaucracy adopted a go-slow approach.[13] For example, until 1991 – that is, five years after framing the rules – out of the 2,279 cases filed with the tribunal in Wayanad district involving 1,534.25 hectares of land, a mere eleven cases that involved 1.23 hectares were adjudicated.[14] Later, the number of cases filed increased to about 5,000 as the *adivasis* became increasingly aware of the law due to the activities of non-governmental organisations (NGOs) and others, including local political activists.[15] Some of the Kurumar said that the go-slow approach was the result of the settlers' 'hold' in 'high places'. The Kerala Congress Party, which represents the interests of the landed classes, had split into four factions in the 1960s. One such faction switched allegiance to the Left coalition and has been sharing power with them, while the other three factions continued to be partners in the conservative coalition. The settlers were therefore in a position to exert power, irrespective of whether the government was formed by the Left or the Congress coalition. The Congress coalition that formed the government in 1991 continued the go-slow approach as an active policy.[16]

In October 1993 the High Court of Kerala directed the government to adjudicate the cases pending within six months. This development was in response to a protracted litigation by a non-*adivasi* activist. While the processing of claims continued, the government repeatedly asked for an extension after every six months, which was granted.[17] In Irulam Village, applications implicating fifty-six settlers were filed by thirty-eight *adivasis* (Case Files, Irulam Village).[18] The adjudication process was completed by 1996. In 80.4% of the cases, the judgements were for restitution of land to the petitioner, and 19.6% of the cases were rejected for various reasons, examined next. Of the total number of cases admitted for restitution, 55.5% were to provide compensation to the present owner since the alienation occurred before 1982. The remaining 44.5%, alienated after 1982, were awarded without compensation. Several reasons for the rejection of the claims are recorded in the case files: failure to produce documents that could establish a petitioner's prior ownership right (28%), failure to appear at the court hearing or failure to present documents that could establish claims (18%), petitions not filed by the rightful heir to the alienated land even though the land belonged to the *adivasi* (18%), previous government orders existing on the petitioned land (18%) or claims on land originally belonging to the *devaswom* (18%).[19] These reasons for rejection further prove the inadequacy of the Act in addressing the land question of the indigenous communities. Moreover, the majority of the *adivasis* who lost land did not even bother to apply, as they did not have any documents to prove prior ownership.[20]

In the cases where the judgements were in favour of the *adivasis*, they were now the de jure owners of the land. However, these lands still had not been physically transferred to them. The defendants continued to be the de facto owners, cultivating the land and reaping the harvests. Nevertheless, the existing title deeds had become invalid, and the revenue department had stopped accepting tax on these lands.[21] The defendants were now unable to get permission to build houses on these lands; could not use the land as collateral; and even if they had repaid earlier loans secured by using the disputed land as collateral, the land would not be redeemed to them.[22] Therefore, many of them did not repay the loans and the interest has been accumulating. They were not able to take advantage of the government programmes for the upliftment of the small and marginal farmers either. The government made some isolated attempts to restore land to the *adivasis*, but these attempts were thwarted by the organised power of the settlers. The settlers organised themselves under the auspices of the *Malayora Karshaka Federation* (Highland Farmers' Federation) and adopted a multi-pronged strategy to prevent restitution.

Settler narratives and strategies

The settlers can be grouped into two factions with regard to the impact of the 1975 Act: those who owned land alienated from *adivasis* during the period 1960–1982 and are eligible for compensation, and those who owned land alienated after 1982 and are not eligible for compensation. The settlers weave their own narratives and arguments regarding the 'implausibility' and 'impossibility' of restitution. For the first category of settlers, the point of departure is memories of a landscape – 'vast, wild and empty' – which they 'nurtured with their sweat' and brought to the present productive condition. They invoke past sufferings to raise moral objections against restitution. As an elderly settler put it:

> We hazarded malaria and other killer diseases here, many families lost several household members to these diseases; we fought against wild animals, slept in huts built on tree-tops, and struggled against poverty to achieve all these. Now, after nearly 40 years the government wants to take away this land from us. Can it be justified?

The same elderly settler described the 'emptiness' of the past landscape in the following words: 'When we arrived here, all these were *empty wastelands* filled with wild trees, bushes, weeds and grasses, where cattle and goats grazed around' (authors' emphasis). The settlers' perception of productive land use informed by their worldview is evident in this statement. For them, only landscapes cultivated with agricultural crops were valuable, and all the rest was 'empty'. The wild trees, bushes, grasses, cattle and goats that constituted the *adivasi* livelihood are not, it would seem, perceived by the settlers as productive land use. The settlers consider the plot of land they own as their accumulated labour or 'materialized labour', as the words used by one of them show: 'This land is created by our sweat. Therefore, it is our right to own this land'. 'Sweat' is the common metaphor for labour. This is reminiscent of Locke's labour-mixing argument to claim private property rights.[23]

The settlers also invoke memories of the struggles to obtain titles to these lands. They remember that both the Left and the Conservative political parties supported them in their struggles and that they were granted legitimate titles by the government in various stages before 1970. Further, with the implementation of the land reforms in 1970, most of them obtained titles to their lands, irrespective of whether it was land that had belonged to the landlords, the *devaswoms* or the *adivasis*. At the time of obtaining these titles, the settlers had to pay the price of the soil (*thara vila*) and the price of the standing trees on the land (*mara vila*) to the government. As a settler asserted:

> Now how can the government ask us to return the lands that we bought after paying the price and following all the lawful procedures stipulated by the government? That too, with effect from 1960. There is no way that we will allow the government to do this to us.

When the issue of the provision for compensation in the 1975 Act was raised, a member of the *Malayora Karshaka Federation* (MKF) responded that this was a nominal gesture on the part of the government. He elaborated by explaining what he called the 'ground truth', which we paraphrase as follows. The first settler who bought land from the *adivasi* may have paid about Rs. 50 per acre in 1962, which was the market price then. Land prices have skyrocketed since then and the plot of land may have undergone several transactions before the present owner bought it in, say, 1981, by paying about Rs. 100,000 per acre to the previous owner. According to the 1975 Act, the compensation for the present owner would be the Rs. 50 that was entered in the records of the first transaction made by the *adivasi* owner. In addition, the present owner would be paid a nominal sum as compensation for the improvements made on the land (*dehanna vila*) as assessed by the RDO. He pointed out that in one case a settler was awarded a sum of Rs. 15 as compensation for eight years' work in a plot of 0.06 hectare (equivalent to 15 cents in the local land measurement unit). Because the Act is included in the Ninth Schedule of the Constitution, the RDO's decision cannot be questioned in the courts. The only possible appeal is to the district collector. Several appeals were made to the collector, but in all cases the collector upheld the RDO's decision. Our informant concluded:

> The 1975 Act and the 1986 rules were formulated without any consideration of the ground truth. These rules have provisions only for penalising the present

owner. Neither the original settler who bought land from the *adivasi*, nor the others who made profits from the transactions are liable to pay any price.

(MKF member)

The second category of settlers, those not eligible for compensation, invoke their own past sufferings to claim their legitimate rights in the land they bought – in some cases directly from the *adivasis* and in many cases from a previous settler. They tell stories of their hardships, of how they skimped and saved and paid for the small plot of land they own now. They also invoke the metaphor of 'sweat'. A typical example might be: 'I paid for this piece of land with my sweat' (a middle-aged settler). They claim that the government would be creating a large population of homeless and destitute if they proceed with restitution, as many of these households have no other lands or money to buy land or houses. They point out that in many cases, an *adivasi*, especially the *Kurumar*, may have sold small plots of land to several settlers, which would mean that when the restitution is effected, there would be several landless settler households for each *adivasi* household whose land was restored. They argue that the government would be creating new injustices –in the name of justice – if it proceeded with the 1975 Act.

The settlers established the MKF in 1975 with the objective of promoting highland farmers' welfare. They have now reorganised themselves to struggle against the 1975 Act, and are actively engaged in resisting the restitution of land. The MKF has adopted a multi-pronged approach to prevent the implementation of the Act. They have been very open about their strategies.[24] These include (1) lobbying at the government level through various representatives, such as elected regional-level representatives, favoured political parties (mainly the various factions of Kerala Congress) and personal 'holds' at higher levels; (2) resorting to judicial means – they have filed a case in the High Court of Kerala pointing out that the 1975 Act is against the Constitution of India, as it violates the fundamental right of the *adivasis* to sell their lands; (3) using the settler-friendly press – newspapers, magazines and television – to publicise their side of the story and gather support; (4) creating awareness about the drawbacks of the Act among the *adivasis*, who are excluded from the benefits of the Act, and prompting them to struggle for a new law that would be beneficial to both parties;[25] and (5) physical resistance to restitution. Under pressure from the *adivasi* organisations and the High Court of Kerala, the government has made an attempt to physically restore land, but this attempt has been successfully resisted by a group of 3,000 settlers organised by the MKF.

Meanwhile, the *adivasis* organised themselves under the *Adivasi Federation* and made an attempt to forcefully harvest the crops from the land that was awarded to an *adivasi* in a tribal land tribunal judgement. This attempt was also foiled by the MKF. The concerned *adivasi* has lodged a fresh complaint with the RDO, demanding physical restoration of his property, physical protection and the right to cultivate the land and harvest the crops. Action has not yet been taken on this petition. Some members of the MKF interviewed said that if a positive decision were made on this petition, it would lead to violent resistance. They claimed that the authorities are aware of this fact.

Changing governments, shifting policies

In 1996, the government of Kerala was given an ultimatum by the High Court of Kerala to implement the 1975 Act. Meanwhile, the settlers had been lobbying to change the cut-off date from 1960 to 1986. Their argument was that the government had framed the rules for the implementation of the 1975 Act as late as 1986 and had allowed lawful land transactions until 31 December of that year. Therefore, they contend that only transactions from 1 January 1987 onwards can be considered illegal. Caught between the judiciary and the settlers' lobby, the Congress coalition government amended the 1975 Act by passing a hasty ordinance just before the state assembly elections in 1996. According to the ordinance, the alienated lands would not be restored and alternative lands would be given to the *adivasis* who had lost land. However, the ordinance did not get the mandatory assent of the governor, as it was promulgated just before the elections, presumably with the intention of canvassing the vote of the settler community.

In the elections that followed, the Left coalition was returned to power. In an earlier section we mentioned the ambivalence of the Left with regard to the *adivasi* land issue. The Left government pleaded in the High Court of Kerala that it was impossible to implement the 1975 Act due to the organised resistance of the settlers. The court, however, did not accept this argument. As a way out of the impasse, the government passed 'The Kerala Scheduled Tribes (Restriction on Transfer of Lands and Restoration of Alienated Lands) Amendment Bill, 1996' in September 1996 (Government of Kerala, 1996). According to this, the cut-off date for restitution was 21 January 1986. The *adivasis* who had lost land between 1960 and 1986 would be provided with alternative land not exceeding one acre, and Rs. 25,000 would be granted as seed money to build a house and to work the new land. The amendment soothed the settlers, but was not acceptable to the *adivasis*, as most of the land alienation occurred before 1986, according to an *adivasi* activist. The amendment, however, did not get the mandatory assent of the President of India and therefore had to be abandoned.

Pressure was mounting on the government of Kerala from various non-*adivasi* activist groups and *adivasi* organisations to implement the 1975 Act. In a meeting convened by the revenue minister on 15 October 1998 and involving the departments concerned, the Left government made a decision to physically restore the lands on which the tribal land tribunals had made judgements, on the strength of the High Court directives.[26] This decision triggered the settler farmers into further action. The state committee of the MKF submitted a long memorandum to the government attacking the 1975 Act and pointing out their grievances. They warned the government of severe resistance and violent unrest in the highlands if any attempt was made to restore lands. The memorandum portrayed the 1975 Act as 'barbaric, impractical, unscientific' and said it 'would pave the way for communal struggles'. The memorandum concludes:

> The settler farmers' house, land and agricultural crops are the products of our lifelong labour. If anyone thinks that we will give up everything in the name of *adivasi* welfare, they are living in a fool's paradise. The *adivasi* land

protection law that would lead to severe unrest in these hills and valleys, where peace and communal harmony co-exist, should be re-written.[27]

This situation forced the Left government to pass another bill on 23 February 1999 – 'The Kerala Scheduled Tribes (Restriction on Land Transfer and Restoration of Lands) Bill' (Government of Kerala, 1999). According to this, the cut-off date for full restitution was 24 January 1986. A settler household could retain up to two hectares of land transacted from the *adivasis* since 1960 and the rest, if any, would be restored. All the *adivasis* who had lost land would be given an equal area of substitute land and Rs. 25,000 each for house building and initial investment in agricultural production. The Act provided for the landless *adivasi* families as well. Each landless family, whether it had lost land or not, would be allotted one acre of land. This was the first legislative attempt to address the land question of the *adivasi* communities who were left out of the ambit of the 1975 Act, and who constituted the majority of the *adivasi* population of Kerala. This Act has been groundbreaking in that respect. Because the bill was passed under the purview of 'agricultural land', a state subject, it did not need concurrence from the government of India and could be implemented after framing the rules. However, a non-*adivasi* activist filed a case in the High Court of Kerala questioning some sections of the Act. Consequently, the High Court ordered a stay in implementation. Following this, the government of Kerala appealed to the Supreme Court of India, and the stay has since been rescinded. The 1999 Act is by far the most comprehensive legislation with regard to *adivasi* lands and represents a breakthrough in the Left's approach to the *adivasi* land question. In this piece of legislation, the Left succeeded, to a large extent, in taking account of the simultaneity of class and ethnic/indigenous dimensions of the *adivasi* land question and at the same time addressing the interests of the marginal and small peasants.

The settlers have hailed the 1999 Act as a positive step. One settler said: 'The Act if implemented will be beneficial to both settlers and *adivasis* and there will be a breakthrough in the stalemate. This is the only way to solve the problem'. The *adivasi* response has been mixed and cautious. Some of the Kurumar who had made land claims under the 1975 Act were skeptical about the 1999 Act, whereas some others shared the view expressed by an elderly Kuruman: 'Finally something will happen. We are getting tired of the long wait'. Yet another group of Kurumar we had discussions with expressed their dilemma as follows:

> Yes, the 1975 Act is good for us as some of us can claim our original land. But many of us were unable to stake claims as we do not have the documents needed to prove our claims. Therefore, about 75 per cent of us who had lost lands did not even file petitions. In principle, we accept the 1975 Act as it asserts our *right* to reclaim our own lands. On the other hand, we know that it is impossible to implement. We feel that the new Act is more practical and we do not have to make enemies of our neighbours. Some of our neighbours have stopped even talking to us as we have filed petitions to claim the land occupied by them.
>
> (A Kuruman, emphasis in original)

As far as the Kurumar are concerned, it would seem the 1975 Act has more symbolic value than practical relevance, as they perceive that its implementation is 'impossible' given the experience of the last two decades. Out of sheer weariness and the added tensions that were brought into their already harsh lives, and seeing the possibility of benefits to more *adivasis*, they cautiously expressed their hopes regarding the 1999 Act. An *adivasi* woman political activist put it this way: 'The 1975 Act has outlived its usefulness. It provided us with a fulcrum around which we could struggle for land rights. Now it is time to let go of it, and move forward with the new Act which seems more beneficial if implemented.'

The 1999 Act elicited a suppressed euphoria among the *adivasi* communities who were excluded from the 1975 Act. This was the first ever opportunity for them to claim lands for cultivation, and they welcomed it. However, they feared that the implementation could be stopped or indefinitely delayed because of the court cases:

> Activists had been doing good by filing cases in the courts. But now they should stop. The tying up of this Act in a court case was completely unwarranted. The Act is radical. It has provisions for the majority of the *adivasis* such as the Paniyar, the Kattunaicker and the Adiyar. The court cases can ruin our chances of getting land. They should forget the 1975 Act, which is of no benefit to us.
>
> (A young Paniyan)

Several Kattunaicker expressed similar sentiments. Some NGOs and activists were quick to denounce the bill as a government ploy to create a split in the *adivasi* interests so as to protect the interests of the settlers. Others, though cautious, have adopted a 'wait-and-see' approach. The indigenous peoples' movement later rejected the provision for alternative lands instead of restitution and extended the demand that the landless *adivasis* should be given lands in the same localities that they live in. Such demands were made possible through a process of re-articulation of *adivasi* identities, which we return to in the next chapter.

The failure of the government to implement the 1975 Act has been posited as a case of betrayal of the *adivasis* by the state (Bijoy, 1999) and as the triumph of the political society over civil society (Sreekumar and Parayil, 2002). We would argue that the process of implementation/non-implementation of the 1975 Act, the contestations and the further amendment and enactment of new legislation were the outcomes of power struggles played out between the settlers and the indigenous communities mediated by the state and the judiciary. This contestation of power on multiple fronts – at the local, regional and national levels and carried through the years – cannot be captured by framing the problem in terms of a binary opposition between what Bernstein (1990: 69) characterises as 'virtuous peasants and vicious states'.[28] Kerala's civil society is a highly heterogeneous arena where communities and social groups repeatedly contest the state and collude with it to promote their own interests. In contesting the issue of land, the settlers and *adivasis*, both constituted by and constitutive of civil society, entered into a struggle mediated through the state and the judiciary. Power was the key factor that determined the outcome of this mediation. The settlers, who commanded multiple sources of power as compared to the *adivasis*, were able to steer state decisions in such a way as to prevent restitution. At the same time, the state enacted new legislations embracing the excluded *adivasi* communities, thus projecting the image of a 'moral state'. As Moore points out, it is important to pay attention to the micro-politics of the struggle over resources at the local level, in order to avoid representations of the 'state' as an undifferentiated actor with a 'unified intentionality, internally consistent in its agenda, structurally and automatically opposed to local interests' (Moore, 1996: 126). Moore concedes that it would be wrong to underestimate the force of political economy, but at the same time he cautions that other important factors may be overlooked by too much emphasis on structural factors. The state in Kerala is undoubtedly a conglomeration of competing interests.

Conclusion

This chapter shows that the land restitution law of 1975 was flawed in that it would benefit only a minority of *adivasis* who had historically owned land and who could provide proof of the same. However, the implementation of this law was contested by the organised power of the settlers. We have discussed the powerful narratives of the settlers and arguments for their hard-earned rights in land, which they defend at any cost. This led to the enactment of a series of legislations, which could be interpreted as being more sensitive to the differential locations of the *adivasis* in the indigeneity–class intersection. However, these interventions generated their own contradictions, which we shall address in the next chapter.

Notes

1. The settlers are the farmers who migrated from the midlands and highlands of Kerala from the 1930s to the early 1980s.
2. See Nossiter (1988).
3. Source: These figures are calculated from the Tables on Panchayat Wise – Community Wise Summary of Scheduled Tribe Habitats in Wayanad District 2001, Records of the Wayanad District Planning Office, Kalpetta.
4. This data is for 1991. Source: Records of Tribal Development Office, Sulthan Bathery.
5. Source: Case Files of Village Office, Irulam.
6. Although these judgements were made in 1994, the lands have not yet been physically restituted to the beneficiaries.
7. See Bijoy (1999).
8. See Sreekumar and Parayil (2002).
9. Discussions with an elderly settler.
10. The early migrants to Wayanad were rich peasants and large planters, whereas the late migrants, that is, after 1960, were largely poor peasants and landless workers (see Tharakan, 1976).
11. Discussions with the village officer, Irulam.
12. Discussions with the village officer, Irulam.
13. Discussions with an *adivasi* activist.
14. Source: Statement filed by government of Kerala on 4 April 1991 to the High Court of Kerala.

15 Source: Solidarity, Mananathavady.
16 Discussion with a Kuruman activist.
17 Discussions with Dr. Nallathampy Thera, the activist who filed the case against the government for its failure to implement the 1975 Act.
18 One *adivasi*'s land may be alienated to two or more settlers.
19 A *devaswom* is a Hindu temple trust.
20 Discussions with the village officer, *adivasi* activists and NGOs.
21 Discussions with village officer, Irulam.
22 Discussion with settlers.
23 See Locke (1924).
24 Discussion with MKF members.
25 The expectation was that the enactment of a new law would present an opportunity to modify the 1975 Act in a direction that would benefit the settlers.
26 *Memorandum Submitted to the Government of Kerala by the State Committee of Malayora Karshaka Federation* in November 1998. Translated from Malayalam by the first author. Source: Office of the MKF, Meenangady, Wayanad.
27 Ibid.
28 See also Moore (1996) and Li (2003).

References

Bernstein, H., 1990, 'Taking the Part of Peasants?', in Bernstein, H., Crow, B.; Mackintosh, M. and Martin, C. (eds.), *The Food Question: Profits Versus People?*, London: Earthscan: 69–79.

Bijoy, C. R., 1999, 'Adivasis Betrayed: Adivasi Land Rights in Kerala', *Economic and Political Weekly*, 34(22): 1329–1335.

District Planning Office, 2001, Tables on Panchayat Wise – Community Wise Summary of Scheduled Tribe Habitats in Wayanad District, Records of Wayanad District Planning Office, Kalpetta.

Government of Kerala, 1975, 'The Kerala Scheduled Tribes (Restriction on Transfer of Lands and Restoration of Alienated Lands) Bill, 1975,' in *Proceedings of the Fourth Kerala Legislative Assembly, Thirteenth Session, August 5,* XXXIX, No. 5, Official Report. Trivandrum: Government of Kerala.

Government of Kerala, 1987, *Kerala Pattikavargakkar (Bhoomi Kaimatta Niynthranavum Anyadheenappeduthiya Bhoomi Thirichukodukkalum) Chattangal 1986*, Government of Kerala. Trivandrum: The Government Press.

Government of Kerala, 1991, Statement filed by the Government of Kerala to the High Court of Kerala, 4 April 1991, Thiruvananthapuram.

Government of Kerala, 1996, The Kerala Scheduled Tribes (Restriction on Transfer of Lands and Restoration of Alienated Lands) Amendment Bill, 1996, Government of Kerala. Trivandrum: The Government Press.

Government of Kerala, 1999, *1999-le Kerala Pattikavarga Bhoomi Kaimatta Niyanthranavum Punaravakasha Sthapanavum Bill*, Government of Kerala. Trivandrum: The Government Press.

Li, T., 2003, 'Situating Resource Struggles: Concepts for Empirical Analysis', *Economic and Political Weekly*, XXXVIII(48): 5120–5128.

Locke, J., 1924, *Two Treatises of Government*. London: J. M. Dent and Sons Ltd.

Malayora Karshaka Federation, 1998, Memorandum Submitted to the Government of Kerala by the State Subcommittee, Meenangady, Wayanad.

Moore, D. S., 1996, 'Marxism, Culture, and Political Ecology: Environmental Struggles in Zimbabwe's Eastern Highlands', in Peets, R. and Watts, M. (eds.), *Liberation Ecologies: Environment, Development and Social Movements*. London: Routledge: 125–147.

Nossiter, T. J., 1988, *Marxist State Governments in India: Politics, Economics and Society*. London: Pinter Publishers.

Solidarity, 1999, Office Records, Mananathavady.

Sreekumar, T. T. and Parayil, G., 2002, 'Democracy, Development and New Forms of Social Movements: A Case Study of Indigenous People's Struggles in Kerala', *The Indian Journal of Labour Economics*, 45(2): 287–309.

Tharakan, P. K. M., 1976, *Migration of Farmers from Travancore to Malabar From 1930 to1960: An Analysis of Its Economic Causes*, M Phil. Thesis. Trivandrum: Centre for Development Studies.

Tribal Development Office, 1991, Records of *Adivasi* Families, Sultan Bathery.

Village Office, Case files for various years, Irulam.

7 Re-articulating *adivasi* land rights and identities

Tensions in the indigeneity–class intersection

Introduction

This chapter provides an account of re-articulating *adivasi* identities and land claims through particular modes of engagement with the state. Our focus is on the *adivasi* land struggles, drawing on the articulation of their identities, the more recent struggles in which land claims were re-framed through a re-articulation and their attempts to project a new politics for an imagined future. Stuart Hall's conceptualisation of identity as an 'articulated positioning' is useful in gaining a theoretical understanding of the *adivasi* land struggles. The term articulation, as defined by Hall, has a dual meaning: articulation as the process of making a collective identity, position or set of interests explicit and comprehensible to an audience; and to the process of linking that position towards achieving definite political ends (Hall, 1990, 1996; Li 2000).

> [A] theory of articulation is both a way of understanding how ideological elements come, under certain conditions, to cohere together within a discourse, and a way of asking how they do or do not become articulated, at specific conjunctures, to certain political subjects.
>
> (Hall, 1996: 141–142)

Hall argues that collective identities can be forged to work towards a political end and then re-articulated in a different conjuncture. Identities are thus 'unstable points of identification or suture ... Not an essence but a *positioning*' (Hall, 1990: 226, emphasis in original). Articulations are therefore open to re-articulation, as the closure of one positioning is merely arbitrary and contingent (Li, 2000). The initial positioning of the indigenous people as a monolithic category – the *adivasis* – can be interpreted as an articulation aimed at projecting a collective identity that would enable them to renegotiate their relations with the state, the settlers and the larger Kerala society in an attempt to reclaim alienated lands. The realisation that government legislation to restore land claims would benefit only certain *adivasi* communities has prompted them to engage in a re-articulation of their sub-identities or micro-identities by positioning themselves in subsequent struggles as particular communities – as Kurumar, Paniyar, Kattunaicker and so on. This has been achieved by highlighting their differential historicities and attachment to place. Such a re-articulation has drawn a favourable response from the state, as reflected in the agreement between the government and the *adivasis* in 2001.

Articulating adivasi *identities*

A people's self-identification as indigenous could be considered 'a *positioning* which draws upon historically sedimented practices, landscapes, and repertoires of meaning, and emerges through particular patterns of engagement and struggle' (Li, 2000: 151). An analysis of the *adivasi* land struggles reveals that their identities were constituted by and are constitutive of the struggles in which they have been engaged.

It could be posited that the ideology implicated in the *adivasi* identity was articulated into the *adivasi* movement in the process of the struggles. In Stuart Hall's view, it is through articulation that ideologies get connected to social groups, thus creating political subjects and transforming them into a social force (Hall, 1996). Hall developed his idea from the theory of articulation developed by Laclau (1977), whose position is that an ideology, although it transforms people's consciousness and awareness of themselves and their historical situation, does not by itself constitute a social or political force. It can, however, become articulated to a social movement so as to recruit sectors of the population who have not been hitherto part of the movement. A movement, by constituting itself as a collective subject within the framework of a common ideology, becomes a social force. It becomes a unified social force – for instance, as a class or cross-class movement – only when it acquires some form of intelligibility that explains a shared collective situation.[1] It is in this moment that a variety of social forces get articulated to that particular ideology. A variety of social groups may enter into and constitute themselves as a social or political force, albeit for a time, partly by 'seeing themselves reflected as a unified force in the ideology which constitutes them' (Hall, 1996: 144). Ideology and social forces thus operate in a dialectical relationship. Hall argues:

> So it is articulation, the non-necessary link, between a social force which is making itself, and the ideology or conceptions of the world which makes intelligible the process they are going through, which begins to bring on to the historical stage a new social position and historical position, a new set of social and political subjects.
>
> (Hall, 1996: 144).

Hall insists that the significance of an 'organic ideology' as a social and political force hinges upon the social groups that can be articulated to and by it. The principle of articulation, therefore, must be located here. The connection, however, is not one '*necessarily* given in socio-economic structures or positions, but precisely as the result of *an articulation*' (Hall, 1996: 145, emphasis in original). Therefore, it may be argued that the articulated ideologies provide the necessary substratum for a social group to tease out the subjective meanings of their objective realities, thus constructing identities that dialectically reinforce ideologies and political action. The development of *adivasi* consciousness and the transformation of the *adivasis* into a social and political force could be understood along these lines.

As we have mentioned in Chapter 1, the term *adivasi* was first articulated in the context of the livelihood struggles of the indigenous communities in central India against the colonial state and its colluders (Bates, 1995). The *adivasi* ideology, which was articulated into the 'tribal movement', helped make sense of the historical marginalisation process and its linkages to the existing socio-economic condition of the *adivasis*, thereby constituting them as political subjects. The articulation of this term by the *adivasis* and activists was undoubtedly a political tactic to forge connections and solidarities among the colonial designates, the 'tribals' inhabiting the fragmented landscape – in geographic and socio-economic terms – that was India. The subsequent struggles of the indigenous peoples in the colonial and post-colonial periods were orchestrated around their identity articulated as *adivasis*.

In India, colonialism had excluded the indigenous people by constructing a 'tribal' other, whereas the post-colonial state created a 'Scheduled Tribe' slot in an attempt to integrate them into the mainstream. In Wayanad, the struggle for land rights has been a simultaneous process of articulation of *adivasi* identities as well. The organic process of shifting strategies in their struggle was linked to their tactical positioning as *adivasis* and/or particular *adivasi* communities at various stages of pauperisation and proletarianisation. In their initial struggles, the pre-constituted heterogeneous and hierarchical formations found a common ideological platform, namely, their identity as indigenous peoples – the *adivasis*. Hierarchies and the politics of difference were strategically played down in a process of articulation that was initially facilitated by non-*adivasi* activists. The image of the *adivasis* as a monolithic entity was projected to the audience – the state and the hegemonic social groups. This was a tactical move to impress upon the audience their (the *adivasis*') imminent power as political subjects and as a social force. 'Original inhabitant' was the lynchpin around which their identities were then articulated. The founding of *Adivasi Aikya Samithi* (The United *Adivasi* Forum), a forum of various indigenous groups at the local level, which coalesced at the regional level to form the *Adivasi Vikasana Pravarthaka Samithi* (The *Adivasi* Development Activists' Forum), was the result of these articulations. It paved the way for the emergence of a critical mass of leadership among the indigenous peoples by the late 1980s. Their positioning as *adivasi* and the rights inherent in that identity supplied the initial impetus for the struggles for land.[2]

The *adivasi* movement gained an added impetus from the developments related to the rights of indigenous peoples in the late 1980s and early 1990s in the international arena. Various developments – the ILO Convention No. 169, 1989; the World Bank's Operational Directive No. 4.20, 1991; the United Nations Working Group on Indigenous Peoples (UNWGIP), Draft Declaration on the Rights of Indigenous Peoples, 1993; the declaration of 1993 as the International Year of the Indigenous Peoples; and 1995–2004 as the UN Decade of the Indigenous Peoples – all provided wider legitimacy to the *adivasi* struggles for land and livelihoods. The international movement of indigenous peoples provided a discursive momentum for Kerala's *adivasi* movement. For instance, Kerala's *adivasi* movement drew upon the discourses of the international indigenous peoples' rights movement to confront the state government, the national government and the judiciary. Idioms and adages employed in distant geographies were co-opted and rephrased in the articulation of *adivasi* identities and their struggles for land. The networking of the *adivasis* with other regions, a weeklong meeting (*sangamom*) of the *adivasis* of south India in Wayanad in 1992, followed by the formation of the *Adivasi* South Zone Forum, served to forge and reinforce their monolithic identity as *adivasis*. Micro-identities were subsumed under the *adivasi* umbrella. This, we would argue, was a tactical positioning adopted by the indigenous movement to swing the conjunctural imperatives of the indigenous politics in the international and national arenas to their advantage. The conjunctures at which some communities position themselves as indigenous are the products of agency and the cultural and political work of articulation. This positioning enables them to renegotiate the ways in which they connect to the nation-state, the government and their own place (Li, 2000).

The politics of place and *adivasi* identity

The Wayanad landscape is being reinterpreted and re-created in the process of articulating *adivasi* identities in the ongoing land struggles. Moore (1998) argues that localities should be conceived of as products of contestations than as inert, fixed backdrops for identity struggles. As Massey says, '[W]e make our space/spatialities in the process of our identities' (Massey, 1995: 285). The cultural politics of place, 'the historically sedimented practices that weave contested meanings into the fabric of the locality' (Moore, 1998: 347), is conjoined with the politics of identity (Jacobs, 1994; Radhakrishnan, 1996; Watts, 1991). In Wayanad, the *adivasi* movement's refusal to accept alternative lands[3] and the insistence on having land in their own localities[4] and their spatially situated livelihood practices all constitute a concrete politics of place. Spatially situated livelihood practices are woven into popular understandings of the relation between locality and identity (Pred, 1986). Gupta and Ferguson (1992) argue that attaching causes to places is important for successful political mobilisation. In articulating attachment to place into the *adivasi* identity, they were tacking their cause – land rights – to the place – Wayanad. A people's attachment to a place, invoking a 'sense of place' (Agnew, 1989), is also constitutive of their identity through history lived in person or experienced in social memories. Therefore, the *adivasi* struggles for place would be simultaneously symbolic – over meanings – and material – over land and livelihoods. The Wayanad landscape can be viewed as a materially and symbolically contested terrain within which the indigeneity–class intersectional experiences of the different *adivasi* communities have played out.

The 1999 Act opened an opportunity for the *adivasis* to re-articulate their identities. The *adivasis* of Wayanad, while hailing the spirit of the Act that provides for alternative land to those who have had their lands alienated and lands to all landless *adivasis*, were concerned about the implementation aspects, and with good reason.[5]

They feared that the government would find lands for them in faraway 'alien' places, where they would be 'out of place'. The Kurumar therefore rejected the Act and its provision for alternative lands.[6] They began to re-articulate their *adivasi* identity by invoking their attachment to place. Their contention was that it was their right to have the lands restored, as they had a historical attachment to the place in a way the settlers could not claim. They declared that the government could give alternative land to the settlers and their own lands should be restituted. The argument was that the settlers' livelihoods could be reproduced elsewhere, unlike the indigenous people's livelihoods that were place situated. As a young Kuruman activist put it:

> If they [the settlers] could leave everything from their native place and live here, it is possible for them to go and live in another place where the government would give them land. It is impossible for us to leave this place.

Another Kuruman who was listening rejoined: 'If you ask a settler where his *nadu* (native place) is, the answer is Pala, Kottayam, Muvattupuzha, Thodupuzha or some other place, never Wayanad'.[7] For him this was an indication of the settlers' lack of attachment to Wayanad. The *adivasis* thus invoke the 'unity of people and place' (Li, 2000: 168). The Kurumar invoked historical narratives to establish their anteriority in the region, such as recounting how their king (the Veda king) was defeated by treachery and their territory was conquered by the neighbouring Kurumbranad and Kottayam kings.

> We have lived in this place from time immemorial. We believe we are the ones who have the right to live here. We were here before the settlers, we were here before the British, we were here before the Nairs and the Nambiars.
> (An elderly Kuruman)

Landscapes can be explored as 'symbolic fields', as 'maps of meaning', as 'ways of seeing'; indeed, they can be read as texts, all of which rests on the assumption that social groups actively produce meanings but do so in ways that can 'pinch out emancipatory impulses' (Thrift, 1989: 151, quoted in Watts, 1992: 122). During the *adivasis*' emancipatory struggles, a mapping of the Wayanad landscape as imbued with spiritual meanings is recognisable. The *adivasis* of Wayanad, whether Kurumar, Paniyar or Kattunaicker, consider their dead ancestors to be gods. The landscape is marked by the presence of these ancestors, who are buried in special burial grounds. Rituals have to be performed for the ancestors on certain days of the year. The life-cycle rituals and ceremonies need the ancestors' presence and blessing. Propitiation of ancestral spirits who watch over their lands is necessary at every stage of their farming activities – sowing, intermediate stage and harvest stage – to get a good crop. Thus ancestors are imbricated in their everyday life:

> This is our ancestral land. If we go away from here how can we perform our rituals and ceremonies? How can we please our ancestors and ask for their guidance? Our existence will be in danger if we go away from this place.
> (Kattunaicken chief)

Problems of death and burial were also invoked by the chief:

> We do not want to die in 'alien' lands. We do not want to be buried with strangers. Our spirits will not have peace. We have to join our ancestors after death. Now do you understand why we do not want to go away?

For the *Paniyar*, too, the ceremonies after death are inextricably interlinked with place. They invoke the necessity of maintaining their social organisation as a prerequisite for performing death ceremonies and propitiating ancestors. They need the services of an *attali* (a specially trained person) to perform the ritual of *Penappattu*, a continuous recital of the story of the *Paniyar* community from the 'beginning'. This ceremony is essential to please the spirit of the dead person before burial and for three years after the burial. There are very few *attalis* in the community, and the *Paniyar* express fears that they may be buried without *Penappattu* if they go away to distant places. The *adivasis*' struggle for land thus assumes a spiritual meaning linked to their identity and attachment to place: '[T]he place is inseparable from the consciousness of those who inhabit it' (Daniels, 1985: 151). The espousing of the spiritual connectedness of the *adivasis* to the Wayanad landscape at this moment of struggle could be understood as a political strategy to reinforce the legitimacy of their claims for land in that region.

In the *adivasi* social memories, the Wayanad landscape is inscribed with political meanings. Their representations of past political sufferings and struggles for the sake of Wayanad are inextricably braided with their present struggles and future aspirations. They invoke their ancestors' role in the Pazhassi *Yudham*, the war of Pazhassi Rajah against the British conquest of Wayanad. In the protracted war that lasted for more than a decade (1792–1805), the *adivasis* fought side by side with the Pazhassi Rajah using bows and arrows, worked as secret intelligence agents and messengers, provided food and other services to the army and protected the Rajah by hiding him in secret places known only to *adivasis* by virtue of their familiarity with the landscape. Thousands of *adivasis* sacrificed their lives for their homeland. In 1805, the Rajah was killed and Wayanad came under British rule. Many *adivasis* fled to the forest interiors, fearing British reprisals. These sufferings of their ancestors are recorded in Wayanad history and inscribed in the *adivasi* social memories, which they invoke to legitimate their land claims in Wayanad. They remember that it was their ancestors who rose up against the British in 1812 to protest against the extraction of high land revenue, while the upper castes – the Nairs and Nambiars – colluded with the British: 'Our ancestors were the ones who shed blood for the Wayanadan soil', said a Kuruman activist. Some of the *adivasis* invoke their more recent memories associated with the 'naxalite' uprising in Wayanad and the suffering for land.[8] Hence, they are not 'a-historic' peoples (cf. Marx, 1853); they have made history – a history invoked in their struggle for land.

The *adivasis*' historical relationship to the Wayanad landscape has not been uniform in nature: they have had historically different relationships with land and forests, leading to the 'coexistence of multiple historicities within any particular locality' (Feierman, 1990: 29). The 1999 Act passed by the Left government presented an opportunity for the historically landless *adivasis* of Wayanad – the Paniyar, Kattunaicker, Adiyar and Uralis – to re-articulate their particular identities that were hitherto subsumed under the pan-*adivasi* identity. The spatially situated livelihood practices stemming from their particular histories were invoked in their insistence on land in the same locality. For instance, the Paniyar were historically agrestic slaves/bonded labourers of landlords and were mostly working in rice fields. A large part of their subsistence needs were obtained by gathering resources from the forest – wood for fuel, roots and tubers, fruits and vegetables. The Wayanad landscape offers rice fields and forests in their vicinity. The Kattunaicker were traditionally hunters and gatherers. Collection of minor forest produce is still a major activity among this community, apart from dependence on forests for food and fuelwood. These communities remember that a large proportion of the vested forestlands of Wayanad were earmarked for distribution to them in the 1970s, considering their specific historical experience. Thus in order to stake their land claims, they began to articulate their sub-*adivasi* identity as Paniyar or Kattunaicker, as distinct from that of the Kurumar, whose struggles hitherto had largely been orchestrated around the 1975 Act for restitution. Micro-identities, however, were articulated within the framework of the larger *adivasi* identity, and these struggles were tactically interlinked.

Although the 1999 Act was contested and recontested in the courts, the Left government proceeded with an assessment of the lands available to be distributed to the *adivasis*.[9] In the May 2001 elections, however, the Congress coalition was elected to power. The *adivasis* were losing patience – a patience that had lasted for more than two decades. Reports of the deaths from starvation of thirty-two *adivasis* in mid-July 2001 triggered them into action. A group of radical *adivasi* women and men enacted a Robin Hood scenario in Wayanad: they captured a mobile food shop belonging to the Civil Supplies Corporation and distributed the food to the *adivasis*. Subsequently, they engaged in a forty-eight-day-long intensive agitation at the state secretariat in the capital, Trivandrum, from 30 August to 16 October 2001. Multiple modes of agitation, including building huts on the premises of the secretariat, *sathyagraham*,[10] relay fasting, indefinite hunger strikes, demonstrations, mass rallies and so on, were adopted to engage the government, the public and the media. The struggle was organised by the *Adivasi Dalith Samara Samithi*, a conglomeration of *adivasi* and *dalith* organisations.[11] This struggle was groundbreaking in that it was the first time the rights to land of the historically landless *adivasi* groups such as the Paniyar, the Kattunaicker, the Adiyar and so on, who constitute the largest section of the *adivasi* population, were projected as the major demand.[12] The slogan of the 2001 struggle was 'land to the landless *adivasis*'.

The new struggle for land rights was layered onto the local cultural politics, the politics of place and the multiple identities of *adivasis* enmeshed in and rearticulated through these politics. A major breakthrough of the struggle was the demand for a settlement outside the ambit of the 1975 Act. This was made possible by the successful re-articulation of the simultaneity of the indigenous identities – their identity as *adivasis*, as well as their sub-identity (micro-identity) as Paniyar,

Kattunaicker, Adiyar and so on. These articulations, however, were closely interlinked with their historical-material conditions of existence. The multiple historicities of the Wayanad *adivasis* were articulated into the struggles in an attempt to break out of the two-and-a-half-decade-long impasse surrounding the 1975 Act that ascribed a single history to the *adivasis*. The mobilisation that ensued was unprecedented in its scale. It would seem that the re-articulation invoking identity politics and the politics of place was forceful enough that the Congress government agreed to grant between one and five acres of land to all *adivasi* families who were landless and to those who had less than one acre of land, in their own localities, depending on availability. The process was to be completed between 1 January and 31 December 2002. The government also agreed to prepare a proposal that would include the *adivasi* regions of Kerala in Schedule 5 of Article 244 of the Indian Constitution and send it to the government of India for notification by the president.[13] Inclusion in Schedule 5 would provide special rights and privileges to the region, including *adivasi* self-rule at the sub-national level through the implementation of the Provisions of the *Panchayats* (Extension to the Scheduled Areas) Bill.

The re-articulations reflected in the 2001 struggle sedimented into a powerful agency of the *adivasis*. This made it possible for them to negotiate a settlement outside the 1975 Act, against the advice of some of the non-*adivasi* supporters of the struggle, including CPI (ML-Red Flag) and the Bharathiya Janatha Party (BJP). This was a tactical and well-considered move by the *adivasis* insofar as the practicalities were concerned, and in consideration of the limitations of the 1975 Act and the protracted stalemate in its implementation. The government, however, agreed to abide by the decision of the Supreme Court with regard to the 1975 Act. The *Adivasi Gothra Maha Sabha* (AGMS), a grand assembly of the various *adivasi* communities with 380 representatives from thirty-one different *adivasi* communities of Kerala, grew out of this struggle. It also serves as a platform for all *adivasi* organisations in Kerala.

Re-imagining indigeneity

A special administrative unit was constituted by the government, which included a tribal mission, a cabinet committee and several other committees for speedy implementation of the 2001 agreement. The tribal mission identified 36,012 acres of land to be distributed, and on 1 January 2002, titles for 370 acres were distributed (Sivanandan and Madhava Menon, 2003). The tribal mission was actively engaged in finding lands and dealing with procedures for obtaining the Central government's permission to distribute vested forestlands to the *adivasis*. The Master Plan Committee proposed the constitution of the *Gothra Sabha* (*Adivasi* Assembly) and *oorukkoottangal* (village assemblies), and formalising this administrative arrangement in the *adivasi* zones – the formation of a sort of autonomous *adivasi* republic (Sivanandan, 2003). However, the government, without giving any explanation, halted all these processes and reduced the tribal mission's status to that of an advisory body and redeployed all the employees who were actively engaged in the

136 Adivasi *land rights and identities*

work. The principal secretary, who was responsible for the implementation of the master plan, was replaced by the forest secretary, who was antagonistic towards the proposals in the plan. The Master Plan Committee was thus sabotaged by the government, and the draft plan was suspended (Sivanandan, 2003).

The *adivasi* activists we had discussions with said that the whole process was sabotaged by vested non-*adivasi* interests, including the Forest Department, the Forest Development Corporation (which controlled many of the plantations that were earmarked to be distributed to *adivasis*), the Agriculture Department (which had some farms under its control), the non-*adivasi* management and the trade unions of other *adivasi* project areas under consideration for distribution. Even the state departments that controlled these project areas were against the distribution of the plantations. Here, the presumption that the state is a monolithic entity with unified interests crumbles; instead, it was revealed to be an internally differentiated entity, itself a site of contestations so much so that 'the state is no longer to be taken as essentially an actor, with the coherence, agency, and subjectivity that term presumes' (Mitchell, 1991: 90). The state could rather be 'opened as a theatre in which resources, property rights and authority are struggled over' (Watts, 1989: 4). In the present context, the state, represented by various administrative departments, state corporations, the bureaucracy and so on, is clearly a differentiated entity contesting for power and control over distribution of property rights. Although the chief minister,[14] certain departments and some bureaucrats were in favor of distribution of certain state lands to the *adivasis*, others were strongly opposed to it, since their interests were dominated by partisan politics, bureaucratic rents and power, and, in some cases, with protecting the class interests of workers who were mostly non-*adivasis*. This situation reveals the dialectical nature of the class–*adivasi* politics as well; a clear mismatch emerges between the interests of non-*adivasi* workers and *adivasi* workers. The opposing forces within the state gained an upper hand, thereby sabotaging the land distribution process and the implementation of the 2001 agreement.

Consequent to this, the left began to play a more active role at the local level. The *adivasis* organised a struggle in Wayanad in May 2002 with the support of the CPI(M) and the *Adivasi Kshema Samithi*, a left-oriented *adivasi* organisation. This was a symbolic struggle in which the *adivasis* built huts on treetops in vested forests to assert their claims to these forestlands. The huts were removed after government assurances to expedite the distribution of land by 1 September 2002. A survey undertaken in Irulam Village as a prelude to implementation showed that 463 *adivasi* families were landless, of which 65% were Paniyar, 22% Kattunaicker, 9% Uralis and 4% Kurumar. The village needed 463 acres of land for distribution to the landless, and an additional 284.52 acres for households that owned less than one acre so that all households could have a minimum of one acre.[15] Thus, the village needed a total of 747.52 acres of land for distribution. The village had 4,676.5 acres of vested forestland within its boundaries. But, after inspection, the Wayanad district collector recommended a mere 50 acres for distribution, as the rest was assessed to be a wildlife movement zone.[16] The village office proposed the two coffee plantations in the vested forest area, constituting 300 acres for distribution.

The labour trade unions protested, however, particularly in one of the plantations where the majority of the workers were non-*adivasis*.[17] The class–*adivasi* contradictions thus came alive at the local level. Although the importance of connecting with broader social forces had been recognised by the *adivasi* movement, the local instantiations of the class–*adivasi* dynamics and conflicts of interest made it difficult to forge an alliance with non-*adivasi* plantation workers in this context. This is related to the *adivasis*' strategic articulation of identity and collective claims to lost land rights in their continuing resistance to pauperisation and proletarianisation. A project to distribute plantation lands to *adivasis* would set them on the path to becoming owner-cultivators of smallholdings of already established cash crops and integrate them more into market relations. This would indeed be a transition of their location in the indigeneity–class intersection. On the other hand, there are instances of the *adivasi* movement collaborating with other movements of subordinated groups such as workers and *dalits*, and even participating in more radical struggles, such as the naxalite uprising in Wayanad in the late 1960s. *Adivasi* workers have also been members of trade unions for many years. In fact, some of the current leaders of the *adivasi* movement had their political schooling in the left trade union movement.

The left, it would seem, was once again caught in a dilemma. Although some left-wing politicians were against distribution of these plantations on the grounds that it would hurt the workers' interests, others were in favour of the move. Discussions with some members of the local unit of the CPI(M) revealed that there was a difference of opinion among them in this matter. They pointed out that the plantation workers were divided into various trade unions, with some having allegiance to the left parties and the others to the Congress parties. The Congress trade unions were against the distribution of the plantations, and since the Congress coalition was in power, there was no chance of distributing the plantations to *adivasis*. Therefore, their position was that it would not make any difference whether the left trade unions were for or against the distribution of these plantations. In their opinion, if the Congress government was genuinely interested in distributing land to the *adivasis*, it was possible to find other lands.

The Irulam Village office informed the government of the available lands and said that an additional 398 acres had to be found elsewhere to meet the requirement. Our field enquiries revealed that there was sufficient land available in the vicinity of the *adivasi* settlements or reasonably close by – lands under the illegal occupation of private/corporate plantations. During the British period, when land was leased out for plantations, a buffer zone of forest area around the plantation site was included, although not officially in the plantation records. The agreement was that when the lease period expired, the buffer zone would be handed back to the government. However, the lands remained in the possession and enjoyment of the private plantations. Given the number and extent of these plantations, such lands would be substantial and, if reclaimed by the government, could be distributed to the *adivasis*. There is a general opinion in the field among the *adivasis*, the peasant settlers, activists, elected peoples' representatives and government officials that this is a good opportunity for the government to expropriate such lands under illegal possession and at the same time solve the *adivasi* land issue. The political will of the state is most crucial for this purpose. There are two private coffee plantations in the village which together account for about 1,000 acres on official records. The local people, however, told us that these plantations, especially one large plantation, may have at least as much area as that of the plantation under illegal possession and that area alone would be sufficient to solve the *adivasi* landlessness in the village.

In spite of the promises, the government discontinued the distribution of land. The *adivasis* reminded the government of the 2001 agreement several times and issued press releases announcing their willingness to wait until the period agreed upon by the chief minister expired, that is, until 31 December 2002. After much deliberation among the *adivasis*, it was decided that the AGMS would assume responsibility for further struggles.[18] On 25 August 2002, thousands of *adivasis* assembled in Mananthavady in Wayanad district to deliberate on the future course of action if the government did not deliver on its promises by December 31 of that year. A 'tribal court' consisting of twenty women and forty men representing the different *adivasi* communities was constituted. The AGMS and the tribal court were reworkings of the erstwhile traditional socio-political institutions of the *adivasis*. In the past, each *adivasi* community had its own such institutions, but the reworked institutions transcend community barriers. One is thus able to discern a further re-articulation of their positioning, which indeed is a political project. The tribal court publicly declared that if the government did not abide by the 2001 agreement, the *adivasis* would go ahead and claim their rights by occupying government lands. Unfortunately, no action was forthcoming from the government side. On 4 January 2003, the two sides entered into a historic struggle that came to be known as the 'Muthanga struggle', named after the site in which the protest was staged. The forty-four-day-long struggle was brutally suppressed by the Congress government using police force, which resulted in the death of an *adivasi* and a policeman. Hundreds of *adivasi* men, women and children were seriously wounded, and the leaders were imprisoned and tortured by the police. This event propelled the leadership of the left parties (in the opposition) to declare open support for the *adivasi* struggle. A CPI(M) member of the legislative assembly engaged in a hunger strike to protest the brutal government action against the *adivasis*.

Pre-living imagined futures: The Muthanga struggle

The physical site of the struggle – the *samara bhoomi* (struggle-land) as they call it – was selected with great care. They purposefully avoided the natural forest areas and selected a degraded section of a eucalyptus plantation in Muthanga owned by the State Forest Department. About 1,100 *adivasi* families of various communities – Kurumar, Kurichiyar, Paniyar, Kattunaicker, Adiyar and Uralis – moved into the site on 4 and 5 January 2003.[19] They had given advance notice to the government that they would be occupying these lands. The selection of the degraded eucalyptus plantation as *samara bhoomi* demonstrated the *adivasis*' ecological concerns and their attempt to avoid direct confrontation with the State Forest Department, which would have arisen had they occupied a natural forest. This, together with the action of giving advance notice to the government, showed that the *adivasis* configured their struggle within what Roseberry (1996) calls the existing fields of force (See also Li, 2001). The *adivasi* actions in Muthanga showed that they acknowledged the legitimacy of the state even in the act and process of challenging it. The land at the *samara bhoomi* was divided into plots of about three hectares each and allotted to individual families. In each plot a house was constructed with bamboo and grasses. The families lived in these houses and cultivated cassava, taro, yams, bananas, and vegetables like amaranthus, bitter gourd and aubergine.[20] Wells were dug to supply drinking water. The plots of the various *adivasi* communities were intermixed so as to allow for closer contact between them, helping to break down the historical hierarchical social practices, promote egalitarian relations and reinforce *adivasi* solidarity. The households were divided into twenty-four *oorukkoottangal* (village collectives), and members were elected from each *oorukkoottam* to form an *oorusabha* (village assembly). About 50% of the members were women. The *oorusabha* was responsible for supervising the day-to-day activities of the community, including the purchase of foodstuffs using money pooled from the households, and solving any problems that might arise. A young Paniyan remembers:

> It was a life we had never experienced before. The various communities were living in harmony and co-operating in various activities. We were busy preparing the field and cultivating crops during the day. At night we kept vigilance to protect the crops from wild animals. Children were reading and studying. We taught our language to the children, told them stories. We sat in groups and remembered our histories. We discussed and debated over future strategies. We had given up alcohol. There was no wife-beating either. We learned to treat women with respect. We were advised and helped by the volunteers. It was a life we had dreamed for our future. But the government shattered it with gunshots.

A middle-aged Kattunaicker woman told us:

> The 44 days in *samara bhoomi* were like a dream. My husband did not drink alcohol. We had no fights at home. My children were happy and read their schoolbooks. We hoped that the government would let us stay there.

The hopes and dreams of the *adivasis* are reflected in these statements. Evidently, *adivasi* lives were changing through the experience at Muthanga. 'Each one reminded the other, this is our self-rule area. So we must set an example with our exemplary behaviour', said a Kuruman elder.

As mentioned earlier, the government crushed the struggle after forty-four days. Although the *adivasis* were forced out of Muthanga, the event marked a historic moment in the *adivasi* life of Kerala. They were able to re-engage the state, the media, the intellectuals and the larger Kerala society in ways that had not been possible before.[21] The image of the *adivasis* had been redefined through this struggle. As Kunhaman (2003: 66) succinctly states: 'The success of that struggle was the struggle itself'. The image of the 'helpless', 'illiterate' and 'uncivilised' *adivasi* has been replaced by the image of an *adivasi* who has been engaging in a militant struggle for their rights.

The Muthanga struggle, therefore, cannot be reduced to a mere struggle for land; it came to symbolise a people's aspiration for a different future. The decision to occupy their ancestral lands in Muthanga had symbolic meanings as well as material implications. In the first place, it was an overt assertion of *adivasi* agency mediated through the reconstituted socio-political institutions, the AGMS and the tribal court. At the same time, it was a symbolic and physical enactment of their autonomy as a people, an expression of their attachment to place and a proclamation of their inalienable rights to ancestral lands. It is important to understand that they were not reproducing the pre-existing *adivasi* institutions, but reconstituting them, after sifting through and retaining what they perceived as the positive features and discarding the regressive ones, and at the same time embracing a new approach that transcended the inter-community hierarchies and incorporated gender concerns. They did not reject the idea of development either, as some 'green orientalists' would like them to.[22] Indeed, visions of modernity were imagined into the struggle. The adoption of modern systems of property rights in land, that is, individual holdings; the demand for individual titles to land; the practice of modern agriculture in the *samara bhoomi* and the importance given to the education of children and youth all encompass visions of a life that would benefit from modernity.[23] Evidently, they do not want to live in a frozen past, but rather in a dynamic future. A new philosophy of life can thus be read into the Muthanga struggle: it was a reflection of their re-imagined future lives and identities orchestrated around the question of land rights. Through the Muthanga struggle, it would seem they were pre-living a new 'social imaginary'. The 'imaginary' accounts for the specific orientation of social institutions, the constitution of motives and needs and the existence of symbolism and tradition (Thompson, 1984, following Castoriadis, 1975).

> This element, which endows the functionality of each institutional system with its specific orientation, which overdetermines the choice and connections of symbolic networks, which creates for each historical period its singular way of living, seeing and making its own existence, its world and its relations to it ... is nothing other than the *imaginary* of the society or period concerned.
> (Castoriadis, 1975: 203 quoted in Thompson, 1984: 23)

The struggle of the *adivasis* continues. Following the Muthanga struggle, the *adivasis* have occupied state lands in various regions of Wayanad. In Irulam Village there are several new *samara bhoomis* located in vested forestland and in the Cheeyambam and Mariyanad coffee plantations under the control of the Kerala

Forest Development Corporation. The government has not taken any action to stop them. It would seem that the government was either trying to regain its moral image following the controversial suppression of the *adivasi* community at Muthanga, or it was paralysed into inaction. The *adivasi* families have divided the *samara bhoomi* into several plots of between one and two hectares each, and each family has built a hut and is living there.[24] In Cheeyambam plantation there were 203 such families who occupied the plantation on 28 March 2003, soon after the Muthanga struggle. They were doing all the agronomic operations in the coffee plantation, such as weeding and pruning. They were not paid any wages by the plantation management. They were also cultivating root and tuber crops, vegetables and other food crops intermixed with the coffee plants in an effort to sustain themselves. Their demand was that the plantation be distributed among them. They were determined to continue the struggle until they received land. 'Come so far, there is no turning back. We have only one way – forward', said a young Paniya woman.

Conclusion

In this chapter we looked into the land struggles of *adivasis* in the changing political contexts in Wayanad and Kerala in the last three decades. The identities came to be reconstituted and articulated as *adivasis* encompassing the different communities, while at the same time projecting their specific identities as Kurumar, Paniyar, Kattunaicker and so on. These articulations, however, were closely interlinked with their historical-material conditions of existence. The chapter highlights the continuing resistance of the indigenous people to pauperisation and proletarianisation and their demand for land as the solution. The *adivasis*' demand for redistribution of state plantation land posed an obstacle to forging alliances with non-*adivasi* sections of plantation workers' unions. Although this was an instance of conflict of interest between the two subordinated groups, there have been other instances of solidarity and collective action across the *adivasi*/non-*adivasi* divide. In the Muthanga struggle, the *adivasis* were projecting an image of their future based on individual land ownership, along with access to opportunities for human development and upward social mobility. Indeed, the struggle was not to reinvent a past, but to secure the material basis and human freedoms for a better future. The legislative and policy interventions of the state and the sustained struggles and aspirations of the *adivasis* continuously impact the dynamics of the indigeneity–class intersection.

Notes

1 Bruno Latour's conceptualisation of politics as a specific discursive regime articulating and performing the transformation of a plurality of voices into one through a work of representation is relevant in this context (Latour, 2003).
2 In the struggles for transformation, Marx makes a distinction between the material realm – that is, the conditions of production – and the ideological realm in which humans become conscious of the inherent conflicts (Marx, 1986).

3 For those who were included in the 1975 Act – mostly Kurumar and Kurichiyar.
4 In the case of the landless communities – mostly Paniyar, Kattunaicker, Adiyar and Uralis – overlooked by the 1975 Act but included in the 1999 Act.
5 Discussions with *adivasi* activists and non-governmental organisations (NGOs).
6 This was the collective stand of the *adivasi* movement. Individual *Kurumar* in discussions told us that they were willing to take alternative lands if they were somewhere near their locality.
7 These were the main regions in Kerala from where large-scale out-migration to Wayanad occurred.
8 This was an uprising organised by the radical left party CPI (ML) – the Communist Party of India (Marxist Leninist) – in the 1960s. Wayanad was a hotbed of naxalite activities in the 1960s, and the *adivasis* played a major role in the uprising against the landlords. The movement's first uprising was in a place called Naxalbari in northeast India and hence the name 'naxalite'.
9 Discussion with village officer in Irulam.
10 Sit-in strikes in front of the secretariat.
11 The struggle was led by C. K. Janu, an *adivasi* woman, and M. Geethanandan, a *dalith* man. *Daliths* are the oppressed castes.
12 See also Ravi Raman (2002).
13 See Bijoy and Ravi Raman (2003) for details of the agreement.
14 Some activists and NGOs told me that the personal commitment of the chief minister was the major factor behind the 2001 agreement. Although a minor section of the bureaucracy supported the agreement, the rest of the government machinery was largely hostile to it.
15 Records of the village office in Irulam.
16 Discussion with village officer.
17 These plantations were initially established to provide employment to *adivasis* (see Kjosavik and Shanmugaratnam, 2004).
18 Discussion with *adivasi* activists.
19 Discussions with an *adivasi* activist.
20 Discussions with *adivasis* who participated in the Muthanga struggle.
21 See Raj (2003) for a compilation of responses of the media, activists and intellectuals.
22 Green orientalists, whether Western or local, view traditional peoples 'as a modernity-free cultural reserve to be fenced off' (Lohmann, 1993: 203). See Said (1978) for the idea of orientalism. Some environmentalists of the mainstream persuasion in Kerala denounced the Muthanga struggle on the grounds that the *samara bhoomi* was part of a wildlife sanctuary, although the site selected by the *adivasis* was in fact a eucalyptus plantation growing cheap wood for the corporate sector.
23 See Veettil, Kjosavik and Ashok (2013) for a study of *adivasi* households' willingness to pay for obtaining individual titles to land.
24 Discussions with the *adivasis* who had occupied the Cheeyambam *samara bhoomi* during field visit in December 2003.

References

Agnew, J. A., 1989, *The Power of Place: Bringing Together Geographical and Sociological Imaginations*. Boston: Unwin Hyman.
Bates, C., 1995, '"Lost Innocents and the Loss of Innocence": Interpreting Adivasi Movements in South Asia,' in Barnes, R. H., Gray, A., and Kingsbury, B. (eds.), *Indigenous Peoples of Asia*. Michigan: The Association for Asian Studies, University of Michigan: 103–119.
Bijoy, C.R., and Ravi Raman, K., 2003, 'Muthanga: The Real Story – Adivasi Movement to Recover Land', *Economic and Political Weekly*, 38 (May 9). www.epw.org.in/showArticles.php?root=2003&leaf=05&filename=5828&filetype=html (accessed 3/3/04).

Castoriadis, C., 1975, *L'Institution imaginaire de la société*. Paris: Seuil.
Daniels, S., 1985, 'Arguments for a Humanistic Geography', in Johnston, R. (ed.), *The Future of Geography*. London: Methuen: 143–158.
Feierman, S., 1990, *Peasant Intellectuals: Anthropology and History in Tanzania*. Madison: University of Wisconsin Press.
Gupta, A. and Ferguson, J., 1992, 'Beyond "Culture": Space, Identity, and the Politics of Difference', *Cultural Anthropology*, 7(1): 6–23.
Hall, S., 1990, 'Cultural Identity and Diaspora,' in Rutherford, J. (ed.), *Identity: Community, Culture, Difference*. London: Lawrence and Wishart: 222–237.
Hall, S. 1996, 'On Postmodernism and Articulation: An Interview with Stuart Hall', edited by Lawrence Grossberg, in Morley, D. and Chen, K-H. (eds.), *Stuart Hall: Critical Dialogues in Cultural Studies*. London: Routledge: 131–150.
Jacobs, J., 1994, *Edge of Empire: Postcolonialism and the City*. London: Routledge.
Kjosavik, D. J. and Shanmugaratnam, N., 2004, 'Integration or Exclusion? Locating Indigenous Peoples in the Development Process of Kerala, South India', *Forum for Development Studies*, 31(2): 232–273.
Kunhaman, M., 2003, Pranthavalkaranavum swathwapunarnirvachanangalum, in Raj, D. (ed.), *Thandedangal: Kerala Samoohapadam Muthanga Samarathinushesham*, (Malayalam). Kottayam: D C Books: 57–67.
Laclau, E., 1977, 'Fascism and Ideology', in Laclau, E. 1977, *Politics and Ideology in Marxist Theory: Capitalism – Fascism – Populism*. London: NLB: 81–142.
Latour, B., 2003, 'What If We Talked Politics a Little?', *Contemporary Political Theory*, 2(2): 143–164.
Li, T. M., 2000, 'Articulating Indigenous Identity in Indonesia: Resource Politics and the Tribal Slot', *Comparative Studies in Society and History*, 42: 149–179.
Li, T. M., 2001, 'Masyarakat Adat, Difference, and the Limits of Recognition in Indonesia's Forest Zone', *Modern Asian Studies*, 35(3): 645–676.
Lohmann, L., 1993, 'Green Orientalism', *The Ecologist*, 23(6): 202–204.
Marx, K., 1853, 'The British Rule in India'. New York Daily Tribune, 10 June 1853. www.marxists.org/archive/marx/works/1853/06/25.htm (accessed 3/3/04).
Marx, K., 1986, 'Preface to the Critique of Political Economy' in Elster, J. (ed.), *Karl Marx: A Reader*. Cambridge: Cambridge University Press: 187–188.
Massey, D., 1995, 'Thinking Radical Democracy Spatially: Environment and Planning', *Society and Space*, 13(3): 283–288.
Mitchell, T., 1991, 'The Limits of the State: Beyond Statist Approaches and Their Critics', *American Political Science Review*, 85(1): 77–96.
Moore, D. S., 1998, 'Subaltern Struggles and the Politics of Place: Remapping Resistance in Zimbabwe's Eastern Highlands', *Cultural Anthropology*, 13(3): 344–381.
Pred, A., 1986, *Place, Practice and Structure*. Cambridge: Polity Press.
Radhakrishnan, R., 1996, *Diasporic Mediations*. Minneapolis: University of Minnesota Press.
Raj, D., ed., 2003, *Thandedangal: Kerala Samoohapadam Muthanga Samarathinushesham*, (Malayalam). Kottayam: D C Books.
Ravi Raman, K., 2002, 'Breaking New Ground: Adivasi Land Struggle in Kerala', *Economic and Political Weekly*, 37(March 9): 916–918.
Roseberry, W., 1996, 'Hegemony, Power, and Language of Contention', in Wilmsen, E. N. and McAllister, P. (eds.), *The Politics of Difference: Ethnic Premises in a World of Power*. Chicago: University of Chicago Press: 71–84.
Said, E. W, 1978, *Orientalism*. London: Routledge & Kegan Paul.

Sivanandan, P, 2003, 'Master Plan Committee Sarkar Attimarichu', in Raj, D. (ed.), *Thandedangal: Kerala Samoohapadam Muthanga Samarathinushesham*, (Malayalam). Kottayam: D C Books: 68–70.

Sivanandan, P. and Madhava Menon, T., 2003, 'Nivedanam', in Raj, D. (ed.), *Thandedangal: Kerala Samoohapadam Muthanga Samarathinushesham*, (Malayalam). Kottayam: D C Books: 68–70.

Thompson, J. B, 1984, *Studies in the Theory of Ideology*. Cambridge: Polity Press.

Thrift, N., 1989, 'Introduction', in Peet, R. and Thrift, N. (eds.), *New Models in Geography*, Vol. 2. London: Unwin Hyman: xiii–xv.

Veettil, P. C., Kjosavik, D. J. and Ashok, A., 2013, 'Valuing the "Bundle of Land Rights": On Formalising Indigenous People's (Adivasis) Land Rights in Kerala, India', *Land Use Policy*, 30: 408–416.

Watts, M., 1989, 'The Agrarian Question in Africa: Debating the Crisis', *Progress in Human Geography*, 13(1): 1–41.

Watts, M., 1991, 'Mapping Meaning, Denoting Difference, Imagining Identity: Dialectical Images and Postmodern Geographies', *Geografiska Annaler*, 73 B(1): 7–16.

Watts, M., 1992, 'Space for Everything (A Commentary)', *Cultural Anthropology*, 7(1): 115–129.

8 Epilogue
The struggle continues: Indigeneity and social change

In this final chapter we provide an update of the recent developments concerning *adivasi* land issues in Wayanad and reflect on the broader problem of indigeneity–class intersection. We revisit the *adivasis*' demand for land in the context of the Forest Rights Act of 2006 (FRA) of the government of India and its implementation, and comment on the recent land struggles. We discuss the National Rural Employment Guarantee Act (NREGA) and the Kerala model in the context of neoliberalisation and their implications for indigeneity and its transition.

The Forest Rights Act of 2006 and the *adivasis*' struggle for land

Contextualising the Forest Rights Act of 2006

The ancestral lands of the *adivasis* in India were appropriated by various means, including a series of Acts, for commercial, conservation and other purposes since the early part of the nineteenth century. In this book, we have documented and analysed the history of dispossession and displacement of the *adivasi* communities of Wayanad, Kerala. We have also discussed the historically diverse nature of *adivasi* land claims in different regions of the country. The FRA of 2006 – officially known as the Scheduled Tribes and Other Traditional Forest Dwellers (Recognition of Forest Rights) Act – arrived six decades after India's independence. Although the Act is generally viewed as a response to the historical demands of the *adivasis* for rights to their ancestral land and territories, it is important to note that it came almost fifteen years after the government of India began implementing neoliberal policies, which remain hegemonic to this day. A defining feature of this policy context is the introduction of property reforms that make land and related resources more readily available to domestic and international capital. On the other hand, there were the ongoing protracted struggles of the *adivasi*s to regain their rights to the lands expropriated in the past and for the protection of their customary rights to forests, which the Central government could not ignore. Moreover, these communities have gained significance as 'vote banks' in the competitive multi-party parliamentary politics in post-independence India. However, the conservation lobby, which had been campaigning for the creation of protected areas, was not in favour of restoration of forest rights to *adivasis*. It has also been critical of tribal development programmes, as it believed that these were harmful to the environment. The FRA would seem to be a legal intervention that sought to accommodate competing demands on the country's forestlands and to manage the conflicting interests behind these demands. It deals specifically with the rights of the Scheduled Tribes and other traditional forest dwellers.

At first glance, the FRA appears to be a document that addresses the economic, social and political rights of the *adivasis* and ensures them a fair degree of social justice. For example, the preamble of The Scheduled Tribes and Other Traditional Forest Dwellers (Recognition of Forest Rights) Bill passed by Lok Sabha on 15 December 2006 (No. 158-C of 2005) states:

> AND WHEREAS the forest rights on ancestral lands and their habitat were not adequately recognized in the consolidation of State forests during the colonial period as well as in independent India resulting in historical injustice to the forest dwelling Scheduled Tribes and other traditional forest dwellers who are integral to the very survival and sustainability of the forest ecosystems.

Chapter II of the FRA deals with forest rights such as the following, which are relevant for the present study:

> 3. (1) For the purpose of this Act, the following rights, which secure individual or community tenure or both, shall be the forest rights of forest dwelling Scheduled Tribes and other traditional forest dwellers on all forest lands, namely:
> *(a)* right to hold and live in the forest land under the individual or common occupation for habitation or self-cultivation for livelihood by a member or members of a forest dwelling Scheduled Tribe or other traditional forest dwellers;
> *(f)* rights in or over disputed lands under any nomenclature in any State where claims are disputed;
> *(g)* rights for conversion of *Pattas* or leases or grants issued by any local authority or any State Government on forest lands to titles.

Chapter III deals with 'Recognition, Restoration and Vesting of Forest Rights and Related Matters'. One of its provisions states:

> 4. (1) Notwithstanding anything contained in any other law for the time being in force, and subject to the provisions of this Act, the Central Government hereby recognises and vests forest rights in:
> *(a)* 'the forest dwelling Scheduled Tribes in States or areas in States where they are declared as Scheduled Tribes in respect of all forest rights mentioned in section 3.

Indeed the general provisions of the FRA, such as the ones quoted earlier, sound fair and promising. The devil, however, is in the detail when it comes to restoration and the limits on entitlement claims in terms of the extent of land and cut-off date. Moreover, so far, the implementation of the FRA has been ineffective to the detriment of the *adivasis* due to legal and bureaucratic constraints, as shown by empirical studies covering different states.[1] The FRA is completely silent on the historical problem of large-scale displacements and the consequent landlessness and livelihood losses suffered by large sections of *adivasis.* However, it recognises the rights of *adivasis* who were occupying forestland before the cut-off date of December 2005. Chapter III, section 4 (3) of the Act states:

> The recognition and vesting of forest rights under this Act to the forest dwelling Scheduled Tribes and other traditional forest dwellers in relation to any State or Union territory in respect of forest land and their habitat shall be subject to the condition that such Scheduled Tribes or tribal communities or other traditional forest dwellers had occupied forest land before the 13th day of December, 2005.

The right granted to a claimant under the Act is heritable but not alienable or transferable. Further, the Act sets an upper limit of four hectares on the extent of actually occupied land claimed by an individual, family or community (Chapter III, Section 4(6)). The enforcement of this provision would redefine boundaries and make surplus forestlands available to the state. Thus the Act can be seen as an intervention with a dual purpose: to confer a degree of forestland entitlement to tribal communities and other traditional forest dwellers, while at the same time freeing a major part of the forests concerned from any future claims from the same groups. In January 2008, the Ministry of Tribal Affairs issued a set of rules to guide the implementation of the FRA at state and sub-state levels.[2] As noted earlier, there have been serious criticisms about the implementation of the Act. According to a countrywide survey published in 2012, a majority of the claims (54%) were rejected on 'frivolous' grounds and the land titles issued were vaguely worded and were often without a clear demarcation of boundaries. Furthermore, the study noted that the high rate of rejection of the claims amounted to a 'perpetuation of the historical injustices' on the intended beneficiaries (Asian Indigenous and Tribal Peoples Network, 2012: 4). Strongly voicing similar concerns in its 'Guide to the Forest Rights Act', the 'Campaign for Survival and Dignity' (undated), states that 'the Act that was finally passed was not the Act that had been fought for. The government is now trying further to damage it by including changes in the Rules to the Act that will undermine it more'.[3] Indeed, the high rate of rejection means denial of land rights to large numbers of genuine claimants. It should be noted that there are wide variations in the applicability of the various provisions of the FRA across the states. We briefly examine the workings of the Act in Kerala.

The FRA in Kerala – The case of Wayanad

The FRA entered the scene when the government of Kerala was grappling with a protracted stalemate in the implementation of its own laws regarding *adivasi* land rights due to organised resistance from non-*adivasi* workers employed in the plantations and from settler farmers, as explained in Chapters 6 and 7. Initially, the FRA did raise hopes among *adivasi* activists and within the Left government that it would help solve the *adivasi* land issue once and for all. In fact, the Left played a major role in lobbying for an extended cut-off date for claims of forest rights. In their usual campaign mode, the Left began to mobilise the huge bureaucratic machinery and to set up the decentralised institutions as stipulated in the rules for implementing the FRA.

However, the FRA's provision that only those *adivasis* who had already occupied forest land before 13 December 2005 were eligible for rights in that land shut the door on those who were displaced from their forests and permanently deprived of the possibility to occupy forestland before the cut-off date. We are referring to those pauperised *adivasis* of Wayanad who remain landless and without opportunities for enhancement of livelihood security and human development. The FRA has failed to deliver justice to a large section of the historically dispossessed *adivasis* of Wayanad. As noted in Chapter 4, access to land is a precondition for the socio-economic stability and development of these *adivasis* who today are among the more seriously affected victims of the exclusionary forces of neoliberalism.

The applicability of the FRA to the land claims of the *adivasis* of Wayanad needs to be seen with reference to three categories of occupied land:

1) The state-owned forest plantations of coffee, pepper and cardamom initially set up to provide employment for *adivasis*. In 2003, the *adivasi* workers stepped up their struggle and took over the plantations, distributing the land among themselves, and have been managing it since.
2) The vested forestlands, that is, private forests vested with the state in 1970. These are mainly degraded teak and eucalyptus plantations. As a part of their struggle, *adivasis* have occupied portions of these lands and created settlements, with each household occupying about half to one acre of land, and have started subsistence cultivation.
3) The reserve forestlands, the fringes of which are occupied by *adivasi* communities, especially *Kattunaicker*. During the formation of reserve forests and protected areas, the Forest Department resettled the *adivasi* communities in their current dwelling sites. Each household has a dwelling site, and they have been cultivating about half an acre to three acres of land for the last several decades.

We had interviews with those belonging to these three categories, in addition to discussions and interviews with activists and local political leaders.

The occupied plantations – The case of Cheeyambam coffee plantation

The first people to receive the record of rights (possession certificate) were the *adivasi* households that occupied plantations in which they were former employees.

Four such plantations in Wayanad have been distributed to the *adivasis*. The account that follows is about the Cheeyambam coffee plantation.

Sixty-two workers were employed in the plantation, of whom the majority were *adivasis*. In 2003, inspired by the Muthanga struggle (see Kjosavik, 2010), they organised themselves and formed a '*samarasamithi*', a struggle committee. Under the leadership of the *samarasamithi*, the workers agreed on a fair way of distributing the land – two acres for the permanent employees and one acre for the temporary employees. They divided the plantation into plots as agreed, constructed small houses and started living there. Each household managed its coffee plot, harvested the produce and sold it for an income. In the first year, the plantation management tried to stop them, but did not succeed. They continued living there, tending the coffee while cultivating some food crops as well. In 2008, during the time of the Left government, they applied for titles to the land under the FRA and received records of rights for the plots of land they were occupying.

This was a positive outcome indeed, as the *adivasis* got security of tenure to the entire land they had occupied. The household incomes have increased, and this gives them increased livelihood security. These households have actually achieved a qualitative shift from being landless permanent and temporary workers to market-oriented smallholders, that is, petty commodity producers. 'Earlier', said an *adivasi* activist, 'we were always living in debt. Now the situation has changed. We get good income from coffee'. Women and elders from many of these households were able to find employment in projects under the NREGA (discussed later). This was an additional source of income. Moreover, several households have also benefitted from the asset-building subsidy granted by the NREGA programme. The children of Cheeyambam are able to complete their secondary and higher secondary education. Some of the households have invested their savings in non-land-based assets such as auto rickshaws, which are a source of additional income. The chances of social mobility for the younger generation seem to have increased for these households.

With the record of rights, these households are entitled to a house number, electricity connection and inclusion in NREGA. The record of rights is heritable but not transferable, and the recipients are not permitted to cut trees, not even the branches of the silver oak shade tree in the coffee plantation. This is clearly against the spirit of the FRA, which provides for cutting up to 75 trees per hectare for constructing houses and related purposes. Moreover, banks and other lending institutions do not accept the record of rights as collateral.

Occupied vested forests

The Left government decided to distribute one acre of land per household to the households occupying the vested forests. However, due to a court case filed by environmentalists, the government was ordered to refrain from this and to distribute only the land actually occupied by the *adivasis*, which in many cases varied from ten cents to fifty cents (one acre is equal to 100 cents). Those who occupied the vested forestlands before December 2005 received records of rights on the same terms and conditions as in the case of the Cheeyambam plantation. However, the majority of the occupations in vested forestlands took place after 2005. Currently, there are about nineteen such *samarabhoomi* ('struggle-land') movements in Wayanad, which are not eligible to receive records of rights under the FRA of 2006.

However, the *adivasis* interviewed by us said that they were hopeful that the government would at some point grant them rights. For example, in the Irulam *samarabhoomi* there are about 3,000 households. Beena, a twenty-eight-year-old, whom we interviewed in December 2013, said that her family (husband and four children) came to live in the *samarabhoomi* two years ago from a crammed colony with fifteen landless households. She said,

> Here also we are suffering. Our old settlement was close to the forest and we were able to collect firewood from the forests for selling. In spite of all the problems we are living in the *samarabhoomi* for the sake of land, especially for our children. We have suffered anyway, but this land struggle is for the sake of our children. Our demand is to get the land we are occupying or an acre of land elsewhere in Wayanad. Only then will we stop our struggle.

Settlements in reserve forestland

These are households settled on the fringes of the forests. They have been living there for decades, settled and resettled by the Forest Department, but without any rights so far. Interviews with them showed that they did not have much awareness about the FRA. As in the case of the vested forests, the Left government's decision to grant them an acre of land surrounding their dwellings was over-ruled by a court order. By this time, the Left had lost power to the Congress coalition in the state. It is relevant to note that these communities were not fully mobilised in the larger *adivasi* struggle for land rights. These *adivasis*, mainly the forest-dependent *Kattunaicker*, were given records of rights merely to their miniscule dwelling sites of three to five cents, even though they were cultivating areas ranging from fifty cents to two acres. Thus, the result was that they were denied rights to most of the land they had occupied.

Our study shows that the nature of rights granted to the *adivasis* is far from the expectations raised by the FRA in 2006. In Kerala, many *adivasis* remain landless and outside the ambit of the FRA. Trapped in a state of deprivation due to lack of human development, employable skills and opportunities for social mobility, this group of *adivasis* sees land as a basic need to build a more stable livelihood. The FRA has not been able to meet that need.

Land, rural labour and the contradictions of neoliberalisation

As demonstrated in this book, the prospects of the *adivasis'* struggle for land and social advancement have varied with the changes of government in Kerala. The *adivasis* and other marginalised groups find themselves in a development triangle of decentralisation, neoliberalism and the Kerala model, as discussed in Chapter 5. The decentralised planning introduced in 1996 by the leftist government sought to contain the 'new social exclusion' through state intervention to make the development process more inclusive of marginalised groups, including the indigenous people. The government launched a People's Planning Campaign (PPC) aimed at the local level to institutionalise a participatory form of decentralisation. The benefits to rural communities included representation in the local bodies, participation in planning, local infrastructure development, subsidies for house construction, provision of drinking water and temporary employment generation. The *Adivasis* of Wayanad were among the beneficiaries. However, the PPC and the decentralised planning did not address the *adivasis*' demand for land. The Congress coalition that came to power in 2001 changed its predecessor's decentralisation programme by substantially reducing the role of the state and the space for people's mobilisation and participation in line with the neoliberal approach. The Left coalition that returned to power in 2006 sought to restore the PPC-based approach to decentralisation, but the policy changed again when the Congress Party regained power in 2011. In the changing national context, neoliberal forces had become more assertive even in a state such as Kerala.

The neoliberal reforms have made significant inroads into the Kerala model and changed its social democratic and transparent character. Drastic cutbacks in public expenditures on education and health and the growing commercialisation of these sectors have severely undermined the egalitarian premises of the model. Rising inequality, persistent rural and urban poverty and the growth of a mafia-type parallel economy[4] represent the other side of the economic growth story of post-reform Kerala (Oommen, 2014, 2010). *Adivasis* (Scheduled Tribes) and Scheduled Castes have the highest head count ratio (HCR) of poverty, at 38.7 and 38.0, respectively (Aravindan, 2006, cited in Oommen, 2014: 23).[5]

The consequences of neoliberalisation, such as rising inequalities and persistent poverty, have created new challenges for the legitimacy of the Indian state and for political parties. Invariably, these challenges necessitate public interventions that may be inconsistent with the economic fundamentals of neoliberalism. Poverty is a highly politicised issue in India. Political parties and alliances seeking governmental power woo the millions of poor voters with promises of poverty reduction programmes. No government could afford to completely ignore the poor because of the sheer magnitude of the latter's numbers as voters. Every Indian government since independence has had its own programmes claiming to attack poverty. In the 1971 national elections, the Congress Party led by Indira Gandhi won an impressive victory with the slogan '*garibi hatao*' (abolish poverty). Nevertheless, poverty remains a major problem in India. In 2005, the Congress-Left alliance (United Progressive Alliance) government at the centre introduced the NREGA as a poverty reduction measure. The Act was renamed the Mahatma Gandhi National Rural Employment Act (MNREGA) in 2009. It guarantees a minimum of 100 days of wage employment per year for each rural household.[6] Employment is generated through public works, as well as subsidised asset building on land or homesteads owned by households belonging to vulnerable sections, including Scheduled Castes, Scheduled Tribes, nomadic tribes, beneficiaries under the FRA, women-headed households and others below the poverty line.[7] The programme covers the labour and material costs for asset building on private lands.

The NREGA represented a significant state intervention under the Congress-led government in post-reform India, although the neoliberal lobby has been opposing it.[8] The Act addresses livelihood issues of large sections of historically marginalised people, who are also the victims of the exclusionary forces of neoliberalisation. It promises to strengthen the productive asset base of vulnerable households and to offer wage employment to the landless and the unskilled who demand work. Its implementation may alter the workings of rural labour markets, as the Act not only guarantees employment to the rural poor, but also prescribes a minimum wage. By legalising the right to work and the right to minimum wages, the NREGA has made these rights justiciable (Dreze and Sen, 2013). These developments are not consistent with the premises of the neoliberal economic policy. However, they reveal the contradictions of neoliberalisation of the state and how conflicting interests are managed to enable capitalist development in a multi-party parliamentary democracy. Before reflecting on the possible implications of the NREGA for our theorisation on the indigeneity–class intersection and its dynamics, we comment on the actual performance of the NREGA programme.

The NREGA's overall impact has been far below the targets in the first five years (July 2006–November 2010) of its implementation. According to a national study of the performance of the NREGA programme during this period, the average annual days of employment provided per participating household was 47.70 (i.e., less than half of the guaranteed minimum), while the average earnings from such employment as a percentage of the rural poverty line was 10.15 (Kannan and Jain, 2013).

In Kerala, the Left government welcomed the NREGA programme and utilised the decentralised local institutions for its implementation. The programme continues to be implemented through the same institutions under the Congress-led government. The beneficiaries were mostly women, the elderly and disabled men who were unskilled and unemployed and belonging to *adivasi* and other marginalised groups, who remained outside or on the fringes of the labour market. Initially, the programme was implemented in the two districts of Palakkad and Wayanad in 2006–2007 (financial year). The number of households provided with employment and the average number of work days per household per year in these districts were 99,107 and 20.66, respectively in 2006–2007. By 2012–2013, the programme had reached all fourteen districts of the state and 1,525,486 households were provided with employment at an average of 54.82 days per household.[9]

The minimum wage offered by the programme was far below the prevailing market wages for men and women, although the gender gap in wages is considerable in the state. Kerala's market wage rates, which keep rising over time, are the highest among Indian states. This is a pull factor for skilled and unskilled workers from other states. However, within Kerala, sections of *adivasis* have remained outside of the state's bourgeoning labour market due to reasons discussed in Chapter 4.

In Wayanad, the Paniyar, who were historically agrestic slaves and bonded labourers, and the Kattunaicker, who were forest dwellers, are among the most excluded from the labour market.

Given their exclusion from the labour market, it was not surprising that the *adivasis* we interviewed in Wayanad in 2012 and 2013 were positive about the NREGA programme as a source of employment.[10] In 2012–2013, the *adivasis*, who accounted for 17% of the district's population, were able to obtain 20% of the total workdays, which increased to 25.64% in 2013–2014.[11] The average number of workdays per *adivasi* household in 2012–2013 in Wayanad district was 55.46, which increased to 59.4 person-days in 2013–2014. In Poothady *Panchayat*, the *adivasis* who constitute 15.03% of the population,[12] had 21.12% of the total workdays in 2012–2013, which increased to 22.61% in 2013–2014. The *adivasi* households in the *Panchayat*, on average, worked for 58.09 days per household in 2012–2013, which increased substantially to 70.93 days in 2013–2014.[13] According to the Noolpuzha *Panchayat* Officer in Wayanad, interviewed in July 2013, 60% of NREGA project workers in her *panchayat* were *adivasis*.[14] These projects offered manual work at a minimum wage to unskilled persons, including women, the elderly and the disabled, who were mostly unemployed.

The data presented here show that the *adivasis* were among the major participants of the NREGA programme in Wayanad. Most of them would have been unemployed in the absence of the programme. However, there is uncertainty about the future of the NREGA with the change of government at the Centre in May 2014. The present government of the Bharatiya Janata Party (BJP) wanted to restructure and limit the programme's coverage to the 'most backward' 200 districts. It also attempted to change the labour-material ratio from 60:40 to 51:49. There were strong objections to these attempts from the opposition and a group of prominent economists. Such changes, if implemented, would go against the basic premises of the Act, pointed out the group of economists in October 2014.[15] However, pro-BJP economists and ideologues would favour a decisive shift away from the NREGA type of public intervention towards market-led programmes of rural development.[16] It is not difficult to see that such a shift would worsen the positions of *adivasis* and other disadvantaged groups.

The struggle continues

> '*Samaram cheithal maathrame bhoomi kittukayollu*'. ('Struggle is the only way to win land rights'.)
>
> An *adivasi* in Wayanad (July 2013)

> 'The lesson from the Cheeyambam struggle is that occupation is the only way to gain access to good land'.
>
> An *adivasi* activist in Wayanad (December 2012)

> 'Jail or land'.
>
> Adivasi Kshema Samiti, Wayanad (*The Hindu*, May 22, 2012)

154 *Struggle continues*

The *adivasis* of Wayanad have a history of mobilisation and struggle for land rights. They have achieved some degree of success, particularly where they dared to occupy forestland or take over state plantations in which they were workers. It is important to note that these struggles generally enjoyed the support of the Left movement of Kerala. However, the outcomes of such struggles have been constrained by the dual-purpose nature of the FRA and the actual practices of its implementation, as shown earlier. This takes us back to the point that the *adivasi* land question cannot be seen in isolation from the ongoing capitalist transition of the Indian economy in which redefining property rights and commodification of land characterise the dynamics of change. And neoliberalisation has intensified the processes of social differentiation in which pauperisation and proletarianisation are the dominant tendencies among *adivasis* and other rural subordinate groups.

The demand for land continues to be the rallying point for the *adivasis'* struggle even though the political circumstances of their deprivation have been changing due to neoliberalisation and the implementation of the FRA. In general, the landless *adivasis'* aspiration is to become land-owning cultivators, which they regard as a starting point for further advancement of their social and economic conditions. According to *adivasi* activists in Wayanad, the records of rights granted under the FRA are less than satisfactory, as they did not meet their demand for full ownership rights. 'We are planning to take forward our struggle', said *adivasi* activist C. K. Janu, 'demanding freehold title to the land received under the FRA'.[17] The struggle is not to return to an 'original' state, but to move towards a state of greater social and economic security in modern Indian society. The *adivasis* of Wayanad are not a passive mass drawn into the dynamics of pauperisation and proletarianisation, but a mobilised political force of resistance exercising its agency, although the outcome of the struggle remains uncertain. Recognition of this is important to understanding our theory of the indigeneity–class intersection and the trajectories of transition it involves.

We would like to reflect on the possible impact of the NREGA programme on the *adivasis* from our theoretical perspective. The NREGA was a major public intervention where market forces had failed to infuse qualitative changes in the dynamics of pauperisation and proletarianisation. Moreover, as already shown in Chapter 4, even though the *adivasis'* dispossession made them potential participants in the labour market, lack of employment opportunities and, more importantly, lack of employable skills pushed them into pauperism. The question is whether the NREGA could succeed where market-led development policies had failed. Could it help the *adivasis* move out of pauperism to become socially and economically secure workers or smallholder farmers, in the case of those who already have access to land? Could it contribute to their intergenerational social mobility?

The NREGA targets the unemployed poor, the majority of whom invariably lack the skills demanded in the labour market. Although it may help reduce income poverty, the programme does not include a skill development component, nor is it linked to any human development or skill development programmes targeting the *adivasis*. Even as a poverty reduction measure, the programme's contribution is limited due to the low wage compared to the average market wage. In such a situation, the opportunities for structural change and social mobility are limited, even in Kerala, as the state no longer plays the role it used to in the human development of low income and marginalised groups. This is particularly the case with the landless *adivasis*, whose position as unskilled workers remains tied to the NREGA programme, the continuity of which is uncertain. This raises the question of their location in the indigeneity–class intersection and the possibilities for them to become competitive in the labour market. In other words, they may remain unemployable outside the NREGA programme, whose future is subject to shifts in the balance of political forces at the national level. On the other hand, *adivasis* with access to cultivable land may benefit more from the opportunities for subsidised asset building on their land, as well as the wage employment provided by the programme. In this regard, the case of the Cheeyambam struggle and its outcome documented earlier could be an example of a particular trajectory of transition, although its connection with the NREGA was rather indirect. The coffee-producing *adivasis* of Cheeyambam benefitted from both the asset-building support and wage employment provided by the NREGA programme.

Stable and adequate income is an absolute precondition for the *adivasi* households to ensure the human development of the younger generations and thereby enhance their life chances and social mobility. The Cheeyambam case represents a specific instance in the indigeneity–class intersection and transition from a state of rural proletarianisation to one of petty commodity production. It exemplifies the complexity and non-linearity of the transitional process in the context of mobilisation and struggle. The argument we reiterate is that given the material deprivation and inability to be competitive in the labour market, the *adivasis* would fall back on land as the central demand for their socio-economic advancement as shown by the widespread land occupation struggles in Wayanad and other *adivasi* areas in Kerala. At the same time, there are compelling objective reasons for them to find a common cause with other subordinate groups such as the working class, whose demands include higher wages, better working conditions, freedoms and opportunities for human development and social mobility. This issue deserves the serious attention of the Left and other emancipatory movements in Kerala.

Notes

1 A study by the Asian Indigenous and Tribal Peoples Network (2012) is highly critical of the actual implementation arrangements and process, and the outcomes of the claims made by members of Scheduled Tribes and other traditional forest dwellers. Another study by the Campaign for Survival and Dignity, which is a network of organisations fighting for the rights of *adivasis* in different states of India, provides a guide to the Act and highlights how mining leases granted to companies such as Pohang Steel Corporation (POSCO) and Vedanta have disregarded the forest rights of tens of thousands of *adivasi*s.
2 The rules are officially known as the Scheduled Tribes and Other Traditional Forest Dwellers (Recognition of Forest Rights) Rules, 2007.
3 www.academia.edu/4506679/A_GUIDE_TO_THE_FOREST_RIGHTS_ACT_CAMPAIGN_FOR_SURVIVAL_AND_DIGNITY

156 *Struggle continues*

4   'The most hazardous economic challenge confronting the state', writes Oommen (2010: 82), 'is the growing parallel economy supported by powerful land mafia, liquor mafia, sand mafia (who supply river and lake sands to the growing construction industry the largest employment provider), the forest mafia (engaged in the fleecing of forest resources) and of late the spiritual/god men mafia and so on. The crime, gangsterism, and insecurity that some of these create are growing into a Frankenstein'.
5   The head count ratio was calculated using the Indian Planning Commission's method (Aravindan, 2006).
6   The Act states: '[T]he State Government shall, in such rural area in the State as may be notified by the Central government, provide every household whose adult members volunteer to do unskilled manual work not less than one hundred days of such work in a financial year' (The National Rural Employment Guarantee Act, 2005, Chapter II,3(I)).
7   For details, see Government of India, Ministry of Rural Development (2013) Notification on Minimum Features of NREGA.
8   In critiquing the NREGA, financial journals and conservative editorials have used terms such as 'expensive gravy train', 'money guzzler', 'costly joke' and 'wonky' (Dreze and Sen, 2013: 199–200).
9   A recent study of the implementation of the programme in the Attapady Tribal Development Block in Palakkad district with reference to adaptation to climate change concludes that, although tackling the proximate causes of vulnerability and fostering some degree of adaptive capacity, it has not been able to promote a 'transformational change'. It shows that, on average, a tribal (*adivasi*) household in the study area had only forty-four days of employment in the 2011–2012 financial year. Further, the study observes that benefits accruing to the *adivasis* were limited due to their disempowerment in terms of land and labour relations (Adam, 2014).
10 The works carried out under the programme that directly benefitted the *adivasis* include renovation and construction of earthen bunds and dams, ponds, irrigation canals and feeder roads.
11 http://mnregaweb4.nic.in/netnrega/dynamic2/dynamicreport_new4.aspx
12 Development Report of Poothady Panchayat, 10th Five Year Plan 2002–2007
13 http://mnregaweb4.nic.in/netnrega/dynamic2/dynamicreport_new4.aspx
14 *Adivasis* account for 39.29% of the *Panchayat's* population (Census of India: Kerala, 2001).
15 The group included Indian economists working in India and abroad. They conveyed their objections in a letter addressed to Prime Minister Narendra Modi in October 2014. www.firstpost.com/india/why-some-economists-are-worried-about-the-fate-of-nrega-under-pm-modi-govt-1760605.html
16 This is the gist of an article by Jagannathan published in Firstpost on November 8, 2014. www.firstpost.com/politics/what-pm-modi-can-learn-from-barack-obamas-loss-dont-forget-the-faithful-1792119.html
17 Interview with C.K. Janu in December 2012.

References

Adam, H. N, 2014, 'Mainstreaming Adaptation in India – The Mahatma Gandhi National Rural Employment Guarantee Act and Climate Change', *Climate and Development*, DOI: 10. 1080/17565529.2014. 934772: 1–11.

Aravindan, K.P. (ed.), 2006, *Kerala Padanam*. Thiruvananthapuram: KSSP.

Asian Indigenous and Tribal Peoples Network, 2012, The State of the Forest Rights Act. Undoing of Historical Injustice Withered. AITPN: New Delhi.

Campaign for Survival and Dignity, undated, A Guide to the Forest Rights Act, New Delhi. Retrieved from www.forestrightsact.com/index.php?option=com_content&view=article&id=73&Itemid=400055 (accessed 11/2/14).

Dreze, J. and Sen, A., 2013, *An Uncertain Glory: India and Its Contradictions*. London: Allen Lane, Penguin Books.

Ghose, D., 2014, Why Some Economists Are Worried about the Fate of NREGA under PM Modi Government, First Post, 17 October 2014. Retrieved from www.firstpost.com/india/why-some-economists-are-worried-about-the-fate-of-nrega-under-pm-modi-govt-1760605.html (accessed 11/2/14).

Government of India, Ministry of Rural Development, 2013, Notification on Minimum Features of NREGA, New Delhi. Retrieved from nrega.nic.in/Netnrega/WriteReaddata/.../Schedule_I_II_MGNREGA.pdf (accessed 11/3/14).

Government of India, 2001, Census of India 2001: Kerala.

Jagannathan, R., 2014, What PM Modi Can Learn From Barack Obama's Loss: Don't Forget the faithful, First Post, 8 November 2014. Retrieved from www.firstpost.com/politics/what-pm-modi-can-learn-from-barack-obamas-loss-dont-forget-the-faithful-1792119.html (accessed 11/9/14).

Kannan, K.P. and Jain, V., 2013, 'Historic Initiative, Limited by Design and Implementation: A National Overview of the Implementation of NREGA', in Kannan, K.P. and Bremen, J. (eds.), *The Long Road to Social Security*. New Delhi: Oxford University Press.

Kjosavik, D.J., 2010, 'Politicising Development: Re-Imagining Indigenous People's Land Rights and Identities in Highland Kerala, South India', *Forum for Development Studies*, 32(2): 243–268.

Ministry of Rural Development, MGNREGA Public Data Portal, 2014. Retrieved from http://mnregaweb4.nic.in/netnrega/dynamic2/dynamicreport_new4.aspx (accessed 11/2/14).

Oommen, M.A., 2010, 'Freedom, Economic Reform and the Kerala 'Model', in Ravi Raman, K. (ed.), *Development, Democracy and the State: Critiquing the Kerala Model of Development*. London: Routledge: 71–86.

Oommen, M.A., 2014, 'Reforms and the Kerala Model'. *Economic and Political Weekly*, 43(2): 22–25.

Poothady Panchayat Office, 2002, 10th Five Year Plan 2002–2007, Report, Poothady, Kerala.

The Hindu, 2012, Tribespeople Evicted from Forestland in Wayanad. http://www.thehindu.com/todays-paper/tp-national/tp-kerala/tribespeople-evicted-from-forestland-in-wayanad/article3444371.ece (accessed 11/2/14).

Index

Tables are indicated by italic page numbers.

aattali (trained person) 23
abolish poverty (*garibi hatao*) 151
aborigine 6
accumulation 2, 4
adhikaris (village revenue officers) 53
Adivasi Aikya Samithi (United *Adivasi* Forum) 82, 130
Adivasi Assembly (*Gothra Sabha*) 135
Adivasi-Dalit Action Council 83, 89n36
Adivasi Dalith Samara Samithi 134
Adivasi Development Activists' Forum (*Adivasi Vikasana Pravarthaka Samithi*) 82, 130
Adivasi Federation 121
Adivasi Gothra Maha Sabha (AGMS) 135, 138
Adivasi Kshema Samithi (AKS) 109
adivasi/non-*adivasi* divide 141
adivasis: assemblies (*oorukkoottams*) 107; background 56–7; communities in Wayanad 11; defined 6–7; empowerment of 100–2; Forest Rights Act and 145–51, 155n1; identities of 128–31, 129–31, 131–5; ideology 130; in the Kerala model of development 9–11, 13, 72–4; and land struggles 14, 145–50; mobilisation process of 81–3; politics and 106–9, 129–30; socio-political institutions of 138; state initiatives for 78–81; *see also* indigenous communities
Adivasi South Zone Forum 131
Adivasi Vikasana Pravarthaka Samithi (*Adivasi* Development Activists' Forum) 82, 130

Adiyar community 11, 74
advancement 3, 7, 15, 150, 154–5
affirmative action 7, 70, 72, 85, 109
African-American women 5
Agarwal, B. 8–9
agency: and advocacy 82, 86, 101; development priorities and 7, 111; information and 43–4
AGMS (*Adivasi Gothra Maha Sabha*) 135, 138
agrarian reforms 58–9, 64, 74–78, 86
Agrarian Relations Bill (1959) 58, 76
agrarian uprisings 39–40
agricultural land, property rights in 36–41, *44*, 50–3, *54*, 56–8, *60*
Agricultural Research Station, Ambalavayal 63
agricultural sector, policies affecting 103–5
Agricultural Workers' Act 71
Agricultural Workers' Welfare Scheme 81
Agriculture Department 136
Aivu (*Kurumar* code of conduct) 23–6, 28, 31
AKS (*Adivasi Kshema Samithi*) 109
alienated land 10, 78, 87, 114–17, 119, 125n10
All-India Muslim League 115
alloted land 25, 30, 55, 57, 59, 79, 123, 139
Alternative Institutionalist School 20
alternative lands 131, 142n3
ancestors 132–3
Anglo-Indian community 70
Area Development Scheme 106–9

articulation 4, 6–7, 128–31, 134–5
Aryans 21
assemblies (*grama sabhas*) 101–2, 112n6
assemblies of *adivasis* (*oorukkoottam*) 107, 139
assessments on occupied land 41–2
assimilation 1, 15n2; *see also* integration
attali (specially trained person) 133
Australoid groups 21
autonomy 9, 13, 98, 111, 140
Azeez, A. 103

backward classes 6–7, 70
Baden-Powell, B. H. 31, 46
beneficiary committees 102, 108
Bernstein, H. 124
Bharatiya Janata Party (BJP) 77, 82, 135, 153
birth rate 8
birthright (*janmam*) 31, 38–9, 41–3
bonded labour (*vallippani*) 42, 65n19, 69
British: legal system 3, 38, 53; plantations 40; policies 20, 36–42, 45–6; rule 3, 28–9, 33n21, 133
bureaucracy 1, 57–8, 77, 79, 97–8, 106

Campaign for Survival and Dignity: 'Guide to the Forest Rights Act' 147
capitalism 7, 10–11, 40
caste–class debate 70
castes: defined 69–70, 87n2; Hindu society 82; indigenous communities and 70, 87–8n3; oppressed 6; upper 38
ceiling laws 76–7
Central Plans (Five-Year Plans) 9
Centre for Development Studies (CDS) 8
centre-state fiscal relations 84
Chasin, B. H. 8
Cheeyambam coffee plantation 148–9, 155
Chera rule 27, 32n19
Chettys 27–8, 30, 39–40, 42–3, 59
chief (*moopan*) 23, 25, 51, 56, 56n35
Chingeri Extension Scheme 62–3
Church-based social service societies 81
Cinchona trees trade 40
civil organizations 81–4, 98–100
Civil Supplies Corporation 134
claims for restitution 114, 117–19, 123, 125n6, 128–9

classes 69, 78–81; backward 6–7, 70; defined 70–1; indigeneity and 4–6, 75
class struggles 115
coalitions 14, 83–5, 96, 98–100, 114–16, 118, 151
Cochin 36, 50, 56–7
coffee trade 40
collateral 42–3, 45, 80, 119
Collectors of Malabar 38–9
College of Dairy Sciences 63
Collingwood, R. G. 22
Collins, P. H. 5
colonial period 36–50; in forests 44–50; and land occupation 42–4, *44*; pre-settler period 36–40; survey and settlement of Wayanad 41–2
colonial policies 12
colonisation programmes 20, 57
coming together (*Sangamom*) 83
common property ownership 25
Communist Parties 7–9, 16n10, 62, 76–7, 83, 96–7, 99, 111n4, 114–15
community use lands (*puramboke*) 41
compensation 115, 118–21
Congress Agrarian Reforms Committee 76
Congress-Left alliance (United Progressive Alliance) 151
Congress Party 9, 14, 57, 62, 66n40, 84, 96–8, 114, 151
conscientizacão, danger of 81, 89n32
conservation lobby 145–6
conservatives 57, 76, 84–6, 114
Consolidated Fund of India 110
Constitution of India 6, 70–2, 96–7, 110; 'Special Provisions Relating to Certain Classes' 70
contract labour 69, 87n1
Convention No. 169 of the International Labour Organisation 82
Coorg territory 36
cost sharing 108
CPI (Communist Party of India) 7–9
CPI-ML (Marxist-Leninist Communist Party of India) 77
CPI-ML Red Flag (Communist Party of India) 83
Crenshaw, K. 5
crisis debate on the Kerala model 84–6

cultivation of land 25–6, 30, 41–3, 46–7, 76
culture, iron-using 21
cumulative disturbances 20

Dalit movement 83, 89n36
decentralisation 10, 13–14, 6-7, 96–102, 106–7, 110–11, 111n1, 151
'Declaration on the Rights of Indigenous Peoples': UN General Assembly 1–2
deforestation 56
delinking 106–7
democratisation 7, 9, 97
desavazhis (overlords) 29
destatisation 96–7
devaswom (temple trust) 119–20, 126n19
development 96–113; debates about 8; and indigenous communities 71–2, 100–2, 104–6; Kerala model of 7–11, 72–4, 86; neoliberal policies and 103–4; overview 96–7; politics and 106–10, 109–10; programmes 4, 6, 71–2, 80, 100–1; rural 76
direct action 78, 89n20
disenfranchisement 4
displacement and dispossession 2–4, 7, 145, 147
documentation 21–2, 28, 41, 58, 61, 117–19, 123
Draft Declaration on the Rights of Indigenous Peoples 82, 130
Dravidians 21

East India Company 36, 40, 45
economic growth 8, 10, 13
Edakkal rock engravings 21, 32n9–10
education 73–4, *73–4*, 104–5
Eldredge, N. 20
embeddedness 19, 59, 75, 87, 98–9
employment 102, 105, 108, 152, 156n9
enfranchisement 2
Engels, F. 22, 26
entrepreneurial class 14, 98–9
Evans, P. 98
evolution 20, 32n7
exclusion: historic 27–31; neoliberalisation and 4, 148, 152; policies 13, 61, 85–7; social 7, 97, 104, 111
exogenous shocks 20

exports 84, 103
external interventions 12, 19–20

Farmer, Mr. 36
farmers 36–7, 105
feminists 5
Ferguson, J. 11, 131
Fifth Schedule of the Constitution 71–2
financial assistance 80
fiscal crisis if Kerala model 84–6
Five-Year Plans 9, 72, 76
food and fuel requirements 55–6, 80, 104
food supplies 84
Forest Conservation Act of 1980 57, 79
Forest Development Corporation 63, 80, 136
Forest Policy (1894) 47
Forest Rights Act of 2006 10, 15, 145–50, 155n1
forests 9, 26–8, 31; fencing of 46–50; occupied vested 149–50; projects for indigenous peoples 62–4; property rights 44–50, *48–9*, 53, 55–6, 59, 61–2; settlements in 150; transfers of 63–4
Franke, R. W. 8
freeholders (*janmis*) 36
Freire, P. 81, 89n32
frozen classes 69–71
fugitive cultivations 42–3, 48
funds allocation 80, 84–6, 99, 101–4, 112n8
future, aspirations for 14, 140

Gandhi, I. 151
garibi hatao (abolish poverty) 151
gender 83, 104, 140, 152
Gender Environment Poverty (Vulnerability) Index 8–9
Gladson, Major 40
globalisation 4, 103
Global South 1–2, 4–6
Gothra Sabha (*Adivasi* Assembly) 135
Gould, S. J. 20
government: coalitions 14, 83–5, 96, 98–100, 114–16, 118, 151; conflicts within 100; decentralisation plans 13–14; land ownership policies 38–9, 47, 78–81; policies in Kerala 71–3, 84–6, 122–5; reforms 8, 10, 13;

162 Index

rehabilitation projects 78–81; spending 103–5
Gownders (Jains) 27–8, 30, 39–40, 42–3, 51–2, 59
grama sabhas (assemblies) 101–2, 112n6
grants-in-aid 110
grassroots level 13, 73, 99, 107, 111
green orientalists 140, 142n22
gross state domestic product (GSDP) 8
'grow more food' campaign 57
GSDP (gross state domestic product) 8
'Guide to the Forest Rights Act' (Campaign for Survival and Dignity) 147
Gupta, A. 131
Gurukkal, R. 100

Hall, S. 128–9
Harijan Welfare Department 63
head count ratio (HCR) of poverty 151
health sectors 104–5
hermeneutics 21
hierarchies: of caste system 69–70, 87n2; of difference 130; and intersectionality 5, 140; of power 11–12, 32; romantic visions of 98; social 32, 116, 139; socio-economic 82
High Court of Kerala 118
Highland Farmers' Federation (MKF) (*Malayora Karshaka Federation*) 119–22
high rent (*melcharthu*) 52
history 3, 21–4, 28, 116–18, 133, 135, 154
Human Development Index 8
Hyder's invasion 29

identity 4–7, 14, 82, 114, 124, 128–35, 137, 141
ideology 129
Idukki district 81
ILO (International Labour Organization) 1, 82, 130
imports 103
inam (revenue-free lands) 41
inclusion rights 27, 32n18
inclusiveness 13–14, 86
India, Marx on 22
Indian Forest Act (1865, 1878) 45–7
indigeneity 1–18; class intersection 4–6, 10, 75, 131, 155; described 1–2; discussions about 3–4; in Indian context 6–7; and Kerala model of development 7–11; re-imagining 135–41; and social change 145–57; and struggle for land 145–50; and Wayanad fieldwork 11–12
indigenous communities 6; civil society organisations and 81–3; colonial interests *versus* welfare of 38–9; and conflicts over natural resources 19–20, 32n2; in decentralised planning 100–2; development of 71–2; forest policies and 45–6, 48; forest projects for 62–4; in-migration effect on 31; Kerala model and 71, 84–6; and land ownership rights 40–1, 51, 74–5, 75, 82; movements 1–2; new social exclusion of 86; oppression of 28; and plantations spread 40–1; property rights of 25–7, 56–7; prospects for 104–6; and work for wages 48, 50; *see also adivasis*
indigenous land and the Kerala model 78–81
industrial sector 103–4
Industrial Workers' Act 71
inequalities 151; and caste 69–70, 87n2; hidden 16n9, 27; historical 10–11
infant mortality rate 8
information 43–4, 103
inheritance systems 25
in-migrations 11, 16n11, 19–21; of Christian populations 81; early (AD 500-1400) 27–8; and the Mysore regime 30–1; in post-independence period 56–62; in settler period 50–6
Innes, C. A. 45
institutionalism 20
Integrated Tribal Development Programme 78, 101
integration 6–7, 13, 15n2, 20, 41, 43, 53, 71–2, 87
internal colonisation 59
International Labour Organization (ILO) 1, 82, 130
International Year of Indigenous Peoples by the United Nations (UN) 82, 130
intersectionality, concept of 5–6
interventions: civil society 81–3; external 12, 19–20, 31–2; state 5, 14–15, 47, 61, 85, 110, 125, 141, 146–7, 151–4
Irulam Village, Wayanad 11–12, 80–1, 83, 116–18, 126n18, 136–8

Index   163

Jains (Gownders) 27–8, 30, 39–40, 42–3, 51–2, 59
Janakeeyasoothranam (Peoples' Planning) 107
janmam (birthright) 31, 38–9, 41–3
Janmis 55–6
janmis (*jelm-kars*) (landlords) 29, 31, 36, 38–43, 41, 45–7, 50–3, 58–61
Janu, C. K. 83, 154
Joint Farming Co-operative Societies 63, 79

Kalimalathampuran (god) 26
kanamkars (mortgagees) 36–8
kanoom-kaars (tenants) 36–8
Karnataka 69
Karnataka Backward Classes Commission Report 70
Kattunaicker community 11–12, 21, 24, 27, 30, 38, 63; agrarian reforms and 74; property rights of 26, 51, 55, 59, 63; restitution filings of 116–17
Kerala: agrarian uprisings 39–40; decentralized planning 97–100; forest rights 147–8; indigenous communities 19; landlessness 75, 77, 88n17; neoliberal policies 103–4; population variations 57; 'tryst with destiny' reforms 8; vulnerability index (1971) 9
Kerala Agricultural University 63
Kerala Agricultural Workers' Act of 1974 76, 88n13
Kerala Communist Party (KCP) 57, 62, 83
Kerala Congress 115
Kerala Congress Party 57, 66n40, 118
Kerala Destitute/Old Age Pension Scheme 81
Kerala Development Programme (*Kerala Vikasana Padhathi*) 107
Kerala Forest Act of 1961 62
Kerala Land Assignment Rules (1964) 75
Kerala Land Reforms Act of 1963 58
Kerala Land Reforms (Amendment) Act of 1969 76
Kerala Legislative Assembly 83
Kerala model 7–11, 69–95; *adivasis* in 9–11; agrarian reforms 74–8; civil organizations and 81–4; crisis of 84–6; development policies 71–4; discussions about 7–8, 15–16n5; 'frozen classes' in 69–71, 86–7; and indigenous land 78–81
Kerala Plantation Labour Act of 1964 76
Kerala Private Forests (Vesting and Assignment) Acts 62–4, 79, 89n23
Kerala Scheduled Tribes (Restriction on Transfer of Lands and Restoration of Alienated Lands) Bill 78, 114–25
Kerala Sthree Vedi (Kerala Women's Forum) 83
Kerala Vikasana Padhathi (Kerala Development Programme) 107
Kerala Widow Pension Scheme 81
Kerala Women's Forum (*Kerala Sthree Vedi*) 83
kin-corporate property rights 26
king (raja) 29
Kjosavik 3, 5, 83, 97, 149
kolkaran (land measurer) 43
Kottayam–Kurumbranad regime *30*
Kottayam regime 28–9
KSSP (People's Science Movement) 102
kudikidappu (squatters) 59, 74, 76, 88n12, 116
Kudumbiya dynasty 21
kudy (settlement) 56
Kurichiyar community 11, 74, 82
Kurumar community 11–12, 20–1, 27–9, 63; agrarian reforms and 74; *Aivu* of 23–6, 28, 31; evictions from land 52; land sales by 55–6; oral history of 28; property rights of 30, 38, 55, 59, 63; and restitution 116–17, 124–5; social position of 25, 82
Kurumbranad regime 28–9

labour market 150–3, 152–3, 156n10
Laclau, E. 129
land: abandonment 42–3; acquisitions 2; alloted 25, 30, 55, 57, 59, 79, 123, 139; alternative 131, 132, 142n3, 142n6–7; dynamics 12; markets 117; ownership 26, 40; prices 50; reforms 58–9, 64, 74–8, 86; resources 12; revenue assessments 31, 41–2; rights 10, 20, 26, 31, 32n16; tax system 39; use conduct 25; *see also* property rights
landlessness 74–5, 75, 77, 77, 87, 88n16, 123

landlord-chieftain regime (1400–1766) 28–30, 32n20
landlords (*janmis*) (*jelm-kars*) 36, 38–9, 41, 51–3
land measurer (*kolkaran*) 43
land restitution law 114–27; implementation of 117–19; legislative measures 114–16, 126n25; policies 122–5; problems with 116–17; settler narratives regarding 119–21
Land Restitution Law of 1975 14
land rush in Travancore 62
landscapes 120, 132
land struggles 15, 78, 83, 130, 141n2
'land to the tiller' slogan 76
land transfers 76, 78, 89n19, 114–16
Langlois, C V. 21–2
Left-leaning governments 13–14, 73, 76, 83–6, 96–100, 122
left movement 136–8
legal issues 38, 41, 47, 53, 78, 117
legislation 114–16
Leprosy and Cancer Patients' Pension Scheme 81
liberalisation 13–14, 85, 87, 97, 99, 103, 111
liberation theology 81
life expectancy 8
line department 106–7, 109
literacy 8–9, 73, *73*
litigation 53, 59, 65n19, 69, 76–8, 118–19, 123–4
localities 131, 142n4
Locke, J. 120
Logan, W. 31, 39–40, 45
Lok Sabha 146

Madhava Menon Commission 79
Madras 47
Madras Forest Act in 1882 47
Madras Preservation of Private Forest (MPPF) Act of 1949 61–2
Mahatma Gandhi National Rural Employment Act (MNREGA) 151–2, 156n6
Malabar: ceded to East India Company 36; colonial interests in 38–9; government forests in 47–8; history 28–9, 31; property rights in 36–41, 45–6; and unification 57, 62

Malabar Tenancy Act of 1930 52, 53, 55
Malayora Karshaka Federation (MKF) (Highland Farmers' Federation) 119–22
Mananthavady, Wayanad 138
Maoist ideology 77, 83, 88n17
Mappilah merchants 44, 45
marginal groups 12–13, 63, 109, 111, 152
marginalisation 1–2, 4, 6, 53, 63, 79, 97; and dispossession 19; historical 6, 10, 23, 31; liberalisation and 12, 14, 111
market-friendly development 4
marupattam agreement 52, 56, 65n35
Marx, K. 21–2, 26; on India 22
Marxist Leninist Communist Party of India (CPI-ML) 7–9, 16n10, 77, 83, 88n17
Massey, D. 131
Master Plan Committee 135–6
materialized labour 120
MDGs (Millennium Development Goals) 4
melcharthu (high rent) 52
member of the legislative assembly (MLA) 106
memory 12, 21
Migdal, J. S. 98
migrations *see* in-migrations
Millennium Development Goals (MDGs) 4
minimum wages 152–3
Ministry of Tribal Affairs 6–7, 147
MKF (*Malayora Karshaka Federation*) (Highland Farmers' Federation) 119–22
MLA (member of the legislative assembly) 106
MNREGA (Mahatma Gandhi National Rural Employment Act) 151–2, 156n6
mobilisation 6, 81–3, 99, 101, 117, 131, 135
modernisation 2, 7
money lenders 51
moopan (chief) 23, 25, 51, 56, 65n35
Moore, D. S. 124, 131
Moplahs (Muslims) 30–1, 42–3, 52
mortgagees (*kanamkars*) 36–8
most backward districts 153
movements 129, 141n1
MPPF (Madras Preservation of Private Forest) Act of 1949 61–2
Muslims (*Moplahs*) 30–1, 42–3, 52
Muthanga struggle 14–15, 138–41, 149
Muthanga Wildlife Sanctuary 83

Mysore regime (1766–1792) 30–1, 39
myths 22

Nair 31, 45
Nair, C. Gopalan 28
Nair/Nambiar families 28, 33n23
Namboothiri Brahmans (upper caste of Kerala) 31
Nannaru (lords of the country) 24
Narayanan, M. G. S. 21
narratives 23–4, 119–21
National Forest Policy 59
National Rural Employment Guarantee Act (NREGA) 15, 149, 151–2, 256n8
National Rural Employment Guarantee Programme 10
naxalite uprising 133, 137, 142n8
neoliberalisation 4, 10, 13, 15, 145, 148, 150–3
neoliberalism 4, 10, 13–14, 85–7, 103–4
New Democratic Initiatives 72
new social exclusion 13, 85–7, 151
Nilambur Rajah 38–9
non-*adivasis* 78–9, 105, 115, 137, 142n17
non-governmental organisations (NGOs) 81–3, 101, 118
non-historic nations 22
North American Indians 6
NREGA (National Rural Employment Guarantee Act) 15, 149, 151–2, 156n8

occupation of land 41–3
Old Institutionalism School 20
Oorali community 11
oorukkoottam (assemblies of *adivasis*) 107, 139
oorukkoottangal (village assemblies) 135, 139
open-access forests 48
oral histories 22–3, 27–8
organic ideology 129
organisations, community based 82
over-politicisation 100
ownership rights 26–7, 32n18, 40, 58, 74, 88n10

Palakkad district 81
Panchayat Presidents' Association 107

Panchayat Raj Act 98
panchayats self-governmental units 11–12, 97–8, 106
Paniyar community 11–12, 21, 23–4, 26–30, 38, 63; agrarian reforms and 74; beliefs of 26; property rights of 53, 55, 59, 63; restitution filings of 116–17
parallel economy 151, 156n4
Parry and Company 40
pattayam land 57, 66n38
pauperisation and proletarianisation of *adivasis* 2, 12–13, 36–68, 71; background 36; colonial period 36–50; forest projects 62–4; post-independence period 56–62; resistance to 141; settler period 50–6
Pazhassi escheats 39
Pazhassi Rajah 36, 39, 133
Pazhassi *Yudham* (war) 133
PDS (public distribution system) 103, 112n9
peasant insurgency 77, 88n17–18
peasant migration 62
peasant unrest 39–40
Penappattu narrative 23, 26, 133
Peoples' Planning (*Janakeeyasoothranam*) 107
People's Planning Campaign (PPC) 13–14, 96–7, 99–100, 151
People's Science Movement (KSSP) 102
personal cultivation 76
Pethiyar (those who arrived before us) 24
Pithalar (fore-fathers) 24
Planning Commission of India 76
Plantation Labour Act of 1964 71, 76, 80
plantations 42–6, 58, 112n11, 136–8; British 2, 20, 40; commercial 12, 40, 46, 58, 63–4; forest conversion to 77; occupied 148–9; state 14, 79, 141; workers 48, 50, 69, 71, 79–80, 105–6
plough agriculture 21
Polanyi, K. 27
policies: affirmative action 7, 70, 84–5; colonial 12, 20, 36, 46–7, 59; decentralisation 96–102; development 4, 8–10, 72–4, 86, 109–10; exclusion 61; forest rights 145–7; government 13–14, 20, 36, 122–125; integration 86–7; land

166 *Index*

64, 74, 78–81; neoliberal 4, 13, 86–7, 103–4; redistribution 8–9; for Scheduled Castes 71; shift in government 122–5
political mobilisation 6, 81–3
politicisation 100
politics: and *adivasi* development 106–9; contestational 100; electoral 84; of land 14; neoliberal 14, 111
Pookot Lake Dairy Project 63
Poothady *Panchayat* 11–12, 24, 102, 107–8, 112n7–8
populations, variation in 57
Porter, D. H. 24
post-colonial development 2
post-independence period, property rights in 56–62
poverty 100–1, 151–2, 154–5
power relations 5, 19, 32n1
PPC (People's Planning Campaign) 13–14, 96–7, 99–100, 151
pre-colonial period, property rights in 19–35; description of 19–21; exclusionary beginnings of 27–30; history of 21–5; of indigenous communities 25–7; Mysore regime influence on 30–1; political economy and 21–5
primitive accumulation 2
primitive tribal communities 72
private forests 47, 61–2
private property rights 40, 43–4, 51
privatisation 48, 71, 85, 96, 104, 109
Priyadarshini Tea Estate 63
professional history 22–3
programmes 85–7; colonisation 20; decentralisation 96–8, 151; development 4, 6, 72–3, 81, 100–2; in Kerala model 13; NREGA 151–5; rehabilitation 78–9; welfare 71, 80–1; *see also* policies
proletarianisation *see* pauperisation and proletarianisation of *adivasis*
property rights: agricultural land 36–41, *44*, 50–3, *54*, 55–62, 56–8; and class 70–1, 88n5; forests 44–50, *48–9*, 53, 55–8; of indigenous communities 25–7; of *Kattunaicker* 55; kin-corporate 26; of *Kurumar* community 30, 38, 55; in Malabar 36–40; of *Paniyar* community 53; in post-independence period 56–62; in pre-colonial period 19–35; private 40,

43–4, 51; of settlers 63; in Wayanad *30, 39, 44, 54*
protected forests 47–8
protests 39–40
public distribution system (PDS) 103, 112n9
punctuated equilibria 20
Punjab 9
puramboke (community use lands) 41, 75, 88n11
Putnam, R. 100

quality of life indicators 8

radicalism 81–2
radical left groups 83
rainfall, annual 9
raja (king) 29
RDO (revenue divisional officer) 118
realism 22
recentralisation 107
redistributive policies 8–9
rehabilitation projects 78–81
reign of King custom, the 29
rent (*pattom*) 37, 52
rent and taxes 12, 29, 37, 39–42, 51–2
rent-tax (*patta-nikuthi*) 39, 41
Report of the Joint Commission (1793) 44–5
Report on the Land Tenures of Malabar (Walker) 29
reserve forests 47–8, 58
restitution 78, *78*, 89n19; *see also* land restitution law
Restriction on Transfer of Lands and Restoration of Alienated Lands (Kerala Scheduled Tribes) Bill 78, 114–25
revenue administration 41
revenue divisional officer (RDO) 118
revenue forests 47, 58
revenue-free lands (*inam*) 41
revenue lands (*ryotwari*) 41, 50–1, 58
revenue villages 11–12
Revolutionary Socialist Party (RSP) 115
rights-holders, British 36
rinderpest disease 42
Robertson, W. 23
Robin Hood scenario 134
Roseberry, W. 139

rules for gathering and hunting 26
rural: development 76; female literacy rate 9; fertility rates 9
ryotwari (revenue lands) 41, 50–1
ryotwari system 41

Sallivan 83
samara bhoomi (struggle-land) 138–41, 150
Sangamom (coming together) 83
sathyagraham (strike) 134
Sathyamurthy, T. V. 84
Scheduled Areas 71–2, 88n7
Scheduled Castes (SCs) 6, 70–1, 83
Scheduled Tribes (ST) (*adivasis*) 5–6, 15n3, 70–2
schools 104–5
scientism 23
Second World War veterans 55, 57
'security of tenure' provision 52
Seignobos, C. 21–2
self-employment 102
self-identification of indigenous people 3
settled agriculture 27–8
settlement (*kudy*) 56
settler communities: and conflicts over natural resources 19, 32n3; narratives 119–21; property rights of 63
settler period, property relations in (1930s-1947) 50–6
settlers 14, 125n1; *see also* in-migrations
sex ratio 8–9
Shanmugaratnam, N. 2, 15n1
slavery 40
social: change 81, 145–57; democratisation 9; development 8; exclusion 13, 86, 97; hierarchies 70–1; imaginary 140; locations 5; memories 133; organisation 24–5; relationships 19
social-sector expenditure and investments 8–9, 103
societies, pre-literate 23
socio-economic advancement 3, 7, 15, 155
South Wayanad Girijan Joint Farming Co-Operative Society (Sugandhagiri Cardamom Project) 63
South Zone *Adivasi* Forum (SZAF) 83
'Special Provisions Relating to Certain Classes' (Constitution of India) 70
spices 27

squatters (*kudikidappu*) 59, 74, 76, 88n12, 116
ST (Scheduled Tribes) (*adivasis*) 5–6, 15n3, 70–2
state: conflicts over natural resources 19, 32n4; development policies 8, 109–10; forests 48; interventions 5, 14–15; land distribution 135–8
State Forest Department 79, 138–9
'state-in-society' approach 98
state-society relations 98–9
statisation 48, 62, 71, 96–7
strike (*sathyagraham*) 134
struggle-land (*samara bhoomi*) 138–41, 150
struggles of indigenous people 2, 7, 10, 14–15, 83, 130, 138–41, 141n2, 153–5
Subrahmanian, K. K. 103
subsidies 74, 103, 112n9, 149, 151, 155
Sugandhagiri Cardamom Project (South Wayanad Girijan Joint Farming Co-Operative Society) 62–3
Sullivan, J. 38–9
surplus land 13, 58–9, 74–7
sweat metaphor 119–21
synoptic judgement 24
SZAF (South Zone *Adivasi* Forum) 83

Tamil Nadu 50, 69
Tamil songs 27
taxes and rent 12, 29, 37, 39–42, 51–2
tax revenues 84, 89n41
teak forests 45–6, 50
tea plantations 40, 50
temple-based economy 27
tenancy rights 39
tenants-at-will (*kanoom-kaars; verumpattamkars*) 36–8, 52
tenure systems 29, 36, 39
Thackeray, W. 29, 37, 44
Tharakan, P. K. M. 100
theeradharam (white paper) 51, 56
Thompson, P. 22–3
tillers 76
timber trade 31, 45–6
Tippu Sultan 31, 36
titles to land 41, 43–4, 57–9, 66n43, 120
Todas, the 39
Tonkin, E. 23

Trade Related Intellectual Property Rights (TRIPS) 105
trade unions 71, 80, 103–4, 137
traditions 21, 23
transition: indigeneity in 1–18; *see also* indigeneity; property rights; social change
transparency 108
Travancore 50, 56–7
Tribal Areas 72
tribal court 138
Tribal Development Blocks 72
Tribal Sub-Plan (TSP) 72, 80, 85, 90n44, 101, 106
tribunals 78, 116, 118
TRIPS (Trade Related Intellectual Property Rights) 105
Trivandrum, agitation in 134
Turner, C. 39

UN (International Year of Indigenous Peoples by the United Nations) 82, 130
UN Commission on Human Rights 82
UN Decade of the Indigenous Peoples 130
UN Declaration of 2007 3
UN General Assembly: 'Declaration on the Rights of Indigenous Peoples' 1–2
UN Human Rights Commission forum on indigenous issues 82
unions 71, 80, 103–4, 137
United *Adivasi* Forum (*Adivasi Aikya Samithi*) 82, 130
United Nations Working Group on Indigenous Populations (UNWGIP) 82, 130
United Progressive Alliance (Congress-Left alliance) 151
upper castes 29, 38
uprisings, agrarian 39–40
Uralis community 24, 116–17

vallippani (bonded labour) 42, 65n19
Veda kings 21, 28
verumpattamkars (tenants-at-will) 36, 38, 52
vested forests 58, 62, 66n44
Vesting and Assignment (Kerala Private Forests) Acts 62–4, 79, 89n23
village assemblies (*oorukkoottangal*) 135, 139
village revenue officers (*adhikaris*) 53
villages 11–12, 46–8, 62
vulnerability index 8–9

wagework 48, 50, 55–6, 59, 63, 85, 102, 105–6
Walker, Major: *Report on the Land Tenures of Malabar* 29, 37
Warden, T. 37–9
Warden *pattam* (Warden rent) 39–40, 39–41
water-contact-birthright (*janmam*) 31
Watson, Captain 45–6
Wayanad: British plantations 40; Church-based social service societies 81; colonization scheme 57–8; conquest of 30–1; fieldwork in 11–12; forest projects 62–3; Forest Rights Act 147–8; history of indigenous communities in 20–1; in-migrations 27–8, 50–6; Irulam Village 11, 79, 83, 116–18; oral traditions 23; place names 24; population variation *57*; property rights *30, 39, 44, 54, 60*; survey and settlement of 41–4; timber trade in 31
Wayanadan Chetty community 27
Wayanad Coffee Plantations 40
WCD (World Commission on Dams) 2
welfare programmes 71, 80, 104
wetlands 24, 26, 43
white paper (*theeradharam*) 51, 56
Winterbotham, H. 45
women: and *adivasi* movement 83; African-American 5; employment opportunities for 102; and gender struggles 83; land rights of 25–6; leaders 102, 124, 138–9; and leadership 83; policies regarding 9, 16n9
Wood, R. B. 28
worker recruitment 50
workers 76, 88n13, 115
working class 70–1
working conditions 40
Working Group on Indigenous Populations 3
World Bank 100
World Bank Operational Directives 82, 130
World Commission on Dams (WCD) 2
World Trade Organization 105

younger generation 102, 110, 140, 149, 155